T0293510

ROUTLEDGE LIBRARY EDITIONS:
INDUSTRIAL ECONOMICS

Volume 11

INDUSTRIAL PROPERTY

INDUSTRIAL PROPERTY

Policy and economic development

Edited by
RICK BALL AND ANDY C. PRATT

Routledge
Taylor & Francis Group

LONDON AND NEW YORK

First published in 1994 by Routledge

This edition first published in 2018
by Routledge
2 Park Square, Milton Park, Abingdon, Oxon OX14 4RN

and by Routledge
711 Third Avenue, New York, NY 10017

Routledge is an imprint of the Taylor & Francis Group, an informa business

British Library Cataloguing in Publication Data
A catalogue record for this book is available from the British Library

ISBN: 978-1-138-30830-5 (Set)
ISBN: 978-1-351-21102-4 (Set) (ebk)
ISBN: 978-1-138-57365-9 (Volume 11) (hbk)
ISBN: 978-0-203-70146-1 (Volume 11) (ebk)

Publisher's Note
The publisher has gone to great lengths to ensure the quality of this reprint but points out that some imperfections in the original copies may be apparent.

Disclaimer
The publisher has made every effort to trace copyright holders and would welcome correspondence from those they have been unable to trace.

Industrial Property

Policy and economic development

Edited by Rick Ball and Andy C. Pratt

London and New York

First published 1994
by Routledge
11 New Fetter Lane, London EC4P 4EE

Simultaneously published in the USA and Canada
by Routledge
29 West 35th Street, New York, NY 10001

Typeset in Times by LaserScript, Mitcham, Surrey
Printed and bound in Great Britain by
Biddles Ltd, Guildford and King's Lynn

British Library Cataloguing in Publication Data
A catalogue record for this book is available from the British
Library.
ISBN 0–415–09152–7

Library of Congress Cataloging in Publication Data
has been applied for.

Contents

Figures

Tables

Preface

This book is the product of a unique collaboration between property professionals and researchers. It is the first ever collection of original research solely devoted to the relationships between industrial property and economic development. It has four key objectives: to provide an overview of the field; to offer practical advice on how to carry out research in this new and difficult area; to report new research findings on a range of current issues; and to set a research agenda for further work in this area.

Industrial property is a vitally important component of the economy, yet it is one that has received little attention in the literature. This book serves to rectify this oversight by offering an analysis of contemporary aspects of industrial property as an investment *and* as a site of production. It focuses on real challenges facing the academic research community, property managers, developers and investors, industrialists and planners in the 1990s.

The book also highlights the information limitations that confront researchers in this field. At a basic level, it is clear that comprehensive information is a key requirement. For example, property investment decisions require detailed, quality information; and that information is clearly not available. Moreover, academics in the industrial property field are increasingly aware of the importance of linking an understanding of industrial activity with that of property development. They cannot do this within the parameters of available information sources.

The contributions to this book, all of them specially commissioned, challenge the conventional view of industrial property as purpose-built factories that are owned by their occupants. Contributors, specialists in their field, highlight an emerging conflict between the users and the providers of industrial premises, a conflict that may undermine economic development potential. A recurrent theme in the book is flexibility; flexibility in the use and in the provision of industrial premises. This is explored in three contexts: in the transformation of the urban fringe; in the development of high-tech premises; and in the redevelopment of old or derelict buildings. In order to survive in the current climate, industrialists are rapidly changing both the organization of work and the layout of factories. An example of this, much referred to in the literature, is flexible special- ization or post-Fordism. Whilst the flexible specialization debate does address the increasingly flexible nature of production, it fails to consider the significance of flexibility in the form of industrial property provision. Neither does it investigate the fact that industrial property is now supplied by developers whose interests are essentially in investment and not in industrial production.

Another area of concern in the book is the policy dimension. All of the contributions represent important current policy issues; from these of high technology industry and its property needs, to the legacies of de- industrialization in the form of redundant factories; and from production issues that draw the attention of regeneration agencies and local authorities, to those of future investment return that concern institutional investors and the private sector. There is discussion, in a variety of contexts, about the changing form of property–state relationships, and in particular about property as a factor in local economic development. In these terms, property is seen not only as a catalyst for change and a basis for regeneration but also as a prime element of public– private interaction in the national space economy.

Moreover, the role of economic and planning policy, at both a local and a national level, is seen as crucial in the resolution of potential conflicts between the users and the providers of industrial premises. The book argues that, whilst industrial property provision by the state has a history almost as long as intervention in industry, it has primarily been viewed as part of a social policy. Given the changing relationship between the provision and the use of industrial buildings, it is argued that it is now time for a dramatic rethink of industrial property provision. There are two aspects to this issue: industrial property *provision* by the public and private sectors and the *consequences* for industrial development.

This book will appeal to those interested in all aspects of industrial property investment, its management and its use; and to both students and researchers from the public and private sectors. More generally, it will be relevant to planning, estate management, surveying and geography students taking courses in industrial location, policy and economic development. Above all, *Industrial property: policy and economic development* is designed to review, critically evaluate and develop policy debates in this field. It is hoped that it will both stimulate and give direction to future research activity.

Twenty-Three Years On

Andy C. Pratt

INTRODUCTION

It is twenty-three years since the first edition of this collection was published. The objective of this new introduction is to argue that the questions originally posed then remain as relevant today. Specifically: first, to provide legitimation and focus for the role of property and its development in industrial location and economic development; second, to problematize the relationship between supply and demand of industrial property, thereby highlighting how development shapes this process; finally, to challenge policy makers in the field of local economic development to understand the challenges and opportunities of industrial property provision.

The simple answers to the questions are: that limited attention has been paid to industrial property, the literature on commercial property development more generally has developed but its focus has overwhelmingly been with the professional concerns of property agents, particularly valuation and procedural matters. Issues around investment strategies, and risk management, and sources of investment and their flow locally and internationally, across and between property, and non-property, sectors remains under-developed. Second, the institutional changes in planning and economic development in the wake of neoliberalism and the small state has meant that the scope of policy to meaningfully change the parameters of investment decisions has been reduced: both in terms of the ever-limited capabilities of local policy makers; and, in terms of the widening disconnect between financial flows and property investment decisions. Finally, the tensions in the relationship of industrial property users and the providers (both investors and landlords) remain, if anything, they are greater. Investment decisions continue to standardization and flexible use. Markets have been slow to respond to demand in either location or style of development (especially on price).

The ultimate ending point for 'industrial property' is 'mixed use, flexible shared workspace', where space and facilities are rented by the hour. Whilst it is often presented as the up-to-the-minute trend, this clearly is a low cost, low risk, property form; moreover, it is a space that can at any moment be re-programmed once it has achieved its 'place making' objective for a new office, or cultural quarter. The point is that specific property, that matches the needs of users is considered too risky an investment: both in terms of internal design, or location. The question that we sought to return to in the collection was 'what is appropriate for the users of industrial space (however defined)'? What makes this question so difficult to resolve is the fact that the cycles of industrial change and those of property provision are out of sync, and of different lengths (and they are changing). The remainder of the introduction seeks to highlight three points: first, what has changed in the last 30 years or so and how has it impacted on property provision and demand; second, has academic and research improved the basic research position, and kept abreast of changes; finally, where should research be looking in the future?

WHAT CHANGED?

Broadly we can identify three phases of industrial property development that occurred in the UK and many North American and European states starting around the early 1970s, a period that saw the extensive process of the 'de-industrialization' of cities and regions which marked a dramatic shift in economic activities away from what had been the norm since the industrial revolution; the 1930s state intervention in industrial property development (in the form of industrial estates) was dwarfed by the deindustrialization process.

It was at the tail end of this cycle that the collection is situated: de-industrialization had become entrenched in inner cities and regions, in many places there were vast stocks of vacant premises that were purpose built for processes not current, or in locations where they were no longer needed. Large scale and extensive manufacturing was replaced by smaller firms, and 'hi-tech' firms. Simply there was a mismatch between supply and demand, as well as over-supplied, or failing property markets. Property development innovation moved to embrace mixed use and smaller units; notably, it was attracted to higher specification 'hi-tech' and 'science park' developments, many of which had tenuous relationship to demand. However, they did resemble a new asset class of property, and hence were over-supplied.

The mid-1990s coincides with a second phase, the state intervention to deal with the obsolete property that was 'blocking' re-development of the inner cities. Quite simply, it was uneconomic to develop property based on the cost of clearing vacant property, and remediating the site (often contaminated with pollutants). This is the era of vast swathes of inner city land lying dormant with negative land values. It is of course a major contributory reason why the idealist urban renaissance plans (Urban Task Force 1999) for re-use of brownfield sites was so often not achieved. The large-scale redevelopment of port areas in many cities, as well as previously industrialised inner cities, was the culmination of the era of urban regeneration. To make these developments viable for private developments, public investment was required. The biggest, and latest, of these mega-developments was the London 2012 Olympic site. The 'pay-off', it was hoped, would be jobs and economic vibrancy, as well as a social and cultural impact for dormant city centres (which were suffering from the property and retail economics of 'out of town' retailing). For investors and developers there was a potential bonanza to be reaped from the revaluing of redundant land, and of previously zoned industrial land, for new uses of office, retail and housing. In most cases industrial uses were at the back of the queue: in one part due to the lower rentals that 'industrial users' can pay; and, in another part because it was not anticipated that industrial uses would need space in a 'post-industrial' landscape.

The latest phase has seen a continued focus on the inner city, in this case much of the development has been concerned with conversion and re-use of industrial spaces. Obviously profitable has been conversion of former industrial and warehouse properties to residential use. A more marginal movement has been an industrial 'co-op' system whereby large industrial units are sub-let into small units or studios. In some cases, notably, the cultural sector (which has undergone a massive growth in the post-1990 period) these developments have been envisaged as the core of a district or regional development (creative clusters), or simply as a as a locus for users in one building (a cultural/creative hub). The question of ownership and management of these 'hubs', often on a not-for-profit basis, has become an important strategy to retain employment, especially cultural employment, in the city.

At the same time, other segments of the property market have noted the 'place making' potential of arts and cultural districts and hence used them as a stepping stone for residential conversion. The consequence in many cases is that the residential development, and associated retail uses, forces up prices, and the artists have to move on. This then is the 'artistic gentrification' process that has captured so much attention recently (Evans 2001). Of course, much popular attention gets paid to 'hipsters' or 'artists' as if they were the cause of the process; little attention is directed to the property development and investment process; or indeed the way in which local authorities get 'regeneration' for 'free' by going with the status quo (Pratt 2010). In reality, it undermines cultural producers, and it pressurises existing residents. Given the economic growth of the cultural sector this 'gentrification' has become an 'industrial problem' as producers can no longer locate in their ideal places, and are disrupted by unstable property conditions. Hence, the mismatch between providers and users is manifest in its contemporary guise.

ACADEMIC RESEARCH

As noted earlier, the rising wave of interest in the relationship to users and local economic development has regrettably broken. The challenges of out of date and inadequate data sources on vacant property and floorspace have not been met in declining public budgets. For example, in 2005 the commercial and industrial property vacancy statistics were discontinued. Moreover, the taxonomies associated with property data have become out of date and quickly surpassed by changes in land use planning classifications, and property marketing, and the shift toward mixed and flexible usage (or, more properly, 'provision': users have to make do with what is provided). The concerns of many planners and policy makers with controlling the employment density of land use/buildings has dwindled to insignificance as any jobs are considered better than no jobs. Moreover, the reform of planning has meant that now planners have fewer powers to reject a planning permission. We still are no closer to having information on the ownership and investment in industrial property; beyond individual case studies, or (incomplete) company data the actual patterns of ownership and investment are obscure, as is the degree that it shapes provision.

Academic work on property development can be divided into two types. First, that which echoes and refines the work of property professionals and investment managers, especially in terms of valuation (Ambrose 1990; Fehribach, Rutherford and Eakin 1993) and investment management (Adair et al. 2003). This area has - generally - received a considerable boost and has developed a number of academic journals and masters level programmes. Second, the usually more critical work on the development process and financial flows, locally and globally, has received less attention (Henneberry 1988; Cook 1989; Jones and Orr 1999). Work in this field has pushed a little further forward with respect to theorising property development within the wider context of economic development and planning (Healey 1994; Ball, Lizieri, and MacGregor 1998). However, there is still very little evidence of property development issues, and in particular industrial property development finding its way into the mainstream economic development and urban studies literature.

The singular exception is perhaps the current concern with gentrification and cultural activities in cities. The international trend in place marketing, the experience economy and 'creative cities' has driven the gentrification of many urban centres, in the sense that not only rents, but wholesale redevelopment and reuse has created adverse effects on those with less money (notably cultural producers, or residents). The gentrification literature is generally not specific and focused enough to explore the property related processes and non-residential users' needs, but this process remains at the core of the re-use and control of urban land uses. As artists leave the city, one is reminded on the killing of 'the goose that laid the golden egg.'

FUTURE DIRECTIONS AND CONCLUSION

So, *plus ca change la meme chose*; however, it is important to see both how the material forms change, and the precise patterns and processes of development change, and who and where their effects impact. Arguably, we have moved on little from a relative ignorance, or neglect, of property development processes, their impacts and questions of how they might be governed. It is important to continue to challenge the naive assumption that provision of property is in response to demand; and, that this mismatch has negative consequence for economic activity.

We are still relatively clueless to the nature, scale and flow of investment into, and across, property classes, locally, regionally and globally. Moreover, how well or poorly, such investment flows shape the (ill-) provision of property; let alone how we might change this. So, the message remains the same as it was originally stated (even if the precise forms and location of industrial property has changed).

There is a raft of other issues that we can pick up on from urban regeneration debates of recent years. Prominent is the issue of environmental sustainability; it remains an open question whether a refurbishment of a building is more energy or environmentally efficient that a new build (the devil is in the detail). There will continue to be superficial debates (in the scope of things) about green roofs and glazing and heating; however, these will continue to be dwarfed by the bigger question of movement in cities. The relationship between residential and industrial location remains fundamental to the generation of transport demand, the major producer of greenhouse gases.

This resolution of home and work seems further from our grasp than ever, and we seem doomed to generate more polluting movement. Moreover, the social consequences of the mis-matches between home and work continue to manifest themselves. The social and cultural values of knowledge exchange and open innovation, and open creativity, are yet another reason why the home-work relation continues to attract attention. Live-work spaces have long been proposed, sadly they are a regulatory nightmare, often providing a loophole for residential users to move into an industrial quarter.

The mixed-use city advocated by writers such as Jane Jacobs (1961) has returned in many case, the strict zoning more an exception than the rule. However, a mixed use dictated by the needs of property investment models is not the same as one dictated by social and cultural objectives, or the effectiveness and efficiency of production. Until we take property development seriously, and in its wider contexts, research and understanding will remain compromised. As usual, more research is needed.

REFERENCES

Adair, A., J. Berry, S. McGreal, N. Hutchison, C. Watkins and K. Gibb (2003). "Urban regeneration and property investment performance." *Journal of Property Research* **20**(4): 371–386.

Ambrose, B. (1990). "An analysis of the factors affecting light industrial property valuation." *Journal of Real Estate Research* **5**(3): 355–370.

Ball, M., C. Lizieri and B. D. MacGregor (1998). *The economics of commercial property markets*, London, Psychology Press.

Cook, G. (1989). "Local authorities and industrial property markets." *Property Management* **7**(1): 3–12.

Evans, G. (2001). Cultural planning: an urban renaissance? London, Routledge.

Fehribach, F., R. Rutherford and M. Eakin (1993). "An analysis of the determinants of industrial property valuation." *Journal of Real Estate Research* **8**(3): 365–376.

Healey, P. (1994). "Urban policy and property development: the institutional relations of real-estate development in an old industrial region." *Environment and Planning A* **26**(2): 177–198.

Henneberry, J. (1988). "Conflict in the industrial property market." *Town Planning Review* **59**(3): 241.

Jacobs, J. (1961). The death and life of great American cities. New York, Random House.

Jones, C. and A. Orr (1999). "Local commercial and industrial rental trends and property market constraints." *Urban Studies* **36**(2): 223–237.

Pratt, A. C. (2010). "Creative cities: Tensions within and between social, cultural and economic development. A critical reading of the UK experience." *City, Culture and Society* **1**(1): 13–20.

Urban Task Force (1999). *Towards an urban renaissance*, London, Spon.

1 Industrial property, policy and economic development

The research agenda

Andy C. Pratt and Rick Ball

INTRODUCTION

Some of the most potent symbols of an industrial age are to be found in its built environment. The literary descriptions of 'dark satanic mills' in Blake's poem or 'Coketown' in Dickens' novel *Hard Times* evoke vivid images. Likewise, in our contemporary media – in video – the standard signifier of 'recession' is either a decaying brick built multi-storey mill or a foundry clad in rusty corrugated iron. Growth and dynamism are signified by a hi-tech, low-rise, glass-fronted building in a lush park or campus setting.

Buildings are important, as is their financing, construction and site planning. Property development, construction, surveying and planning are major professions. It is not surprising that some attention has been paid to the needs and problems of commercial property development (see for example Rose 1985; Radcliffe 1978; Darlow 1982; Scarrett 1983; Ball 1988; Healey and Nabarro 1990; Healey *et al.* 1992). What is surprising is that so little attention has been paid specifically to industrial property. Recent books have acknowledged this oversight (Cadman and Austin-Crowe 1983; Fothergill *et al.* 1987; Morley *et al.* 1989; Wood and Williams 1992). However, their focus has been predominantly a procedural one, whether they are written from the perspective of the planner, surveyor or developer. What they fail to fully acknowledge is the significance of the activities that these buildings house and exactly what the needs of their occupants might be.

Clearly, industry is more than a collection of buildings. Researchers have, quite rightly, concerned themselves with attempting to understand the activities that are carried out within these buildings. However, in doing so, they have perhaps excluded all consideration of buildings. Most work on industrial location, organization and activity makes the unwritten assumption that a 'demand' for an industrial building will be met, unproblematically, with a 'supply'. We are not disputing that, in many cases, this assumption has held good. However, we want to argue in this book that there are an increasing number of cases where such an assumption is no longer valid. Furthermore, we believe that this fact has important consequences for our understanding of industrial development.

The breakdown of the relationship between the 'supply' of and 'demand' for industrial property can be illustrated by a few examples. First, in reports of the shortage of small industrial premises (Coopers and Lybrand Associates/Drivers Jonas Associates 1980). Second, by the work by Fothergill *et al.* (1985) highlighting the constraints of much of the existing stock of industrial buildings in inner urban areas. Third, with the long-running provision – since the 1930s – of industrial premises (advance factory units and industrial estates) by both central and local government (Slowe 1981; Loebl 1988).

This last example does remind us that this is not a new issue. Harvey (1989: 88) reminds us that, 'the geographical landscape that results is the crowning glory of past capitalist development. But at the same time . . . it imprisons and inhibits the accumulation process within a set of physical constraints.' There is constantly a need to overcome the limitations of the old, worn out, or inappropriate built environment. While Harvey is referring to the process of urbanization more generally, this view has particular resonance for those interested in the industrial built environment. Surprisingly, few have explored this issue in any detail.

A less obvious point, but one that this book is based upon, is that the interests of property development and investment may not, at any particular site, coincide with the needs of industrialists. It is this fact that results in the breakdown between 'supply' and 'demand'. It is this new set of relationships which, we would argue, needs to be investigated. We would stress that we are not suggesting some sort of 'gestalt shift', where concern is focused solely on property developers and investors at the expense of industrialists or planners. We are calling for new conceptualizations of both the uneven process of development and the unevenness of the property development process. This will require account to be taken of new 'actors' and 'institutions'.

It is, we would argue, the dramatic restructuring of the British economy in the post-war period – particularly post-1975 – that has pushed the consideration of industrial property to the forefront. But, of course, the property sector has itself undergone a period of restructuring. One of the distinctive developments in the last twenty-five years has been the emergence in the UK of a distinct and separate property development and investment sector that has had an increasing influence on the location decisions and activities that may be carried out within buildings. The indications are that the UK property market is one of the most advanced in this process; as such, the eyes of those in neighbouring European states must be upon it. If our argument is valid, the implication is that researchers and planners interested in industrial development and policy will need to consider the production of property as well as the traditional aspects of industrial organization. We would argue that this has not been done before. This book is an attempt to develop such an understanding.

If research is to be promoted in this field some sort of institutional focus will also be required. It is perhaps significant that, historically, research on industrial property and economic development has occupied a 'half world' between several disciplines and professional areas of expertise. The Society of Property Researchers (SPR) was established in 1987 as a professional body concerned with raising the profile of the commercial property researcher more generally.[1] The SPR has close links with the Royal Institute of Chartered Surveyors (RICS). It is a positive sign that two of the current SPR committee members (Colin Lizieri and Nick Axford) are contributors to this book. Nevertheless, property research continues to be dominated by the concerns of retail and office property investment. Academics – mainly geographers, estate managers and planners – have been primarily concerned with aspects of industrial location and regional development. Recently, academic research groups, notably the 'Economic Geography Study Group' of the Institute of British Geographers (IBG), have organized meetings on the theme of industrial property and economic development;[2] the editors of this book have been committee members of this group. More generally, as can be noted from the institutional and professional affiliations of the contributors, a broad range of research interests and professional expertise has been brought together in this book. It is our collective hope that it will encourage, by example, further work in the field.

Another important forum for debate about issues related to property production and economic development is the Bartlett International Summer School (BISS). BISS aims to develop an interdisciplinary perspective on the development of the built environment, with particular emphasis on the production process. It was established in 1979 and has met annually since. The conference proceedings are published.[3] However, few contributions to BISS have, as yet, focused primarily on industrial property. We are glad that one of the contributors to this book – Dick Pratt – has been active in BISS.

Research work also needs a publication outlet and a forum for debate. In this context the establishment of *Land Development Studies* in 1984 (now renamed *Journal of Property Research*) is to be welcomed. However, the index of published articles reveals just two specifically on industrial property.

The remainder of this chapter is dedicated to setting the context for research in industrial property and economic development. First, a set of issues surrounding the restructuring of industrial production, primarily resulting in employment loss in manufacturing production (de-industrialization), and gain in high-tech and office activities, are discussed. The significance of organizational changes that affect the use of individual industrial spaces – flexible specialization and post-Fordism – are also highlighted. Second, the restructuring of the property production sector is considered. Here a set of issues is raised concerning the use and suitability of property for occupants as provided by developers and investors. Third, the implications of the increasing flexibility of both industrial property production and industrial property use are considered as a research problem in itself. Fourth, the contribution of industrial property to British regional and local economic policy is reviewed. The general failure to consider the role of property in economic development in the context of an industrial strategy is highlighted as both a problem and an area for future research.

INDUSTRIAL RESTRUCTURING

The most obvious place from which to begin investigating the changing nature of industrial property and its relationship to industrial activity is to consider the changes that have occurred with regards to the organization of industrial production in the last two decades. In the 1970s, Britain, along with much of western Europe and the United States, experienced a progressive contraction of the manufacturing sector. This is commonly referred to as de-industrialization. De-industrialization is strictly a descriptive term. Nevertheless, it has generated considerable debate about its causes and possible implications for both local, regional and national economies (see Blackaby 1981; Martin and Rowthorn 1986).

It is not difficult to imagine what the implications of this de-industrialization are for the industrial buildings of Britain – dereliction and vacancy (see Chapter 8; and figures from King & Co. in Chapter 2). This state of affairs should not surprise us. After all, previous periods of industrial change have left behind their own legacy in the form of derelict industrial environments. Some have now received a new lease of life as tourist attractions, for example, Coalbrookedale, near Telford, or the Jewellery Quarter in Birmingham (see Chapter 5).

Some researchers have sought to point out that the existing building stock – or rather the restrictions placed on it by planning or landownership – has in fact been a causal factor itself in urban de-industrialization (Fothergill, Kitson and Monk 1985). Others have sought to place de-industrialization within a broader frame of reference. Here, explanation turns upon the longer-term consideration of organizational changes. First, in terms of the organization of the production process within firms – for example, the organization of the labour process or the factory layout. Second, in terms of the scale and operation of the firm, both through the nature of linkages and alliances with other firms and the spatial scale of operations – local, regional, national or transnational.

A particularly useful conceptualization of this organizational change is that broadly termed 'Regulation Theory' (see Dunford and Perrons 1983; Allen and Massey 1989; Lipietz 1992). A central idea is that of 'Fordism' which refers to a particular set of relationships linking a form of industrial organization and a form of state organization. The industrial organization comprises a Tayloristic labour process, i.e. one in which each job is broken down into small tasks. These are timed and measured, and an employee is allocated to completing one task. These various tasks are linked via the production line. There is a strict division between the 'thought work' of designers and managers, and the 'hand work' of the production line operatives. Efficient mass production of goods is the goal. The state organization comprises of a welfare state and arrangements for collective bargaining. The goal is mass consumption. The balance of mass consumption and mass production makes the system work.

It has been argued that the Fordist 'compromise' which produced such impressive growth in the post-war years broke down in the mid-1970s with underfunding of the welfare state and the end of collective wage bargaining. Underconsumption and falling profitability followed. Attempts were made by producers to lower wage costs by setting up branch plants (using state subsidies and exploiting lower wages in peripheral areas). In the late 1980s this strategy too was in disarray.

The emergence of mass production techniques and Tayloristic labour processes to make them work required new spaces and buildings. The old premises were clearly incompatible. Some of these were developed in towns and the largest examples were invariably on new sites. The emergent planning system, and central government's attempts to disperse industry, clearly assisted in this process. The peculiarity of these new buildings, perhaps, militated against anything but owner-occupation for the most. Private industrial estates were developed at Trafford Park (Manchester) in the 1890s, at Slough in the 1920s, and at various locations around London in the 1930s (see Pratt 1994). On these estates it was the smaller units that were rented; larger units were built by occupants. The state also emerged as a provider of industrial premises at the local and central scale from the 1930s onwards. It was not until the 1970s that industrial buildings emerged as an investment vehicle, beyond the interest of specialist developers.

Recently, the debate has highlighted the emergence of other solutions to the Fordist problem: post-Fordism and Flexible Accumulation. Post-Fordism is based upon batch, not mass, production. It is characterized by a social division of labour within a local economy or industrial district (as opposed to within a firm). Piore and Sabel (1984) argue that these new industrial districts bear a strong similarity to those identified in nineteenth century England by Alfred Marshall. Northern Italy and southern Germany are often cited as contemporary examples of these new industrial spaces. Other authors point to the emergence of 'high-tech' new industrial spaces in southern California, and near Boston (Scott 1988).

Harvey's (1987) work on Flexible Accumulation is relevant here. He refers to what he terms the 'switching crises' whereby investments are shifted from one industrial sector and/or location to another more profitable one in the pursuit of profits. We might highlight a particular example of this process; disinvestment in manufacturing stock and re-investment in property dealing. The obvious consequences that Harvey picks up on are the draining of investment from particular locations and sectors and the increasing competition between cities and regions for a dwindling pool of investors.

What is conspicuous by its absence from these contemporary debates is any concern with the industrial built environment (but see Pratt 1991). The assumption would seem to be that supply simply follows demand. However, this assumption does not hold. The contemporary discussion of industrial districts in Italy refers to 'collective' property (see Murray 1991: 48). There is evidence from the economic history of the English industrial districts that property was important. Those in Birmingham are perhaps the best documented (see Allen 1929; Wise 1945; Rogers 1983). Such research highlights the fact that the industrial district was based upon a distinct built environment, which depended upon the availability of rented accommodation, of buildings and parts of buildings.

The emergent built environment to accompany either post-Fordism or Flexible Accumulation is as yet still emerging; some authors point to high-tech industrial spaces and science parks. Perhaps the significant point to note here is the changing form of the provision of industrial property that is accompanying such a shift in production. Here we would agree with Harvey's observation concerning the increasing penetration of industrial production by financial institutions and investors. One theme of recent years in Britain has been the increasing involvement of both the state and financial institutions in the ownership and control of industrial property. To fully appreciate the dimensions of this change it is necessary to explore these arenas in more detail. We turn our attention first to the property sector.

RESTRUCTURING IN THE PROPERTY SECTOR

The key characteristic of the nature of commercial property provision in Britain – the dominance by large financial institutions – has its roots in the early 1970s. It should not be surprising that restructuring has been as significant for the organization and output of the property and financial sector as it has been to the manufacturing sector. Furthermore, as one of the growing sectors of the economy, it deserves attention in its own right. This restructuring has had significant implications for the manufacturing sector, primarily because a growing proportion of the prime industrial building stock is controlled by the financial institutions.

It is important to note that the independent commercial property developer did not really exist in any significant sense until after the Second World War. Commercial developers grew in prominence (and notoriety) through retail and office developments in the 1960s. Industrial property development had always played a very minor role in commercial property development. Perhaps the most significant period for property development has been the growth on investment interests, primarily from the large financial institutions. To understand this we need to consider the period after the 1973 property crash. What took place was effectively a 'mopping up' of the surplus commercial property on the market by the surviving developers and investors. The result was a large-scale takeover of the minor property companies that had survived the changes in corporate taxation in the mid-1960s. This time the main beneficiaries were not the larger property companies but the institutional investors (see Pratt 1993).

Cadman (1984: 77) estimates that by the early 1980s the pension funds and insurance companies controlled some 83 per cent of all property investment. To get some indication of the total property assets held, we should note that the institutions' assets grew two-fold between 1980–8 (CSO 1991a). However, over the same period corporate property sector assets grew three-fold (Debenham, Tewson and Chinnocks 1989: 11). This indicates that the latest property boom has led to the re-emergence of the property company. This expansion has been funded by a huge injection of bank lending to property companies which grew more than five-fold during the period 1981–8. Currently, outstanding loans surpass even those of the 1973–4 period (CSO 1991b). Over the same period the net annual investment by financial institutions has declined, especially that of pension funds. What little investment that did take place was solely in retailing.

Looking more closely at the institutions, one of the key characteristics is the concentration of power. A 1984 survey indicated that 59 per cent of pension schemes are managed by a small number of merchant and clearing banks (Greater London Council 1986: 29). With regard to the property holdings of the institutions, further concentration is evident. It is estimated that some 60–5 per cent of the institutional sector's UK property holdings are controlled by just thirty-seven of the larger institutional funds (each holding assets in excess of £1,000 million) (Debenham, Tewson and

Chinnocks 1989: 16). These larger funds currently dedicate on average 11–12 per cent of their investment portfolios by value into property (Debenham, Tewson and Chinnocks 1989: 16). It should be noted that this figure is both lower for the smaller funds and has been, on average, much higher in the past: for example, 30 per cent for the larger funds in 1981 (Debenham, Tewson and Chinnocks 1982: 11).

Of their property portfolio, on average some 10 per cent is currently dedicated to industrials, and this has fallen from 16 per cent in 1980. The influence of the institutions goes beyond the property held at any one time in a portfolio as the institutions like to 'turn over' their investments to maintain a balanced and up-to-date portfolio. Despite generally being considered to be a long-term investment, approximately 10 per cent of property is annually turned over compared with 45 per cent of gilts and 14 per cent of equities (Debenham, Tewson and Chinnocks 1989: 15). Interestingly, prior to 1980 less than 2 per cent of property was turned over by institutions, suggesting that property is becoming an increasingly volatile investment. Thus, not only is a substantial share of property directly developed and owned by institutions, but also an increasing proportion of all property is passing through institutional hands at one time or another.

The implications of this shift in the relationships and structure of industrial property development are three-fold. First, there is the concentration of this institutionally funded property in areas that are already experiencing economic growth. In effect this compounds the disadvantage of economically depressed localities. Second, the design of buildings is shifting towards standardized units (or 'sheds'). The logic here is that investors approve of the design, and that they can accommodate the greatest range of potential occupants thereby reducing the risk of a building lying empty. There is also a tendency to build units in groups as this provides comparable properties for valuation purposes. Standardization of design also reduces the risk of low valuation. Third, developers and investors are developing a significant percentage of 'high-tech properties' or science parks. There was some initial reluctance on the part of the financial institutions, borne out of conservativism, to enter such a new market. However, the advantages are that, for a given unit of floorspace, higher rentals can be demanded for high-tech property. As a consequence, greater financial returns flow from a given development. The significant question remains: do the interests of property developers and investors coincide with the needs of industrialists? As we point out elsewhere in this book, this important question is relatively underresearched.

CONCEPTUALIZING INDUSTRIAL PROPERTY

A fundamental problem for anyone concerned with industrial property is its definition or, more broadly, its conceptualization. The previous sections have highlighted recent shifts both in the nature of industrial property provision and its location and use. There are current tendencies for industrial property to become similar to, or interchangeable with, offices (see Chapters 5 and 9) or even houses and churches (see Chapter 8). At this level the point is that any built structure is capable of being used to accommodate economic activity. Some users are less demanding in their requirements and are thus able to utilize older premises, or those designed for other (or no specific) purpose, without too many problems. However, in some cases non-specific property can be a disadvantage, occasionally actually impeding production or innovation.

There is some value in developing the concept of industrial property; not simply as a taxonomic device, but as evidence of the resolution of particular social and economic relationships at a point in space and time. Such a conceptualization will encompass changes in the nature of the manufacturing (and property development) process and changes in the role of the state. This is a dynamic representation of the production process, the outcome of which is specific buildings, or groups of buildings, at specific places and times. The conventional 'factory' – purpose built, and its design closely related to a specific production process which is accommodated within it – is but one example of industrial property, one that is perhaps becoming less common in the UK.

The point is to highlight the different purposes of the definition of industrial property. This issue is addressed later in this book (see Chapter 3) in relation to information sources. So, for example, the Valuation Office's definition of industrial property for rating purposes will be different from that used by local planners for development control, and different again from definitions used by property developers to market their developments. Here we might refer to the list of names that have been attached to industrial estates: trading estates; business parks; and science parks. In short, the definitions tell us more about the definer, or purpose of definition, than the object that they define.

Various contributors to this book show how, in a practical sense, the social and economic relations of economic development and property development are constantly being renegotiated with respect to the redefinition of derelict and urban fringe land, and vacant property (see Chapters 4, 5 and 8), high-tech property (Chapters 5 and 6), intra-state and public–private agency relationships (Chapter 7), and leasehold and contractual arrangements (Chapter 9).

The increasing flexibility of industrial buildings and the changing uses that are made of them and the consequential 'slipperiness' of the concept itself pose particular problems for systematic research. This is particularly acute with respect to standardized information sources. Categories that might have been relevant at one time period are less so at another. The consequence is that attention needs to be focused on the dynamic nature of industrial property rather than as a static or idealized form. As we have pointed out above, the implications of flexibility by developers may be inflexibility for occupants. Detailed analyses of the existence or lack of restrictions for producers engaged in different production processes in a variety of buildings are clearly required. Furthermore, such issues have to be taken account of by policy makers, both in accommodating changes in the production process and in the provision of new or refurbished property. It is to the issue of the role of industrial buildings in industrial policy that we now turn.

INDUSTRIAL PROPERTY PROVISION AND ITS RELATIONSHIP WITH INDUSTRIAL, REGIONAL AND LOCAL POLICY

Direct intervention in the property market by the state has been practiced since the early part of this century. Intervention was clearly linked to the achievement of economic, sanitary and social goals. Not surprisingly, public housing provision has been the focus of considerable policy generation, evaluation and critique. In contrast, the public provision of industrial property has had a very low profile. We would argue that the structure of industrial property provision has relevance to the aims of regional policy; but these aims are based in social not industrial policy. As such, the provision of industrial premises by the state has been particularly problematic.

As with housing, intervention in the industrial property market can be related to the resolution of a form of market failure. In the case of industrial property the lack was in areas seeking to promote economic development. Local government has a long history of economic promotion since the 1920s (see Ward 1990). In some cases special powers were sought to develop land and buildings (Camina 1974). More general powers were made available to local authorities from 1963 onwards (Boddy 1983). Since then, particularly in the period 1970–85, district and former metropolitan, and in some cases county, authorities have been extensively involved in the activities of general economic promotion and the specific servicing of industrial land and the development of industrial buildings (see Sellgren 1989; Armstrong and Fildes 1989). The economic development activities of local authorities have been severely curtailed in the late 1980s and early

1990s through a combination of central government-imposed financial constraints and changed legislation (see Hayton 1990).

Central government has been involved in industrial property development since the dawn of regional policy in the mid-1930s. A characteristic activity was the development of Team Valley industrial estate in Tyne and Wear (see Loebl 1988). A key component of regional policy ever since has been the construction of advance factory units (see Slowe 1981). Urban policy, dating from 1978, has also included a component of industrial property provision and improvement (Fothergill *et al.* 1985). Likewise rural policy, through the agency of the Rural Development Commission (RDC), has been developing industrial buildings in significant numbers since the mid-1970s (see Minay 1985).

The point to note about the various forms of industrial property provision by both the local and central arms of the state has been the fact that they have fitted into what has primarily been social, and not economic or industrial, policy. The main objective has invariably been to reduce unemployment, the preferred policy being the relocation of existing or newly emerging employment (Pratt and Totterdill 1992). Unlike housing, where there was considerable concern with improving inadequate or dilapidated stock, industrial property provision has been to facilitate the relocation of firms. Industrial estates provide a good example of the inadequacy of such a policy for real economic development.

A key idea behind the development of industrial estates is that they will either propagate or facilitate production linkages between firms engaged in similar production processes (see Pratt 1994). Such benefits are normally referred to by economists as agglomeration economies. The development of industrial estates by practically every local authority in Britain has been primarily pursued as a social policy. Precious little attention has been paid to the industrial policy dimension that would imply filtering and selecting firms who might locate on industrial estates; ensuring that the property was suitable for the production processes involved; or providing a range of 'real services' (such as office and secretarial support, accountancy and book-keeping services, etc.).

Some commentators, apologists for such a 'property only' strategy, have claimed that property development, like all other infrastructure projects, creates jobs and promotes a positive image of the local area (see Turok 1992). While the job generation claim is indisputable, it is a rather limited and short-term conception of the real potential of industrial development. As for image, it may be claimed that a vacant new building is a better advert for an area than a vacant old building; the point is that it is still vacant and unused.

The failure to develop proper industrial policies – policies that address problems to do with the structure of particular sectors of industry and the workforce – and to link these with industrial property provision is a key problem. Such a policy agenda requires research, highlighted by the contributors to this book, into the exact nature of the relationship between the changing nature of the organization of manufacturing production, property provision and use. If the state is to intervene in this area agencies will have to be aware of these relationships.

A further distinction between industrial property and residential property is the structure of provision. Historically, the dominant form has been owner-occupation. In part, as Lizieri (Chapter 9) points out, this was due to the restrictions of the leasehold structure for industrial property prior to 1954. Since that date there has been a massive shift in tenure towards rented or leased accommodation (see Chapter 3). This has been fuelled in the prosperous regions by pension fund and insurance company investments, and in the depressed regions by local and central state provision. Of course, this is precisely the opposite trend to that in housing. A further contrast is in the provision; whereas housing is provided at a local scale, industrial property is provided by both local and central government.

This diverse public sector provision has led to a multiplication of agencies developing industrial property. Each policy programme area has its own providers. There have been recent attempts to merge agencies; for example, the merging of the activities of the RDC's factory building programme into that of English Estates (EE); followed, more recently, by the merging of the development of industrial buildings under the Urban Programme with that of EE's former concern in the new Urban Regeneration Agency. Although this rationalization has improved matters, there is still a lack of co-ordination and great potential for conflict, as Imrie and Thomas (Chapter 7) highlight, both within public sector agencies and between public and private agencies.

The motive force behind these policies and agencies has been the changing role of the state. A key aspect of this in the post-1979 period has been termed 'the rolling back of the state' (Thompson 1984). This attempt to withdraw as much state intervention as possible has inevitably given rise to changing relations of industrial property provision. The main criticism laid at the door of government agencies by the Right is that they might be 'crowding out' the private sector (see Bacon and Eltis 1978). The activities of EE were much scrutinized in the 1980s and it was pushed to operate along the lines of a private sector agency. Inevitably this meant focusing on the return on investment rather than specifically appropriate provision. Where areas of no private participation were identified (for example the provision of small industrial units) partnerships were proposed (see Coopers and Lybrand 1980).

What is clear then is the fact that industrial property provision has been primarily considered in the context of a social policy framework; simply as an assistance to relocation. As yet, policy makers have failed to grasp the relationship between economic development and property. It is suggested that this issue will only be addressed if property is considered within an industrial, not a social, policy framework. However, such a policy agenda is reliant upon a clarification of the relationship between industrial activity and industrial property. This activity–property interdependency forms the focus of the contributions to this book.

THE STRUCTURE OF THE BOOK

The eight chapters that comprise the main part of this book focus on a range of topical issues confronting practitioners and academics in the 1990s, from questions concerning the information base to those involving the processes of property development. In all cases, the aim is to draw out some of the practical research and policy issues. The intention is to provide a perspective on the scope of concerns that pioneering researchers in the field have identified. The hope is that this book will both form a basis for, and encourage, future research.

Chapters 2 and 3 focus on the problem of industrial property data information from private sector and from public sector perspectives. The important point is that the information sources, and the uses made of them, are different in both cases and have little overlap. Nick Axford evaluates the quality of the available industrial property data base, focusing in particular on the information requirements of the private sector. Various sources of information are reviewed and the quality prognosis on such data is used as the basis for a discussion of gaps in the information. In addition, and building on this critique, the chapter uses several sources of data to document recent trends in industrial property investment. In particular, it reviews major changes in the property market during the 1980s, commenting on the impact of the B1 use class and the development boom in business parks. The different components of the collapse of the property investment market in 1989 are analysed and the early stages of market recovery are discussed. Finally, in combining the basic arguments from earlier sections, the chapter suggests ways in which future research can help to generate information which is of value to both academics and practitioners who are concerned with the operation of the UK property market.

Andy Pratt looks in detail at the various components of the industrial property information base from the public sector perspective. His chapter considers the information needs and use of three public sector agencies:

central government, local planners and academics. It attempts to identify information that links industrial property and the economic activities that are carried out within it. The chapter stresses that the information collected by one agency may well not be suitable for the use of another. Moreover, it argues that information requirements are dynamic and changing; not simply in response to changing property use but also with respect to changing public sector policy goals and academic theoretical debates. While the public sector is identified as a very useful source of comprehensive data, the various funding cutbacks of the 1980s and 1990s are lamented as they are progressively destroying important data series. In some cases, private sector bodies are taking over such data collection. However, in these cases the information collected is being focused on more narrow market criteria.

The reclamation and re-use of derelict and contaminated sites is a major problem for planners and developers. Paul Syms looks at some of the practical issues in bringing land and existing buildings in such areas back into use. Elements of the case for giving priority to 'brownfield' sites over new development in 'greenfield' locations are established. However, the redevelopment of such sites is seen as far from straightforward, especially when funding issues are raised. Some of these matters are explored in the chapter, which argues that valuation surveyors tend to overvalue many derelict and contaminated sites. The chapter also discusses the development constraints of, and options for, contaminated sites, concluding with a plea for more research on methods of reclamation and suitable future uses of those sites and on the social and economic issues attached to such reclamation and redevelopment.

In essence, Syms relates the problems confronting the productive re-generation of 'brownfield' sites to the constraints that ensue, setting this needs–constraints position into the context of recent environmental legislation and thinking through the implications for conventional public funding sources. The conclusion is that there is a tension between environmental legislation and the drive to forge new productive activity on such 'brownfield' sites in Britain's urban areas. The hesitancy of lending institutions, coupled with the limited existence (Chapter 8) or modest coverage of centrally-financed urban aid programmes, leads Syms to the conclusion that there is a need for the central state to really investigate ways in which it might encourage re-use by swinging the balance in favour of 'brownfield' development. Of course, the patent unattractiveness of such locations for the private development industry renders that a challenge of gigantic proportions.

Dick Pratt discusses the process whereby new land uses are generated for land in 'city fringe' locations. He argues for the necessity of a well-theorized approach to this problem that accounts for the changing relations of the state and capital. Pratt suggests that long before the changes to the

Use Classes Order of 1986, new land uses – business parks, high-tech offices, science park offices/laboratories and inner city 'studio offices' – had begun to appear. A market for such uses had not, however, been strongly established and institutional investors were deterred by high yields in all except highly favoured areas of the south east. The new B1 use class may have come to the assistance of developers. The recession has blighted the possibility of a recommodification of inner city land with negative value in the immediate future. However, some patterns have already been established which would facilitate the recommodification of the 'city fringe'. In some areas of under-utilization this will be welcome. In other areas of established industrial communities, existing land uses will be threatened. This chapter critically explores the prospects of establishing a new land use in areas of struggling industrial communities. The Birmingham Jewellery Quarter provides the case study setting.

John Henneberry looks at the relationships between the character and development of property and manufacturing activity. Initially, he focuses on the general importance of property in the performance of manufacturing firms, reviewing different ways of conceptualizing firm–property relationships: industry-based; behaviouralist; and life-cycle perspectives. Consideration is then given to the characteristics of high technology firms which distinguish them from 'conventional' firms. The implications for the former's property-using behaviour are then described and empirical evidence is reviewed before conclusions are drawn concerning the impact of high technology firms on the property market.

The property supply industry's response to the growing property requirements of high technology firms is shown to have been inadequate. The perceived changes in demand were used as a lever to relax control over the supply industry. The outcome – the introduction of the business use class (B1) in 1987 – benefited property developers and investors and was detrimental to manufacturing firms generally and high technology firms in particular. The strength of supply-side influence on the behaviour of the property market raises significant issues for economic and land use policy makers. These are discussed in the conclusion to the chapter.

Rob Imrie and Huw Thomas focus on the changing public–private background to property-led urban regeneration. They suggest that the actors and agencies involved in contemporary property development are forging new organizational and procedural associations with a re-orientation of interests, strategies, working methods and relationships underpinned and characterized by new forms of public–private coalition. Focusing particularly on Cardiff's dockland, the authors trace the 'dynamic flux in contemporary property development' and the changing character of the property development industry, together with newly-emerging forms of local state–private sector alliance and interaction. The chapter is rich in the exemplification of important issues such as 'coalitions of interest', inter-authority conflicts, and the two-way dependency of the 'public' and the 'private' in local industrial property development.

Perhaps the most notable legacy of Britain's de-industrialization over the 1970s and 1980s was the problem of the abandonment of much of the older industrial space and the emergent problem of vacant industrial premises. Not only has the problem been a major burden on the development prospects of many 'old industrial areas', but it has also affected the institutional investment scene. Rick Ball charts this problem in the late 1980s using Stoke-on-Trent's Potteries as the area of focus. The chapter draws on some recent survey work conducted in this classic 'old industrial area' in order to chart the nature of industrial property dynamics. It uses the notion that some key market trends can be documented by focusing on variations in the level and nature of vacant industrial premises at several points in time. The analysis covers not only standard, conventional industrial buildings but also the more marginal premises that tend to be drawn into the inventory of local industrial property and to be used as a base for production activities in mature industrial places.

In addition to the detailed documentation of local market trends, the chapter analyses the three major components of industrial property market change – reoccupations, persistent vacancies and redevelopments – occurring over time. These are assessed on two spatial scales: first, from an aggregate locality perspective, and second, by documenting and evaluating the micro-geography of vacant industrial premises dynamics. As with all the other chapters, Ball considers the policy implications of the survey findings – in the general sense and in terms of variations in local industrial property problems within the locality. These are related to the actual policy initiatives developed and pursued by the local authority in the area.

Another important contemporary property issue concerns the lack of attention given to the detailed mechanics of property markets. This apparent research gap is tackled by Colin Lizieri. As noted at the beginning of the chapter, considerable economic and technical change has impacted commercial property markets since the mid-1970s. Amongst the forces of change that affect the patterns of ownership and leasehold are the restructuring of economic activity on a global scale, changing technical conditions of production, the internationalization of property markets and changes in the nature of financing and investment. These would be expected to result in the development of more flexible arrangements in occupational and investment markets. However, the process of adjustment in the UK appears to be hampered by institutional arrangements in the UK market – in particular the presentation of the standard institutional lease with its contractual basis and restrictive covenants. This chapter, drawing on recent research into leasehold forms, suggests that innate, institutional conservatism and valuation/legal practice act as an inertial force hindering the development of flexibility and the implementation of industrial policy.

CONCLUSION

The role of property in economic development and policy is an important one. We have highlighted the significance of placing the consideration of property into the wider context of economic restructuring for both the industries occupying property and the producers of that property. In so doing we have stressed the potential for conflict between the needs of the users and those of the providers of industrial property. This conflict has potential strategic importance; hence, it is worthy of urgent consideration by planners and policy makers. However, it is clear that the relationship between the users and providers of industrial property is a dynamic one and that, as yet, we have only sketchy outlines of both the processes and the issues involved. Our aim in this book is to highlight a research need and to promote that research. Appropriately, we turn in the following two chapters to a consideration of the information base and the research context.

NOTES

1 The Society of Property Researchers can be contacted through Ms Fiona Trott, St Mary's, Gandish Road, East Bergholt, Suffolk CO7 6UR.
2 The Economic Geography Study Group of the Institute of British Geographers can be contacted through the honorary secretary, Dr David Sadler, Department of Geography, University of Durham, Science Laboratories, South Road, Durham DH1 3LE.
3 The proceedings and details of the annual meetings of BISS are available from BISS, Bartlett School of Architecture and Planning, University College London, 22 Gordon Street, London WC1H 0QB.

REFERENCES

Allen, G. (1929) *The Industrial Development of Birmingham and the Black Country, 1860–1927*, London: George Allen & Unwin.
Allen, J. and Massey, D. (eds) (1989) *The Economy in Question*, London: Sage.
Armstrong, H. and Fildes, S. (1989) 'Industrial development initiatives in England and Wales: the role of the district councils', *Progress in Planning* 30(2): 91–156.
Bacon, R. and Eltis, W. (1978) *Britain's Economic Problem: Too Few Producers*, 2nd edn, London: Macmillan.
Ball, M. (1988) *Rebuilding Construction*, London: Routledge.
Blackaby, F. (ed.) (1981) *Deindustrialisation*, London: Heinemann.
Boddy, M. (1983) 'Changing public–private sector relationships in the industrial

development process', in K. Young and C. Mason (eds) *Urban Economic Development*, London: Macmillan.

Cadman, D. (1984) 'Property finance in the UK in the post-war period', *Land Development Studies* 1(1): 61–82.

—— and Austin-Crowe, L. (1983) *Property Development*, 2nd edn, London: Spon.

Camina, M. (1974) 'Local authorities and the attraction of industry', *Progress in Planning* 3(2): 83–182.

Coopers and Lybrand Associates/Drivers Jonas Associates (1980) *Provision of Small Industrial Premises*, London: Department of Industry.

CSO (1991a) *Business Monitor MQ5: Insurance companies' and pension funds' investments*, Third Quarter, Tables 4 and 17, London: HMSO.

—— (1991b) *Financial Statistics*, May, London: HMSO.

Darlow, C. (ed.) (1982) *Valuation and Development Appraisal*, London: Estates Gazette.

Debenham, Tewson and Chinnocks (1982) *Money into Property 1970–1982*, London: Debenham, Tewson and Chinnocks.

—— (1989) *Money into Property*, London: Debenham, Tewson and Chinnocks.

Dunford, M. and Perrons, D. (1983) *The Arena of Capital*, London: Macmillan.

Fothergill, S., Kitson, M. and Monk, S. (1985) *Urban Industrial Change*, Inner Cities Research Programme, Report No. 11, London: Department of the Environment.

——, Monk, S. and Perry, M. (1987) *Property and Industrial Development*, London: Hutchinson.

Greater London Council (1986) *The London Financial Strategy*, London: Greater London Council.

Harvey, D. (1987) 'Flexible accumulation through urbanism: reflections on "post-modernism" in the American city', *Antipode*, 19: 260–86.

—— (1989) *The Urban Experience,* Oxford: Blackwell.

Hayton, K. (1990) 'The future of local economic development', *Regional Studies* 23: 549–57.

Healey, P. and Nabarro, R. (eds) (1990) *Land and Property Development: a Changing Context*, Aldershot: Gower.

——, Usher, D., Davoudi, S., Tavsanoglu, S. and O'Toole, M. (1992) *Rebuilding the City: Property-Led Urban Regeneration*, London: Spon.

Lipietz, A. (1992) *Towards a New Economic Order,* Cambridge: Polity.

Loebl, H. (1988) *Government Factories and the Origins of British Regional Policy, 1934–48*, Aldershot: Avebury.

Martin, R. and Rowthorn, B. (eds) (1986) *The Geography of Deindustrialisation*, London: Macmillan.

Minay, C. (1985) 'The Development Commission's Rural Industrial Development Programme', Working Paper No. 87, Oxford: Department of Town Planning, Oxford Polytechnic.

Morley, S., Marsh, C., McIntosh, A. and Martinos, H. (1989) *Industrial Land and Business Space Development*, London: Spon.

Murray, R. (1991) *Local Space: Europe and the New Regionalism*, Manchester and London: CLES/SEEDS.

Piore, M. and Sabel, C. (1984) *The Second Industrial Divide*, New York: Basic Books.

Pratt, A.C. (1991) 'Industrial districts and the flexible local economy', *Planning Practice and Research* 6(1): 4–8.

Pratt, A.C. (1993) 'Property, finance and industrial location', in E. Schamp, and C. Rogerson, (eds) *Finance, Markets and Industrial Change*, Berlin: Walter de Gruyter.
—— (1994) *Uneven Reproduction: industry, space and society*, Oxford: Pergamon.
—— and Totterdill, P. (1992) 'Industrial policy in a period of organisational and institutional change: the case of inward investment and the electronics sector', *Environment and Planning C: Government and Policy*, 10: 375–85.
Radcliffe, J. (1978) *An Introduction to Urban Land Administration*, London: Estates Gazette.
Rogers, N. (1983) 'Industrial decline, restructuring and relocation: Aston and the Great Victorian depression', in J. Anderson, S. Duncan and R. Hudson (eds) *Redundant Spaces in Cities and Regions?*, London: Academic Press.
Rose, J. (1985) *The Dynamics of Urban Property Development*, London: Spon.
Scarrett, D. (1983) *Property Management*, London: Spon.
Scott, A. (1988) *New Industrial Spaces*, London: Pion.
Sellgren, J.M. (1989) 'Assisting local economies: an assessment of emerging patterns of local authority economic development initiatives', in D. Gibbs (ed.) *Government Policy and Industrial Change*, London: Routledge.
Slowe, P. (1981) *The Advance Factory in Regional Development*, Aldershot: Gower.
Thompson, G. (1984) '"Rolling back" the state?: economic intervention 1975–82', in G. McLennan, D. Held and S. Hall (eds) *State and Society in Contemporary Britain*, Cambridge: Polity.
Turok, I. (1992) 'Property led regeneration: panacea or placebo?', *Environment and Planning, A* 24: 361–79.
Ward, S. (1990) 'Local industrial promotion and development policies, 1899–1940', *Local Economy* 5(2): 100–18.
Wise, M. (1945) 'On the evolution of the jewellery and gun quarters in Birmingham', *Transactions of the Institute of British Geographers* 15: 57–72.
Wood, B. and Williams, R. (eds) (1992) *Industrial Property Markets in Western Europe*, London: Spon.

2 Documenting recent trends in industrial property investment
The information requirements of the private sector from a practitioner perspective

Nick Axford

INTRODUCTION

This chapter considers two issues which are central to analysis of the UK industrial property market: the information base which exists to inform such analysis; and the fundamental principles which govern the way in which the market operates. These issues are viewed from the perspective of practitioners, a perspective which is in fact somewhat distorted. Although not exclusively so, much practitioner activity relates to the higher quality properties which make up the investment market representing around 20 per cent by value of the total property stock (Crosby 1988). The remainder of the market is of interest, but it is investment property which has come to dominate the consumption, and therefore the provision, of property market information. This is not least because it is in the investment market that the level of provision of new floorspace is determined. Property development, on the whole, takes place only when there is bank finance available and evidence of investor willingness to purchase a newly-completed building. Investors, in turn, will only purchase properties when they are confident that sufficient occupier demand exists. Information concerning the supply and demand characteristics of the market is therefore required on a regular basis, and has particularly high commercial value.

The second section examines the information sources currently used to monitor trends in the investment market, commenting upon the utility (and problems) of each. The chapter then moves on to consider the changes which have taken place in the industrial property market since the mid-1980s; the transition from boom to recession exemplifies the need for better quality information to facilitate a more detailed understanding of the inter-action between industrial property investment and the wider economy. The concluding section draws together the various arguments advanced and suggests ways in which future research may generate information which will be of value to both academics and practitioners. Initially, however, it may be helpful to examine some of the fundamental characteristics of the market and those who invest in it.

THE INDUSTRIAL PROPERTY MARKET

The principal investors in the property market are the property companies and institutions such as pension funds, insurance and life assurance companies. They view property not just as a factor of production, but as an investment medium. The criteria which they use to analyse the property market reflect their desire to compare the investment value of property with that of the alternative forms of investment which are available to them, principally government stock (gilts) and company shares (equities). The principal measure of comparison between these media is known as the yield, a measure of the rate of return given by an investment on the capital expended in purchasing it.

The simplest form is the initial yield, calculated by dividing the annual income from an investment by its purchase price. Thus, an investment which generates an income of £1,000 per annum and which cost £10,000 to buy gives an annual rate of return of 0.1, a yield of 10 per cent. This process is also used to value investments; the inverse of the required yield, when multiplied by the annual income, gives the purchase price at which that annual income represents the desired rate of return. Thus an investor who requires a return of 20 per cent per annum would only be prepared to pay £5,000 to purchase the investment in the example above. The yield incorporates a number of considerations as to the quality and likely future performance of an investment, and particularly the level of risk associated with its purchase. The greater the degree of risk involved, the more rapidly the investor will wish to recoup the initial outlay and the greater the 'risk premium' (additional return) required. Because of the way in which investments are valued, raising the yield to reflect additional risk has the effect of reducing the purchase price of the investment, so a perception of increased risk in the market as a whole will reduce capital values across the board.

These basic principles are reflected in the yields associated with different investment media. Gilts (fixed-interest government stock) are attractive to investors because they offer a high degree of security, regular income and are a 'liquid' (easily traded) investment medium. But they offer no long-term prospect of capital appreciation and the value of their income is constant over time. The yield which they attract (around 9 per cent on long-dated issues in early 1993) reflects this combination of low risk and no income growth, and provides the benchmark against which yields on other investments are determined. The extent to which any investment yield falls below the average gilt yield may be taken to represent the income growth which the investment is expected to see in the future.

The attraction of equities (shares in companies) is that the income which they generate by way of dividends may increase over time. When a company is expected to improve its performance in the future, the initial yield required by investors will be lowered to reflect this growth potential, which has the effect of raising the value of shares in the company. Income from equities was about 5 per cent at the start of 1993 and is typically 4 or 5 per cent below the level of gilt yields, but this relationship is clearly not cast in stone.

The third major form of institutional investment is in direct property. The high costs of transfer of ownership (compared with equities or gilts), the indivisibility and illiquidity of the unit of investment (i.e. buildings) and the high level of capital expenditure required to purchase such investments mean that property is generally regarded as a long-term investment. While variation in income (changes in rents) are possible, the historic expectation has been that rents and capital values will rise over time due to economic growth. Indeed, such has been the dominance of the major investors over the provision of new property that the terms on which they are let to tenants are designed to protect the interests of such investors. The institutional lease includes clauses which provide for, amongst other things, upward-only rent reviews. This means that when the rent is reviewed (usually every five years in current leases) it will not decrease, thereby ensuring a minimum income for the investor who owns the building. These lease terms were developed during the 1960s when rental growth was assumed to be inevitable and tenants did not then object to them. However, they have been the subject of much controversy since the late 1980s because rents achievable on a new letting have fallen rapidly in many areas, with the consequence that occupiers locked into an institutional lease have been forced to pay rents well above current market levels.

The attractions of rental growth mean that average property yields have in the past been below those on gilts, but above those on equities because of the disadvantages of property as an investment medium. However, the 1980s saw gradual changes in this pattern, with a general convergence of gilt and property yields due to growing awareness that rental growth is far from inevitable. As the property market has declined since 1989 prospects of rental growth have become more remote, with the result that by the end of 1992 average property yields were 0.5 per cent above gilt yields. This makes property exceptionally cheap in historic terms, but reflects the fact that investors are currently taking a very pessimistic view of the prospects for rental growth.

Looking at the property market in more detail, it is important to note that rents and yields vary widely across the UK and between different classes of property. Figures from the Investors' Chronicle Hillier Parker ICHP *Average Yields* for November 1992 reveal that the all property average

Table 2.1 Average property yields by sector and region, November 1992

Region	Retail (%)	Office (%)	Industrial (%)
Average	7.4	9.3	10.3
Central London	6.2	7.7	–
Greater London	9.0	9.5	9.4
South east	6.6	9.4	9.2
South west	6.5	9.8	9.9
East Anglia	6.6	9.9	9.8
East Midlands	6.9	10.1	9.7
West Midlands	6.5	9.7	10.1
North west	7.0	10.9	10.5
Yorks and Humberside	7.1	10.4	10.5
North	7.4	10.9	10.9
Scotland	7.4	8.3	11.4
Wales	7.9	11.3	10.5

Source: ICHP 1992

yield is 9.2 per cent. This incorporates the three main sector averages of 9.3 per cent for offices, 7.4 per cent for shops and 10.3 per cent on industrials. As Table 2.1 shows, there is further variation between the averages for these sectors in different regions.

This leads to the question of what factors are responsible for this variation. As has been discussed, the value of a property is a function of the annual income stream which it generates (in the form of rent) and the yield (which incorporates investor assessment of future prospects for rental growth). Variation in the yield on property investments is therefore principally the result of differential perceptions of past and future rental performance. Investors generally look for buildings and towns with a history of strong rental growth, although outperformance (above average growth) may not result in low yields if, for some reason, the trend is unlikely to continue.

But what is it that determines rental growth? In fundamental terms, rent on a property reflects straightforward supply and demand. However, the need for property is a derived demand, in that it arises as a by-product of the operation of the wider economy. Many different factors must be taken into account before the future demand for property may be assessed. It is generally true that a new property in good condition and built to modern specifications tends to be the most attractive to a potential occupier and thus is the most likely to see rental growth. Such property is also generally easier to re-let or sell, satisfying investors' requirements in this respect. Location is also important; an industrial property located next to a motorway junction or intersection is always likely to be in demand and property in south-east England has traditionally been favoured by the institutions because rents have risen faster in this region due to the greater robustness of its economy.

However, the location and quality of a property are not the only considerations for an investor. The recession of the early 1990s placed new importance on tenant quality (or covenant) in determining the yield on a property investment. A good building which is empty because the tenant has gone out of business does not generate any income. All these factors, and many more, must be taken into account by an investor when considering whether to invest in the property sector at all and, if so, which buildings to purchase. Investors, property developers and their professional advisors therefore require a wide range of information relating to current and likely future supplies of particular classes of floorspace; trends in the local, regional, national and even international economy which might influence current and future demand; and likely future occupier requirements, to avoid investing in a building which may become obsolete due to trends in production technology, for example. The process of bringing together all these pieces of information is a complex one, particularly where the investment involves the provision of funding for a new building in anticipation of future occupier demand. By virtue of the nature of the product, there is a long lead time involved in a new property development. The problems involved in assessing levels of demand some years into the future are considerable, particularly bearing in mind that a new property is expected to have an investment life in excess of twenty years. As a result, there is potential for considerable mismatch between property supply and demand.

The above discussion, while perhaps slightly peripheral to the main themes of this chapter, is crucial to the following discussion of the information sources used to analyse the property market and the ensuing appraisal of the performance of the industrial market over the last decade.

THE PROPERTY INFORMATION BASE

In this section, the major sources of information relating to various aspects of the industrial property market are reviewed. The intention is not to be unduly negative, but given that the focus of this publication is upon improving our understanding and our information base, it is inevitable that greater emphasis will tend to be placed upon those areas where deficiencies are apparent and further research is required.

Given the discussion above it is hardly surprising that, although it represents a relatively small proportion of the total stock of property, it is the needs of the investment market which have tended to dominate the provision of information concerning industrial property. What is surprising is that the property industry has for so long relied upon information sources which fall far short of what is required. It is only comparatively recently that specialists have entered this field in an attempt to improve upon existing data sources. As a result, a wide variety of types of information are used and these are reviewed below.

Press surveys

As in any profession, there are a substantial number of publications which deal specifically with the property market; the best known are the *Estates Gazette, Estates Times* and *Chartered Surveyor Weekly*. The quality daily papers also contribute to the body of this literature, carrying weekly commercial property sections, and many local areas have their own property publications (for example, *Property News* which covers the south west and south Wales). These all serve a variety of purposes, informing professionals of current property news and issues of general interest. However, they are also important vehicles for the circulation of analysis and comment relating to the market as a whole, to particular sectors or to specific regions.

Such surveys play an important role in helping property professionals to keep abreast of changes in the market. The difficulty is that very little of the information which they contain is entirely objective. Articles are submitted by those who have a particular interest in the topic or area. Thus in a survey of a city, the local economic development officer may provide an overview of recent economic growth and excellent future prospects, while the agents responsible for marketing the new industrial park will comment on the revival of manufacturing activity in the area! This process of 'talking up the market' is widespread and it is the job of the researcher to determine the reality which lies behind the claims made. However, it should be recognized that the property press does exert an influence over general perceptions within the market; an area that receives 'a good press' is likely to benefit as a result, due not simply to agents' extravagant claims but because attention is directed towards the location.

A further problem is that even where press articles offer genuinely objective assessment, they usually lack the detail required for research purposes. Furthermore, no standard areas of analysis or measures of market change and performance are used and information given is often difficult to check at source and thus problematic for the purposes of any secondary analysis.

Research by industrial agents and surveyors

Many commercial property organizations publish information concerning the property market, generally as a marketing tool. Examples include the King Sturge and Co. *Industrial Floorspace Survey* (giving details of industrial floorspace availability in different regions); the Hillier Parker, Richard Ellis, Healey & Baker and Jones Lang Wootton rental indices (which depict trends in rental values across the UK); and the Investors' Chronicle Hillier Parker (ICHP) *Yield Indices* (which give estimates of current yields in different regions and sectors of the market).

These data sets are of great value in providing specific information to the property industry and, if interpreted correctly, they can provide an excellent insight into various dimensions of change in the market. However, as a group they do suffer from a number of problems.

The UK data sets give average figures, usually only to a regional level of disaggregation, and thus they may conceal potentially important trends at the local level. More problematically, the exceptional performance of one particular area may significantly distort the regional picture.

The various measures available which appear to represent the same thing are in fact produced in very different ways, using different methods of assessment, different sample sizes and a variety of valuation methods. While some are based on analysis of actual transactions, others are based upon agents' assessments of current value. Information on transactions may be particularly difficult to obtain and may be flawed. Confidentiality clauses applied to property deals and new lettings prevent details being released to the market and 'headline' rents quoted will often conceal letting incentives (which may dramatically reduce the 'effective' level of rent being paid). A detailed understanding of the method of composition of a particular data set is therefore necessary before it can be used and many would be regarded as entirely inappropriate for use in academic research.

When only one organization produces a particular type of information, it is difficult to authenticate and check the validity of the data. Where more than one organization produces similar information, there is often a discrepancy between the figures produced which, for the reasons outlined above, it can be problematic for the consumer to understand.

Many agents also produce local market information: for example Chestertons (local *Business Space Briefs*); King Sturge and Co. (*Southern Hampshire Property Market Report*); and Drivers Jonas (East Anglia data of various types). But again it is difficult to make best use of such data, despite much of it being excellent quality and reflecting specialist local knowledge. This is because it is not available in the same format for all areas; agents produce reports for locations with which they are familiar and so spatial coverage is incomplete. Reports by the same agent on different areas may not be produced using standard definitions and those on the same location by different agents will almost certainly vary widely in methodology and findings.

When these various problems are taken together, they present a considerable barrier to analysis. For example, the task of assessing available industrial floorspace and property values in Portsmouth and Southampton is not as straightforward as it might seem. Most published sources deal with regional rather than sub-regional data. Various agents produce commentaries on the local markets involved, but use different definitions. Should business parks outside the city boundary be included in its floorspace figures? How are office buildings distinguished from industrial properties on the same business park? Does the data relate to net useable area or gross floorspace? How has value been determined? What accounts for variation between surveys taken at different dates – change in the market or differences in methodology? The problems involved in simply assembling a comprehensive and reliable data set using such information are substantial.

The difficulty, of course, is that few commercial organizations are willing to disclose valuable information freely to their competitors. Indices, analyses and commentaries are published in summary form for marketing purposes, to indicate the expertise of the organization in a particular field. Detailed information remains confidential to the producers and their clients, and inaccessible to the market as a whole. Those who possess the data actually have a vested interest in maintaining the current imperfections and inconsistencies.

Commercial data bases and information organizations

In recognition of the difficulties associated with the above data sources, the growing desire of the market for higher quality information to inform decision-making has led to the emergence of a number of organizations which produce property-related data of different types. These may specialize in particular types of information (such as property performance) or they may produce data on a range of topics for particular areas or locations.

Examples of the latter are Property Market Analysis (PMA) and Property Intelligence, both of which offer a broad range of economic, demographic and property-specific data on particular towns and cities. A major drawback of such services is that comprehensive coverage is achieved at the expense of information quality and detail, and information is not always up to date.

The leading source of information on property market performance is the Investment Property Databank (IPD). By the end of 1992 it contained details of the property holdings of over 150 of the largest funds with a total value of approximately £43 billion and representing over 50 per cent of the total investment market. The function of IPD is to provide a portfolio analysis service to individual institutions, but they also generate aggregate data showing changes in property value since 1980 in different areas and sectors down to town level. However, the data relates only to investment properties. IPD contains more high yielding (lower quality) property than might be expected (Knight Frank & Rutley 1990), but accounts for less than 2 per cent of total UK property stock, and is inevitably biased towards the quality end of the market. Furthermore, the distribution of IPD property reflects the tendency for institutions to concentrate their investments within south east England. Coverage of centres outside this region is less comprehensive, particularly in the industrial sector where small sample sizes preclude publication of data for many sizeable towns and cities. A further drawback from the researcher's point of view is that IPD data is expensive to purchase, making it unsuitable for much *ad hoc* or low budget research.

However, the major advantage of these sources is that they are broadly standardized across space, so even if they contain inaccurate data at least information can be obtained at a uniform level of inaccuracy across the country! A further positive feature is that primary data generated by specialist organizations tends to be less prone to errors than the information produced by other sources.

Local authorities

The information produced by local authorities exhibits considerable variation in both quality and quantity. Authorities are gradually becoming more aware of the need to generate accurate information, both for their own purposes and for external consumption. At present, some produce an excellent range of information of high quality and reliability. At its best, data of this type exhibits a detailed local knowledge which few other sources can match. However, local authority data is possibly more problematic than any other when attempting to identify spatial patterns which extend beyond administrative boundaries. Comparisons between authorities are impossible in many cases because of variation in methods of data collection, analysis and presentation.

Local authorities as a group produce information on a variety of topics including the local economy, demographics, existing commercial and industrial business space, site and property availability, and planning policy. In recent years many authorities have also begun to produce business directories, although the information contained within these may be incomplete or of questionable accuracy.

However, very few authorities make effective use of the vast information store that they have available to them in the form of planning and rating records. Local authorities have often collected information over a very long period, which is important in itself. Most researchers encounter difficulty not only in obtaining reliable data, but also in obtaining a time-series of sufficient length to enable statistical analysis to be undertaken. Yet authorities do not (or for reasons of confidentiality cannot) make this information easily available and it is often difficult to discover precisely what information is held. Local authority floorspace data is particularly problematic in this respect, precisely due to the issue of confidentiality. On other occasions, however, the problem is that authorities do not recognize the commercial value of the information which they hold. As a result, it is not 'packaged' for general distribution – a lost opportunity and wasteful of time and resources for both public and private sectors.

Central government

The Central Statistical Office (CSO) and other government departments produce a variety of information indirectly related to the property market, such as the annual *Inland Revenue Statistics* and the *Census of Production*. But overall, central government generates virtually no information relating to property and, within that which is produced, major gaps and problems exist. The *Census of Production* provides no information on the service sector and no equivalent data for the service industries is produced. The decisions to end publication of the *Retail Floorspace Statistics* in 1972 and the *Commercial and Industrial Floorspace Statistics* (CIFS) in 1985 resulted in the loss of major data series. There is also considerable variation in the format in which government information generally is made available. Some is published in relation to local authority administrative areas, some for local health authority areas, some for travel-to-work areas (TTWAs), while much is only available publicly at regional or national levels. Again, confidentiality restrictions and the cost of providing detailed local information are major problems.

The fundamental issue is that the government does not give sufficient priority to the routine collection of such information and that which does get collected is not always accessible to researchers. This is not peculiar to the property industry. Better access to government statistics would be welcomed by researchers in most fields. For the property market, the opening up of the land registry provides a welcome source of data on land ownership, even if it is not particularly 'user friendly'. In general the CSO appears to be adopting a more commercial approach to the provision of information. This may lead to an improvement in their service and a wider range of information being made available, but only to those who are able to pay for it. The end result will mirror the situation in the private sector, where a premium is placed not on ability to use information but on simply obtaining reliable data in the first place.

Concerns have also surfaced in recent years over the quality of some central government information. The best example of this is the CSO quarterly analysis of pension fund property investments. It had previously been scrutinized in some detail by market analysts, yet it was withdrawn for over a year when it became apparent that there were major inaccuracies in the data. This series has now been restored, in a substantially revised form, but with the loss of much of the time-series and previous consumer confidence.

In view of the problems in obtaining reliable information about property, it is not surprising that the recent history of the property market illustrates some significant deficiencies in judgement and decision-making.

RECENT TRENDS IN INDUSTRIAL PROPERTY INVESTMENT

There have been a number of major changes in the UK property market since 1980, with the 'boom and bust' cycle typical of the industry strongly evident. Following the recession of the late 1970s, the market as a whole picked up gradually in the early 1980s before the start of the developer-led boom in 1986–7. The rate of growth in property rents peaked in early 1989, but had fallen away substantially by the start of 1990. Since then, the property market as a whole has remained depressed, the lack of activity accentuated by national economic recession. During the last five years, a number of trends have been particularly apparent within the industrial sector.

The 1987 Use Classes Order introduced the B1 class (removing the planning distinction between office and light industrial properties) which aimed to promote the development of buildings and business parks which could combine a variety of different manufacturing and office uses without the need for planning permission for change of use. The motivation for this was a perception that 'high-tech' or 'sunrise' industries required properties which combined office, research and production facilities under one roof, or at least were adjacent to each other. From an investor point of view such properties offered the advantage that, being appropriate for use by a variety of different types of tenant, they were attractive to a much wider range of potential occupiers. The practical consequence was that a substantial amount of land scheduled for industrial use was developed for purely office functions, because rental values on office space (particularly in the south east) were substantially higher than those for industrial properties. As a result, offices came to dominate many areas traditionally regarded as manufacturing locations, most often at out-of-town sites with good accessibility, for example around Heathrow and Bristol.

Many of these supposedly 'mixed use' parks successfully precluded the development of any non-office space. Genuine high-tech occupiers had to resort to substantial fitting out of speculative developments, or had suitable accommodation purpose-built, both at considerable expense. The result was an undersupply of traditional manufacturing 'sheds' in many areas, which forced up rents (and thus manufacturing overheads).

But in the autumn of 1989, there was a sudden dramatic decline in the level of activity in the property market. The rate of growth in the economy had fallen off and interest rates reached 15 per cent, leading to a sharp reduction in demand for new industrial space. Since that time, out-of-town B1 land prices have fallen by 40 per cent or more in most areas and premiums for leases have been replaced by rent-free periods and a host of other letting incentives. This in itself has substantial implications for many landowners who had hoped to sell off large quantities of secondary quality but (previously) high value B1 land for business park development. Landowners who might be most affected include numerous public bodies such as local authorities, health authorities, the Ministry of Defence and British Rail.

Some investors who purchased high-tech B1 buildings made substantial windfall profits as rental values rose due to their conversion to office usage. However, many more developers paid office prices for industrial sites which proved unattractive to occupiers or which they were unable to develop before the collapse of the market. Many were located in areas which are demographically unsuited to office development due to the lack of a suitable labour force and they have proved difficult or impossible to let. The situation continued to deteriorate through 1991 and into 1992 as developments started during the latter stages of the boom continued to emerge from the pipeline. It is entirely possible that many of the developments undertaken at that time will not be let for several years and even then only at rents well below prime levels as they are superseded by newer properties built to higher specifications.

It should be noted that in many areas, particularly outside the south east, an apparent oversupply of property conceals a genuine shortage of quality new industrial floorspace and there is a significant geographical component within this pattern. Industrial floorspace figures from King Sturge & Co (1992) show that the amount of available space in England and Wales has now been increasing for nearly four years, with significant variation between regions. Figure 2.1 plots the results of a shift–share analysis carried out on this data, indicating the level of vacancy within different types of industrial property relative to that which would be expected if total vacancy were distributed across the regions in proportion to their share of

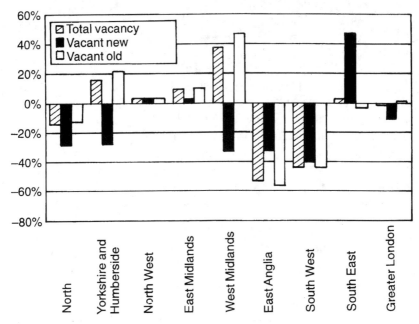

Figure 2.1 Industrial floorspace shift–share analysis: vacancy relative to regional expectation
Sources: Gerald Eve (1993), King Sturge & Co. (1992) and Inland Revenue (1992)

national industrial stock (Gerald Eve 1993). This reveals the legacy of the development boom in the south east, where the amount of vacant new floorspace is particularly high relative to total stock, while the supply picture is healthiest in East Anglia and the south west. The high level of vacancy in the West Midlands, it would appear, is due to company failure during the recession rather than overdevelopment; vacancy is predominantly in second-hand rather than new property.

Since the market began to decline, the majority of the investment deals which have been completed have been finance driven; that is to say, they have been bought off such high yields that they are financially viable at the initial rental level without assuming any subsequent increase. Pessimism about low levels of rental growth in the future resulted in yields rising to reflect the additional risk associated with industrial property investments during a period of national economic recession. Figure 2.2 illustrates in very general terms how real rental growth (i.e. stripping out inflation) during the late 1980s was associated with falling average yields, the latter subsequently moving out sharply as the market declined, to a peak in excess of 11 per cent in the first quarter of 1991. That industrial yields have

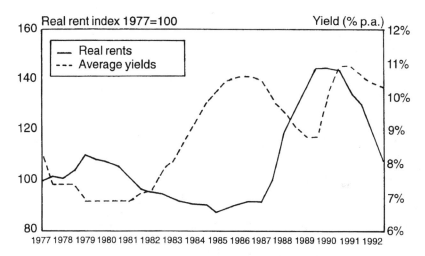

Figure 2.2 UK industrial property market: movements in average yields and real
rents, 1977 to 1992
Sources: Gerald Eve (1993) and Investors' Chronicle Hillier Parker (1992)

subsequently fallen back is not an indication that rental growth is expected;
in large part, it is a measure of the decline in interest rates, the extent to
which investors have already discounted future growth and the fact that
rents have fallen so sharply that further yield rises would have reduced
capital values too far.

It is important to recognize that even during the depths of the recession,
investor demand for certain properties has remained firm. High yielding
properties with tenants of first class covenant (i.e. well able to pay the rent
both now and in the future) have continued to attract investors. However,
very few such properties came onto the market during this period because
the only sellers were those forced by the recession into relinquishing their
holdings. As the market begins to improve, covenant strength will remain
the determining factor when judging the quality (and the value) of an
investment, although there are signs that some investors might be prepared
to reduce their covenant criteria when they judge that values are so low that
the prospects for longer-term growth outweigh the risks involved. The
recessionary market has seen a substantial number of sale and leaseback
deals. A number of companies found themselves needing to generate
capital and had to do so by realizing some of the value tied up in their
property assets. They did this by selling their freehold property to an
investor and then renting it back on an 'institutional' lease. However, they
found that the leaseback arrangements had to offer significant benefits to

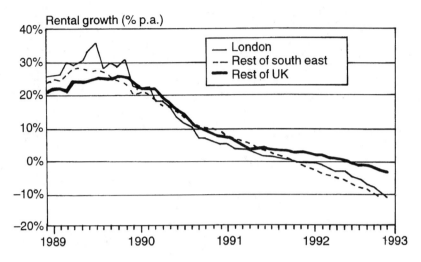

Figure 2.3 UK industrial property market: rental growth by region, 1989 to 1992

investors in order to generate any interest. As the economy recovers, many firms who have weathered the recession may yet be forced into similar deals. While a stronger market would enable them to negotiate more favourable leases as competition grows for the higher quality investments, investors have become more wary of such deals as the level of company failures has risen during the recession.

So what are the prospects for the future? The trends which became apparent in the industrial sector led many to predict that it would lead the property market out of the slump during the early 1990s for two main reasons. First, the occupational supply–demand equation was more beneficial in industrials than in the other sectors. The construction of B1 offices as opposed to sheds has led to a supply shortage of the latter, particularly at the quality end of the market. Figure 2.3 reveals that this shortage sustained low levels of industrial rental growth almost everywhere during the slump, with rents not starting to decline until December 1991 in the south east and June 1992 elsewhere. Total return (the overall effect of changes in rental and capital value) remained positive throughout 1992 (IPD 1992). Second, deals have been done on financial rather than property criteria. They have been yield driven, and have not been based on expectations of long-term rental growth. This has a number of implications. Most notably the majority of institutional investors have stayed out of the market because the prime properties which they favour are not generally available. However, the non-institutional purchasers who are doing deals do so on the basis of borrowed funds, involving loans which they must be able to service from the outset. Such investors do not restrict themselves to dealing with prime properties, so it is not surprising that the highest yielding properties have seen the highest levels of trading. Deals conducted on the property elements of an investment are only likely to become predominant in the market once there is a renewed prospect of longer-term rental growth and it has been argued that this was likely to be seen first in the industrial sector due to the supply–demand mismatch.

However, the longevity of the property slump and the accompanying economic recession have called this viewpoint into question. The recession has forced many industrial occupiers to cut back production (and employment) to levels well below the capacity of their existing facilities. A sustained period of economic growth will be required before these occupiers begin searching for new premises. Second, banks over-exposed themselves to the property sector during the late 1980s and many have suffered heavy losses as a result. The pain has been compounded as record numbers of firms have been forced into liquidation, leaving banks holding large amounts of property which they took as security for loans. While the state of the market has prevented them from selling these properties to date, the banks are unlikely to show such restraint once values start to rise. A steady flow of such properties onto the market in the early stages of recovery will reduce prospects of capital growth, with yields being pushed out as supply increases. At the same time, bank willingness to fund all but the very best finance-driven deals has been significantly eroded, leaving the market in a state of stagnation with little chance of a rapid recovery. Third, after several years of rental outperformance, values in the industrial sector are now at an historically high level and already reflect investors' assumptions regarding future rental growth arising from the recovery of the market.

What is quite clear is that many of the problems experienced since the mid-1980s could have been avoided had development and investment decision-making been of a higher quality. Furthermore, as noted by the Governor of the Bank of England (*Estates Times* 1993), quality of decision-making is in large part dependent upon the level of research and information available. It is worth considering briefly the major shortcomings which have been highlighted in recent years.

In seeking to capitalize on an apparently booming market, many developers proceeded to construct office properties of poor quality in inadequate locations. The resulting oversupply contributed to the collapse in rental values and the consequent failure of many schemes which could otherwise have been profitable. The banks, in their anxiety to secure a share in the profits which had been seen in previous years, were prepared to fund sub-standard schemes which would have been rejected during anything other than boom conditions. There can be no question that inadequacies in both information and analysis contributed significantly to the collapse of the market. Conditions of falling demand and oversupply should have been anticipated before they became apparent in the marketplace.

It will be interesting to see how the financial institutions behave in the coming years as the market recovers. Just as an inability to read the market led to heavy losses in the early part of the decade, so the same shortcomings may lead to opportunities in the mid-1990s being missed. The falls in value over the last four years have meant that property is now cheap in historic terms, although this may not be true of much of the industrial sector. While there may be few genuine bargains, investors and funding institutions which adopt a prudent purchasing strategy could see significant dividends in the medium term. Yet thus far, the harsh experiences of the recession have discouraged many banks from involvement in deals which deserved closer scrutiny. The real lesson to be learned is not that property should be avoided, but that investment decisions require better analysis of a wider range of quality information. It is to this issue that we finally turn: how can one define and put into practice a prudent purchasing strategy?

IMPLICATIONS FOR FUTURE RESEARCH

The difficulties associated with sources of information relating to the property market are part of a much wider problem relating to a scarcity of accurate, reliable time-series data on economic and social issues across the UK, particularly at the local level. Indeed, demand for property is a derived demand which can only be estimated once many other economic factors have been taken into consideration. However, in many cases what is needed is not more information, but a clarification and standardization of that which already exists. It must be accepted that some information (particularly that relating to the detailed financial aspects of property transactions) is never likely to become public on a large scale. However, we do need to take stock of what is currently available and attempts should be made to standardize some aspects of research and information gathering to prevent wasteful repetition and make better use of the material that is generated. Definitions of property types (such as 'high-tech' for example) and market areas, and the adoption of standard terminology would be a useful starting point.

An initial requirement, therefore, is information regarding who is collecting data on what. There is a particular need to promote greater awareness of the links between academic and private sector research, and the extent to which these may be combined to satisfy the information needs of both the market and academia. A step forward in this direction was the establishment of the Society of Property Researchers in 1988, which is making some headway in breaking down the public–private boundary and lobbying for increased provision of information by central government. The Society has launched a number of important initiatives and research projects which aim to evaluate existing information sources, co-ordinate future research and generate some standard definitions of property terminology.

In terms of specific research requirements, a number of areas may be identified where further work is needed. While these may be somewhat idealistic objectives, the intention is to set out goals towards which attention may be directed and hence some progress made.

There is a fundamental need for better information on the geographical distribution of economic activity at the local level, relating to property and to more general economic characteristics of standard areas. Academic researchers should play a key role in determining precisely what information would be most beneficial and how it could best be gathered and utilized.

There is a shortage of information on property transactions. Data bases and other mechanisms for the sharing of information do exist, but they are not sufficiently comprehensive to generate maximum benefit for those who use them. The current combination of formal recording systems and informal information exchange between property professionals is wasteful of time and resources and has somewhat worrying implications for the reliability of some of the information. A standard data base of property values would be of enormous benefit. Subdivided into property sectors and organized by geographical areas, such a data base could include information on date of transaction, property floorspace details, rental or capital values; and the basis of transaction (sale of freehold/leasehold, lease renewal, rent review, etc.).

In the UK, there is currently a lack of information on land prices. Currently, the market may be aware of the 'going rate' for particular categories of land in an area, but such values are very difficult to authenticate. This would seem to be one area where co-operation in data collection could produce benefits across both public and private sectors with no significant disadvantages to those involved.

The general problem is that, at present, the ability to utilize data effectively is less important than possession of data in the first instance. Even the most rudimentary analysis of privileged data gives significant advantages over competitors without any need for sophisticated or innovative research. If the information 'playing field' were levelled out, a premium would then be placed on understanding and interpretation to generate competitive advantage.

Beyond these specific requirements, there are a number of more general issues which are worthy of further research. On the whole, an assessment of current and future property supply can generally be made by reference to existing published information and by talking to local planners, at least to the level of detail currently demanded by investors and analysts. Although central and local government initiatives would be more effective and most welcome, improvement on these information sources is likely to remain the responsibility of private sector researchers. However, there is a severe problem in assessing levels of demand for property and this reflects an absence of analytical frameworks as much as a shortage of data. What is needed is a better understanding of the way in which the industrial property market works under given circumstances. For example, when is the market supply-led and when are demand levels the dominant factor? Such an understanding is required by the private sector to assist in the development of research-led investment strategies. Property professionals have clearly revealed their inability to understand the fundamental ways in which the market operates and the assistance of academics is required in order to take a broader view which places property within its economic context.

Further research is also needed into the way in which the property market may interact with wider political and social objectives such as regional development, regeneration and urban revitalization. Blithely referring to the need for private sector involvement in government initiatives is insufficient. The true nature of that role must be researched and demonstrated to the private sector in the form of economically viable schemes. Academic research is capable of playing a major role in developing our understanding and a number of contributions have already been made in this respect (see, for example, Healey 1991). However, ongoing relationships with the private sector are essential to ensure that academic solutions incorporate an appreciation of business realities (Dijkstra 1991).

In conclusion, many of the information needs of the property industry relate to the acquisition of a detailed knowledge of the market in particular areas. It is clearly unrealistic to expect the development of a complete data base of property information relating to every location in the country. However, two areas do exist where improvements in the current situation can be made. First, there is a need to develop comparable basic information sources on industrial property and development issues at regional and appropriate local levels. Second, it is essential to develop and refine methodologies for evaluating local economies and markets. A major issue in this respect is the determination of an appropriate scale of analysis. A useful starting point for addressing these issues has been made by the Department of the Environment's *Area Economic Studies* project (Department of the Environment, 1990).

It is to be hoped that academics, private sector researchers and government bodies at every level will begin to recognize more clearly the advantages to be gained from closer co-operation in researching such issues and will act accordingly.

REFERENCES

Crosby, N. (1988) 'An analysis of property market indices with emphasis on shop rent change', *Land Development Studies* 5: 145–77.

Department of the Environment (1990) *Area Economic Studies: An Evaluation*, School of Urban and Regional Studies, Sheffield City Polytechnic, London: HMSO.

Dijkstra, F. (1991) 'Urban redevelopment and regeneration: using the property industry to do the job', paper presented at the Annual Conference of the Institute of British Geographers, University of Sheffield, January 1991.

Estates Times (1993) 'Bank slams lease practices', *Estates Times*, 1173, 22 January: 1.

Gerald Eve (1993) *Investment Brief* 4, 2 (April), London: Gerald Eve Chartered Surveyors.

Healey, P. (1991) 'Urban regeneration and the development industry', *Regional Studies* 25(2): 97–110.

Inland Revenue (1992 and annual) *Inland Revenue Statistics*, London: HMSO.

Investors' Chronicle Hillier Parker (1992) *Rent and Yield Indices*, London: Hillier Parker.

Investment Property Databank (IPD) (1992) *1992 Property Investors' Digest*, London: Investment Property Databank.

King Sturge & Co. (1992) *Industrial Floorspace Survey*, London: King Sturge & Co.

Knight Frank & Rutley (1990) *The High Yield Report*, London: Knight Frank Kolpron Research.

3 Information sources for non-commercial research on industrial property and industrial activity

Andy C. Pratt

INTRODUCTION

All information gathering is carried out with a purpose in mind. The purpose will delimit and characterize what and how information is collected and, in turn, how it is analysed. As we have seen in the previous chapter, information collection for commercial industrial property research has an immediate objective: to satisfy a particular market need. Invariably the requirement is monitoring; commonly a role subservient to – or dictated by – the needs of property management, investment or transaction. When non-commercial researchers need this type of information then the inevitable constraints of the data collected will not be a problem. However, where the need for, and use of, information differs there is likely to be a necessity for new information gathering. The two areas of non-commercial information gathering focused on in this chapter are those carried out by three groups: central government; town planners; and academics. The aim of the chapter is to set the information collected by these groups into the context of their – changing – needs. It is hoped that this will highlight both the potential and the limitations of the available information.

What characterizes non-commercial information gathering is that it requires comprehensive rather than partial information collection. For example, rather than gathering indicators of market activity from selected transactions, planners may need to know precisely which land is developed, which buildings are being built, which are vacant and what existing buildings are used for and by whom. In the case of each group – central government, planners and academics – new roles and responsibilities, or new theoretical and methodological traditions, create demands for new types of information.

The information collected by central government plays an important role in national policy making and monitoring. This information can be considered in three ways. First, much of the key information collected feeds directly into the preparation of the *UK National Accounts* (the 'blue book'). This statistical collection, updated annually, forms a crucial barometer of the economic performance of the economy. Generally, the information collected refers to aggregate national trends. Related to the preparation of the *UK National Accounts* are several other separately available, sectorally specific, publications including the *Business Monitors*, the *Housing and Construction Statistics*, and the *Financial Statistics*. Second, central government organizes occasional censuses, most notably the census of production, and the census of employment. These sources are most valuable both in terms of their comprehensiveness (response is obligatory) and detail. Third, there are the nationally collated statistics that support local authorities' activities, in particular rating and valuation and planning. The relevant information refers to industrial floorspace and land use.

The increasing concern with economic development and land use has led to a growth in planners' interest in relationships between industrial buildings and their occupants. This concern can be considered in four ways. The first three of these flow from the statutory responsibilities of planning authorities. First, in terms of a desire to calculate the likely land or building space needed for any population and employment growth in an area. Second, from a concern with the monitoring and promotion of the most efficient use of particular parcels of land. In recent years aspects of this task have become computerized. Information can be stored in data bases, geographical information systems (GIS) and land information systems (LIS). Third, from an interest in the type of work and industrial activity carried out at particular sites. This may be important not just in terms of land-use zoning, but also with respect to the potential linkages with both other firms and labour market skills in the locality. Fourth, there are the non-statutorily generated activities, namely the role of local authorities as industrial property developers and landlords in their own right. In this latter respect the interest in property information collection may overlap with that of commercial operators. In many cases this role is carried out by estates departments of local authorities. In recent years there has been a merging of planning and estates departments. In any case the point is that ready access to this information can be afforded by planners.

For academics, the interest in industrial development was in order to first describe and then to explain industrial location. Not surprisingly there has been both an ongoing dialogue between planners and academics, mainly geographers and planners, and an actual movement of personnel between the two professions. Academic studies have shifted away from concern with abstract or idealized industrial location models and have grown more interested both in actual locational forms (for example, science parks or industrial districts) and in the local employment and labour market implications of such developments. Attention has turned first, from patterns of employment and industrial locations, to industries and their organization and later to the relationship between industries and their localities, and labour processes and labour markets.

Relatively neglected areas of concern have been those of the actual production of the built environment itself and the relationship of the building form to the activity carried out within it. It is primarily through the work of Stephen Fothergill and his colleagues (1982, 1985, 1987) that the latter issue has been raised as an explanation of the urban to rural shift of the manufacturing industry. This work is as yet in its early stages. One thing holding back empirical development is the lack of availability of appropriate detailed information. The general problem is that, although information has been gathered separately on employment and (to a lesser extent) property, few attempts have been made to marry them up at the site scale. One of the obstacles has been information storage and retrieval, another is confidentiality. However, the development of new software linked to both GIS and LIS being developed within the planning context may well solve the technical problems of information storage and retrieval. The problem of confidentiality is rather more intractable.

It is not the objective of this chapter to give an exhaustive evaluation of the individual information sources as this is covered elsewhere (see Axford in this volume; Perry 1991). Rather, the intention is to stress the relevance, use and limitation of the information for exploring the problems in which academics and planners are interested. The structure of the chapter is as follows. First, information collected by central government is considered. Second, the availability of planning-related information sources by scale of collection and topic of concern is assessed. Third, stressing the link between theoretical developments and research interests, the main strands of academic research on employment and property are reviewed.

The final section considers the future for research and data collection in this field. The difficulty of carrying out research on property using public sources is emphasised. They are collected for a variety of different uses and they are not integrated. The purposes of collection in many cases militate against any systematic use. Furthermore, data is seldom available for small spatial units. These are basic problems for researchers who have an interest in this area. The obvious solution is new data collection. The following sections consider data collection by central government, local planners and academics. All are shaped by their own research agendas.

INFORMATION GENERATED BY CENTRAL GOVERNMENT

The information collected by central government relating to property and economic development can best be considered under five headings: land area and floorspace; development; ownership; investment; and market intelligence. While strictly a centrally generated source, employment will be dealt with in the following section. This is for two reasons: first, the output is available at a very localized level; second, its use has been closely linked to local planning and policy making.

Floorspace

Perhaps the best known, most comprehensive and immediately accessible source, *Commercial and Industrial Floorspace Statistics (CIFS)*, was first published in 1964 as *Statistics for Town and Country Planning*. The name was changed in 1974 and it was produced on an annual basis by the Department of the Environment. The information derives from the Inland Revenue Valuation Office's 118 district offices.[1] The information and its categorizations are particularly relevant to the purposes of rating. This source is not ideally suited to the needs of academic research on property development, employment or the specific nature of economic activity carried on within the buildings.

Information is collected for eight separate use classes: central government; local government; shops and restaurants; shops with living accommodation (the residential component is excluded); warehouses, stores and workshops; commercial offices; industrial; and open warehousing. In the case of warehousing and industrials, information is collected in each case by the floorspace of the buildings and by the site area (called a hereditament).[2] The total floorspace is listed by local authority district, county and regional spatial unit in England and Wales.[3] Change is reflected in four components, the first three relate to additions to the stock: completely new buildings; extensions to existing buildings; and change of use. The final component relates to the depletion of the stock: demolitions. The information is also classified by both the numbers of units and the total floorspace falling into four size bands: less than 500 square metres; 500 square metres to 2,499 square metres; 2,500 square metres to 9,999 square metres; 10,000 square metres and above.

There are several points worth making here concerning the utility and interpretation of these statistics. First, there is no distinction between occupied and vacant buildings. As the commercially collected vacant floorspace statistics published by King & Co. suggest (see Chapter 2), the distribution of vacant premises is not even but is closely related to the age and design of buildings (see Chapter 8).[4] Thus, statistics for the older industrial areas are likely to include a greater than average number of both vacant and substandard buildings. The latter may never come onto the market as they are substandard; the classic example is a disused multi-storey mill building.

Second, as Perry (1991) notes in his review of the *CIFS* as a research source, buildings are classified by current or intended occupant rather than those for which they may be ideally suited. Third, the data categorizes floorspace by the dominant use by hereditament. Clearly, there is a danger of misrepresentation of activity. However, the difficulties do not stop here.

To fully appreciate what problems these classification issues may cause the analyst, it is important to sketch in a little context. The operation of the planning system and the nature of the property development market has rather muddied the waters regarding the interpretation of the *CIFS*. The problem for developers in the 1970s and 1980s was that, at the time, the Use Classes Order (UCO) (1972) designated warehousing as a separate use class (class X) from other industrial uses. Planners were thus able to restrict the development of warehousing (usually for reasons related to employment density – see below – and traffic generation) by excluding the permission for class X uses on a site. This regulatory arrangement seemed to encourage developers to build flexible 'sheds'. These buildings were simple boxes that were in effect the lowest common denominator of industrial space. On the one hand it could be seen as a way for developers to circumvent the UCO. It was often possible to build a 'shed' on a site with planning permission for manufacturing only and later to obtain a 'change of use' permission to class X. On the other hand, 'flexible sheds' reduced the risk of developments being unlet or unsold by positioning them in two markets at once.

In 1987 the UCO was changed and, along with later changes in planning legislation (the 1988 General Development Order), a new liberal classification was created. The less significant consequence of such modifications was that the manufacturing/warehousing division was effectively erased for buildings smaller than 235 square metres. The most significant consequence was the creation of a new 'business class' (termed B1) that, in effect, allowed a high office content in industrial buildings. Again there are two interpretations possible here. First, that the old UCO was creating difficulties for developers trying to build for the 'high-tech' market. The new UCO allowed the creation of the flexible spaces that modern industry required. Second, that change gave developers further leeway to 'hedge their bets' with developments, thereby reducing their risk. Furthermore, it allowed some developers to extract high 'office level rents' from low 'industrial value' land.

The consequence of this upheaval is that it is difficult to specify from figures such as the *CIFS* whether the building lies in the warehouse/distribution sector or the industrial/manufacturing sector. In some cases there is also a question as to whether the development is an office or not. This is not yet a practical question as the last *CIFS* published by the

Department of the Environment covered 1985. No further information has been published for England,[5] however, it does continue to be available for Wales.

Development

A further problem with the *CIFS* is that it does not identify the developer of the land or building. There are two routes to obtaining some indication of developer type. First, there is the information gathered in the *Housing and Construction Statistics* (*HCS*). Some indication of output/construction of industrial buildings can be gleaned from this source. Published tables relate the value of contractors' annual output by 'type of work' and by public or private sector client. It should be noted that the public sector component is an amalgam of uses. However, nowadays it also represents a very small proportion of construction work compared to the private sector. The private sector 'industrial' component is broken down between factories, warehouses and others. Regional data is also published for the private sector 'industrial' output. Unfortunately, as the *HCS* data refers to value of work and the *CIFS* to floorspace, it is not possible to match up the data adequately, for example on 'new constructions' in the *HCS* and 'new additions' in the *CIFS*.

The second route to obtaining information on developer type is to obtain developers' annual reports. Private sector reports are generally unhelpful. However, public sector developers in Britain (English Estates,[6] the Scottish Development Agency (now part of Scottish Enterprise), the Welsh Development Agency, the Highlands and Islands Development Board, the Development Board for Rural Wales and the Commission for New Towns) do publish reports that furnish the researcher with a significant amount of information on floorspace developed and the proportion vacant by region. Regional offices of English Estates (EE) have, in the past, been willing to release general information on the numbers employed in their units. The shift towards a more market-led style of operation in recent years has made EE less sympathetic to the researcher. Nevertheless, historical records may be made available by personal application and a visit to the head offices in Tyne and Wear.

Ownership

A further component of information relates to ownership, both of land and buildings. Information on ownership, though crucial to research on property development, is notoriously difficult to obtain in Britain. General statements about land ownership are also difficult (but see Massey and Catalano (1978) for a classic, if dated, account, and Kivell (1993) for

partial, though contemporary, coverage). Even with the easing of confidentiality, records from the British Land Registry will only be available
on individual plots, in effect obstructing any general statement about
ownership in a locality.

The only published information concerning land use has been produced
by the Department of the Environment from records collected by the
Ordnance Surveyors between 1985–9 (CSO 1991). Two tabulations have
been produced, one for land changing from agricultural uses (by new use)
and one for land changing to industrial use (by previous use). Both tables
give a regional breakdown of information. The Valuation Office does
collect information on industrial land transaction prices, by region and by
major town. However, due to publication restrictions (see below) these
cannot be reproduced. Private sector monitoring of national variation in
industrial land prices has been carried out by Healey and Baker (1991) for
the years 1977 and 1990.

There does not seem to be any reliable source of information about
ownership or tenure of industrial buildings. Estimates suggest that a shift
has occurred in the post-war period from almost entirely owner occupied to
the current situation where a considerable proportion of industrial firms are
renting premises. Fothergill, Monk and Perry (1987: Table 2.4) estimate
that a quarter of all industrial property is rented nationally. A more rigorous
sample survey of 501 establishments in urban areas carried out for the
Department of the Environment (McIntosh and Keddie 1979: 17) indicates
that half were renting property compared with just over a third in an earlier
DTI survey (HMSO 1973: 651).[7] The 1979 survey indicated two issues:
first, that two-thirds of all firms renting or leasing accommodation did so
from private landlords; and second, that the smaller the firm the less likely
it was to be an owner-occupier. Clearly, there is a need for further data
collection in this area.

Investment

Obtaining information on the financial dealings of any company, especially
those involved in property investment, is fraught with difficulties. Fortunately, some information is collected by the Central Statistical Office on a
systematic basis. The first source worth consideration – *Business Monitor
MQ5 Insurance companies' and pension funds' investment* – sheds light on
the role of financial institutions (insurance companies and pension funds)
in commercial property investment. Unfortunately, statistics are only available on a national scale for 'investment in land, buildings, property and
ground rents' for the property sector as a whole. Regional investment or
investments in industrials are not separated out.[8] A wider perspective on

investment can be obtained from the *Commercial and Industrial Property Statistics* (*CIPS*) which detail the 'net capital stock of buildings and works' by sector (including industrial and commercial, public corporations and financial companies). Using these figures it is possible to get a rough indication of the relative importance, in value terms, of the net capital stock of buildings owned by what the *CIPS* terms 'financial' companies 'which is growing' compared with that of which the *CIPS* terms 'industrial and commercial' companies.

Statistics collected for the *UK National Accounts* include details of fixed investment in new buildings and works by manufacturing industry. The annual, seasonally adjusted, level of gross investment in real terms has been remarkably stable in the post-war period (see CSO 1993: Table 10). Ideally, if such information were linked with that on gross fixed investment in plant and machinery it would be possible to get an indication of the shifting priorities of investment. This is a very important relationship to explore if one is interested in the role that property plays in industrial development. For example, whether companies have taken the opportunity to rent property instead of owning it in order to free up capital to invest in new plant and machinery could be investigated. The ratio of investment has shifted in favour of plant and machinery in the post-war period. While this gives an indication of the changing annual picture, the net fixed assets held by companies at the end of year would, perhaps, provide a better indication.

Statistics on this topic can be found in *Business Monitor MA3 Company Financing*. The statistics would suggest that the ratio between buildings and plant and machinery assets over the period 1980–90 has tended towards property and away from plant and machinery – quite opposite to the gross statistics presented above. However, there are some problems with this source in relation to its use in this manner. The information available is rather general, as *MA3* does not provide detail of land and buildings disaggregated beyond what are termed 'all companies: manufacturing and non-manufacturing' (which includes a company's overseas assets too). Furthermore, these net figures are estimates. We cannot read too much significance into such statistics as there are several factors that obscure the relationship between investment in either buildings and works or plant and machinery. These factors include inflation in land prices, land and property revaluations, and changing accounting practices in the 1980s. Clearly, more detailed research is required here if a real insight is to be gained into this important relationship.

Some general points can be made about financial and investment information. First, the information tends to be available only at a very aggregated scale. Second, the differential price changes of plant and machinery and property are both regionally and temporally variable and are difficult to account for. Third, information on fixed capital and assets does not take account of 'investment' in leasing or renting of property. It is for this reason that one hypothesis worth exploring is the relationship between investment in plant and machinery and tenure of industrial property. Fourth, the information is not collected with the property or industrial researcher in mind. It is neither available at a local scale nor disaggregated by sector. Furthermore, the actual reported information feeds into the *UK National Accounts*. A practical consequence of this is that in 1992 the CSO announced the cessation of *MA3* because it was not used for the *UK National Accounts* and was not profitable on a subscription only basis.

Market Intelligence

The Valuation Office produces a very useful *Property Market Report* (*PMR*) which draws upon its local offices to report various aspects of property market trends, including those in Northern Ireland and Scotland. The report was first produced in 1983 and is published bi-annually. There is a section of the report that deals specifically with industrial property. As has already been noted above, information is available on land values. Additionally, data is available on capital and rental values by region and major town. The capital values are broken down into four categories: small starter units (25–75 square metres); nursery units (150–200 square metres); industrial/warehouse units (circa 500 square metres); and industrial/warehouse units (circa 1,000 square metres). The rental values are broken into the same four categories, with the addition of a fifth; converted multi-storey ex-mill units. These categories do not correspond to those of the *CIFS*, hence comparison of regional values and floorspace is impossible. While it is comprehensive, the *PMR* has one major drawback. It is not available through the usual channels but only produced on a restricted circulation basis and the information contained within it cannot be quoted or published.[9]

Scottish Enterprise produces the very useful *Scottish Property Market Report*. This was produced for the first time in 1992.[10] The report was prepared by private sector agents and consultants (PMA, IPD and BSL). The scope of the report is very much like a private sector report focusing on investment and returns. No detailed information on floorspace is included.

LOCAL PLANNING

The information sources related to local planning practice can usefully be broken down into three categories: land use; employment; and property and economic promotion. Information plays an important role in the planning process; from policy formulation, through to implementation, monitoring and evaluation. The range and extent of information collection is determined by planning legislation currently in place.

Land use

Generally, planning can be divided into two types of activity: development control and strategic and local – or forward – planning. The most intensive information requirements are generated by the need to monitor planning applications. Until recently this information, the approved use for any plot of land and its history (in terms of previous planning applications), was kept in simple paper filing systems. In the last decade the adoption of computerized data bases has enabled the automation of this process. Crucially, computerization has also made possible the interrogation of both past and outstanding planning applications cross-referenced by particular land use, time period and location.

Strategic planning, at least in the early phase, was less dependent on intensive data collection. The modification of the Development Plans system in 1968, giving rise to the preparation of structure plans with a twenty-five-year time horizon, created a need for forecasting land uses. In order to forecast future land use, more information had to be collected on current land uses. Basically, all county planning authorities had to identify land with current permission as well as that likely to come 'on stream' within the plan period and subsequently, in the light of population and employment projections, predict whether there would be sufficient land. If new land was required it had to be allocated by activity and broadly by where it would be required. The detail of land use allocation was taken up by the local plan. Both the local and structure plan formed the material basis for the determination of future planning applications.

The legacy of the post-war planning system was a rudimentary data base prepared by county planning authorities containing information on land use and land-use change. This information is held locally in the form of actual planning application forms. These have been computerized by many local authorities. Fortunately for the researcher, there is a statutory right of access to the 'register' of applications and decisions. There was no incentive for planning authorities to collate information on the specific buildings developed on site aside from the satisfaction of basic building and planning regulations. Specific analyses – that would yield information on property 'in the pipeline' – require unique and time consuming interrogation of the planning applications data base. Some regional scale statistics, focusing on broad changes of land use to industrial activity were collected by the Department of the Environment and published in *Regional Trends* in 1990 and 1991 covering the period 1985–9. This information originates from a rather peculiar source – map changes recorded by the Ordnance Survey – and not from planning applications and notification of changes of use.

Employment

The collection of employment information by local authorities is carried out as a central part of plan making; all structure plans have an 'employment' chapter. The main source of information is the Census of Employment (CE). This was begun in 1971 and carried out on an annual basis until 1978. The great benefit is that response to the CE is compulsory. In recent years central government cutbacks have led to an irregular periodicity of collection – currently averaging a census every three years – and a retreat from 100 per cent coverage (see Townsend 1991). This source is particularly useful for local authorities as, unlike the decennial Census of Population, the actual returns are available for use for 'planning purposes'. Researchers may also gain access to these statistics at the local district level, but only with the permission of the Secretary of State and with suitable restrictions on confidentiality that suppress the reporting of information that identifies individual firms. The storage of CE information on computer (the NOMIS system, see Townsend 1991) has made this a key source for information on local employment. However, as the information is not linked to specific properties it is of limited use in the generation of detailed analyses of employment density.

Accurate information on the 'employment density' (measured in persons per hectare) of industrial land by particular users is necessary for the accurate forecasting of likely needs of industrial land use. This is not simply a matter of adding in a static 'density factor' to employment projections. The complexity is related to dynamic changes in employment densities which are in turn related to both cyclical factors and the restructuring of industry more generally.

Significantly for those interested in the relationship between employment and the built environment, there is also a recognition of the variation in employment generated by different industrial activities. In particular, it is argued that if allocated industrial land is occupied by storage or warehousing companies, which generate fewer jobs than a manufacturing counterpart, more land will be required in the long term (Tempest 1982). Planners have been concerned on two counts: first, the potential use of agricultural land for non-agricultural activities; second, the use of costly local authority 'serviced' industrial sites for low employment-yielding developments. This concern has generated research interest in actual employment density figures by location, particularly with respect to warehousing (see Bone 1987; Burden 1990). Significantly, this information is very difficult to collate as it requires matching specific sites and the specific employment generated there (but see information collected by McKinnon and Pratt 1984, 1986).

Generally, the availability of local level information on land, buildings and employment is fragmented. Collection and availability is patchy and *ad hoc*. Consequently, attempts to link up information sources is particularly difficult, primarily because of the need to link particular buildings with particular employment and land use. A few local authorities have sought to establish land and employment information systems to link together information on land use, buildings, economic activity and employment. The key is the use of unique spatial reference codes for all information sources (see Pattison 1981; Dale 1991; and Worrall 1991). However, these are resource intensive as they are dependent upon primary data collection by the local authority. It is clear that there is considerable potential for further development in this area utilizing both land, and more general geographical, information systems. Until such systems are developed, and the software infrastructure is increasingly in place, even basic research on the relationship between property and employment is going to be slow, localized and labour intensive.

Property and economic promotion

The changing role of planning authorities from the 1960s onwards emphasised the significance of the promotion of economic activities. Specific 'loop holes' in planning legislation were exploited for the purpose of 'employment generation' or 'activities to benefit the local area'. Boddy (1983) notes that few local authorities actually got involved in economic development activities until the 1970s. A crucial element of this concern with economic promotion was direct intervention in the local industrial property market; first by servicing sites with basic utilities, then by building industrial units for rent (Mills and Young 1986). Several surveys covering this period of activity have documented the extent of local authority involvement in advance factory building and the provision of industrial estates (see Camina 1974; Armstrong and Fildes 1989; and Sellgren 1989). These analyses focus on the expenditure of local government and not on the physical outcomes of their policies. The role of local authorities was severely curtailed in the late 1980s: first, by spending restrictions on local government more generally; second, by the curtailment of local authority participation in local economic development by the Local Government and Housing Act 1989 (see Hayton 1990).

In the normal course of events local authorities hold information for monitoring purposes on the buildings that they have actually been responsible for developing. In many cases this information may be held by the estates department rather than the planning department. Aside from the statistics on floorspace there may also be information available on rental levels and occupancy rates. Access, as usual, has to be negotiated locally. There is no national collation of data on the nature, extent and occupancy of factory building initiatives. Estimates can only be made by direct survey of local authorities (see Perry 1986). There are differences between local authorities and commercial developers in terms of the data that they collect for their property development activities. The main motivation for local authority activity is employment creation, not yield on capital invested (although this is a consideration). Invariably the goal has been the satisfaction of the needs of a particular group of industrialists – usually local small businesses – for whom market rents are too high or suitable properties or sites are not available.

In practical terms there are two main potential sources of information generated by local authorities in the pursuance of such policies that may be of use to the researcher. First, local authorities develop 'lists', very much as commercial estate agents do, of enquiries for sites and premises. These lists of general enquiries may be supplemented by the mailing or enquiry list generated in response to advertising or other promotional activities of local authorities. While such lists appear to offer an insight into the 'pressure of demand' in an area they are notoriously difficult to interpret with respect to the 'conversion' rate into actual occupations. The availability of such lists for the researcher is very limited; obviously the enquiry information is private and may be considered sensitive. Nevertheless, quarterly figures for enquiries (possibly disaggregated by size band) may be available either in reports prepared for the industrial promotion unit or minutes of employment and planning committees of local authorities.

Second, some local authorities have developed a 'vacant property list'. Essentially these documents list vacant property by size, location and rent or price. They are usually compiled by collecting lists from local estate agents and individual referrals, as well as lists from other public bodies (English Estates, the Rural Development Commission, New Town and Urban Development Corporations) or local and sometimes county and former metropolitan districts. These documents offer a quick and easy way of getting an indication of the state of the vacant property market in an area. However, investigation as to the accuracy ought to be carried out particularly with respect to a cross-check on the currency of the information. Inevitably, property is missed off such lists. These lists are readily available from county or district planning or estates departments as they are prepared as part of their overall planning and promotional activities. Once again, they are developed on local initiative and there is by no means nationwide coverage of the UK. There is no centralized collection of information.

Occasionally local authorities may carry out or commission analyses of such information (see Ball 1989). Generally collection, retention and analysis of historic information is only carried out on an *ad hoc* basis.

ACADEMIC RESEARCH

The information requirements of the academic researcher are different from those of central government statisticians, local planners and commercial researchers. The principal difference is that the academic researcher is concerned with the nature of the institutions and agencies of property development and employment themselves; explaining how and why they act in the way they do, as well as chronicling the outcomes of their actions. So even where there is a concern with buildings themselves, it is common that academic researchers will be interested in the relationship of those buildings both to the particular institutions that produced them and to the industrial activities carried out within them. In short, the *process* element of property development and employment change characterizes the particular nature of academic research information needs. Of course, many of the information sources cited earlier in this chapter – as well as those in the previous chapter – will be of interest to the academic researcher. However, additional information will also be required. It is only recently that the potential relationships between employment and property development have been fully recognized by academic researchers. It is the collation of information linking these two concerns that presents particular problems for the academic researcher.

The specific information needs are closely intertwined with particular theoretical concerns; these have changed and developed in the last twenty years. In academia, to an even greater extent than in the planning field, the concerns of property and employment have been kept apart. Three different themes can be identified. First, research on 'establishment level' industrial employment change. Second, research on the evaluation of local economic policy. Third, research specifically on the development process. None of these themes has drawn solely upon established sources of information. However, in the case of 'establishment level' research new sources were created. To a great extent what follows is a literature review of the diverse information collected on issues that relate to our central concern. This stresses the need for systematic work in the future that both links together and fills in the gaps in this research area.

Establishment level information

Dissatisfaction with aggregate employment statistics as an indicator of economic activity which only indicates *net changes* has led researchers to explore

disaggregated sources. The most disaggregated level is that of the manufacturing establishment.[11] The research that highlighted the utility of this
approach was that on de-industrialization (see Lloyd 1979; Healey 1984). This
technique is termed 'components of change analysis' and allows the identification of *gross changes*. Characteristically, employment data is collected, by
direct survey, on all of the firms in a locality. The locality is resurveyed after a
time period. The data generated in such an exercise makes possible the
disaggregation of employment change into that attributed to new firms, movement out of the area and existing firm expansion and contraction. Lloyd's work
(see Lloyd 1979; Lloyd and Dicken 1981; Lloyd and Shutt 1985) showed that
much of the employment decline in inner city manufacturing establishments
was *in situ* decline, not relocation. This supported the hypothesis that 'de-
industrialization' was due to a structural weakness in the manufacturing sector
(see Massey and Meegan 1982).

Research sponsored by the Department of the Environment Inner Cities
Programme was innovative in that, unlike most establishment level
surveys,[12] property was considered. As part of the work, a sample survey of
industrial employment and property was carried out (see McIntosh and
Keddie 1979). Besides employment and floorspace data, information was
also collected on the form of buildings and their tenure (see above). Further
research by Joint Unit for Research on the Urban Environment (JURUE)
(1980) and Fothergill, Kitson and Monk (1985), also funded under the
Department of the Environment Inner Cities Programme, collected similar
data for Birmingham and the East Midlands respectively (see summary
table 5.7 in Fothergill, Monk and Perry, 1987). This work further emphasised the 'property mismatch' theory.[13]

What is lacking in this research is a systematic attempt to explain why
locations are constrained for manufacturing industry. While the data
gathering is at the establishment level, the conceptualization – of the land
development process – is at the institutional level. Thus, work by Perry
(1986), Fothergill, Monk and Perry (1987) and Cameron, Dabinett and
Gillard (1985) highlights the role of developers as 'gatekeepers' of the
industrial built environment, regulating access to sites and buildings.[14]
However, it does not consider the variation in the actual provision of
property. This last issue is taken up in the discussion about property
development research below.

Local economic policy evaluation

The dominant interpretation of local economic activity by local authorities
has been 'property led' regeneration. It is not surprising that analyses of
these policies by academics offer some insight into the property–

employment relationship. Turok (1990), reviewing the debate about policy evaluation, suggests two dominant modes. First, those stressing administrative efficiency which is measured in terms of the physical output of buildings by an agency. Second, the mode most popular since the early 1980s, those stressing financial efficiency which is measured in terms of the internal rate of return of investment; 'cost-per-job generated' is commonly used as a surrogate for this measure.

Financial efficiency calculations have been applied in several cases to advance factory building by the public sector (see Willis 1983, 1985; Thomas and Drudy 1987). The drawback with such 'cost-per-job' calculations is that they tend to have a very narrow focus which tends to ignore the wider significance of industrial buildings. Clearly, there is some employment created in the construction of the buildings themselves. More significantly, Thomas and Drudy (1988: 535) acknowledge that firms would not have located in mid-Wales (their study area) if advance factories had not been available. Other researchers have also stressed the importance of property availability in economic development. Valente and Leigh (1982), for example, highlight the importance of the availability of local 'property chains' for small firms to progress along in their early stages of development. Furthermore, Newman's (1982) research on small advance factories in rural areas stresses the importance of the consideration of the interaction of factory design and individual user requirements in the success of such schemes.

Narrow accounting procedures such as 'cost-per-job' calculations do not distinguish either whether the jobs created are new jobs (i.e. not substitutes for redundancy elsewhere) or what the quality/skill level is. Furthermore, these techniques only narrowly define the costs and benefits of job creation or loss. Significant progress has been made in developing skills and social audits recently, the aim being to consider the impact of investment for both the wider community and for longer time periods (see Geddes 1988).

The research cited above does seem to indicate that the significance of industrial property goes well beyond that captured by narrow 'cost-per-job' calculations. Furthermore, it suggests that there is an important inter-relationship between firms, development and property. As we noted, most of the research has only concerned itself with factory units provided by public bodies. Clearly, there is a need to expand this research, preferably taking up the issue of property provision and use more centrally, with respect to all sectors of property provision.

The development process

We have already noted the extension of work on the establishment-level technique into a consideration of property. While this must be praised for its attempt to link property and industrial activity, the property development aspect is under-theorized. Research on the relationship between industrial development and property development is hampered by the paucity of research on property development more generally, and industrial property in particular. Recent reviews of the conceptualization of the development process demonstrate this point (see Gore and Nicholson 1991; Healey, P. 1991, 1992). Approaches have developed from a focus on individual agents and the 'property pipeline', to a concern with particular agents – landowners, builders or developers – to negotiation between agents, or the structural context of capital accumulation. Much of this research has its roots in, and is applied to, residential and office property.

As we have already noted, the work of Perry (1986), taking a managerialist approach to the consideration of industrial property, has its limitations due to its narrow conceptualization of the property development process. Structural approaches, stressing the contradiction between the interests in the capital accumulation strategies of developers (as representatives of 'finance capital') and those of the occupants of industrial premises (as representatives of 'manufacturing capital') are an attempt to make up for such deficiencies (see Boddy 1981).[15] These approaches have also been adopted in research on industrial property by Henneberry (1988), and Massey, Quintas and Wield (1992, Chapter 7).[16]

The problem with the structural approach, in general terms, is the tendency to see developers as functionaries of capital. A more satisfactory approach takes into account the broad context of the social relations of building provision. This leaves space to consider the internal relationships between builders, developers, financiers and industrialists. (See Ball 1986, 1988 for an application to housing and the construction industry. A similar approach is developed by Pratt 1993, 1994 with respect to industrial property.) Once again, more research is needed in this area. One of the major problems that researchers face is information collection. As we noted above, and as is noted in the previous chapter, both the official and the commercially available statistics on these issues are rather limited. There is a need for extensive and intensive information gathering to pursue this research agenda.

CONCLUSION

In this chapter information gathered on industrial property and local economic activity has been evaluated with reference to the context in which it was originally collected. As such, many of the available sources duplicate the conceptual division of buildings and the activities that are carried out within them. This presents a major barrier for the researcher. Potentially, some of these problems might be overcome by the use of GIS to link site-specific data on employment and floorspace. However, this would only be a first step in research into a key relationship.

A less optimistic note is that the national information base is fast becoming depleted, information collected by central government has been subject to the same financial 'cutbacks' as all public spending in the post-1975 era. In some cases this has latterly led to the non-publication of statistics (for example, the *Commercial and Industrial Floorspace Statistics*); in others it has meant the cessation of collection altogether. The *Business Monitor MA3 Company Financing* is a case in point. *MA3* was recently discontinued because the data was not considered to be directly relevant to the *UK National Accounts*. Furthermore, because the data was not adjudged to be self-financing either by private subscription or private publication, it was withdrawn. In other cases (for example, the *Scottish Property Market Report*), reports are being contracted out; produced by the private sector for central government. This trend does not bode well for non-commercial researchers.

It is encouraging to note that research starting from a prior concern with industrial property development has thrown up some interesting issues with respect to possible needs for future research. Two interrelated areas in particular can be identified. First, the changing nature of the relationship between firms' relative investment in property and that in plant and machinery (and training) and its impact on productivity. Second, the changing nature of industrial tenure in Britain and the potential impact – in terms of spatial distribution, design and leasehold conditions – of continued large-scale investment by financial institutions in this market. Both research areas would require detailed and sensitive localized research on the changing nature of property developers and their activities, the roles of investors and the impact upon particular tenants and users of industrial premises.

At the other end of the spectrum, property development and investment has been a key element in the globalization of economic activities that has gathered pace in the last twenty-five years. The implications of the globalization of production and global industrial property trading have yet to be evaluated. Some indications can be gleaned from Thrift's (1986, 1987) work on the emergence of an international property market (for offices), and Wood and Williams' (1992) overview of industrial property development in western Europe. This research is still in its very early stages and is currently very dependent on commercially generated sources. However, it does offer a pointer to yet another area of future research. Without a doubt, all research in the foreseeable future on the relationship between industrial property and industrial activity is going to be considerably limited by questions of data availability.

ACKNOWLEDGEMENTS

I would like to thank Mike Edwards and Dan Graham for their useful comments on an earlier version of this chapter. The usual disclaimers apply.

NOTES

1   The preparation and maintenance of Valuation Lists by the Inland Revenue has been a statutory duty since 1950. Previously local authorities made their own valuations for rating purposes. Prior to 1974, the statistics were updated from stock counts in 1963 and 1967. From 1974 to 1985 the stock details are updated annually (see also note 5).

2   Some very large-scale, and some small-scale, manufacturing plants are excluded (iron and steel plants, glass works, refineries, cement works, silos, flour mills and concrete batching plants). The exclusion is due to the type of plant and its building, not to the type of industry involved.

3   This information is not available for Scotland or Northern Ireland.

4   There are no published figures relating to the age or design of industrial building. Fothergill, Monk and Perry (1987: Table 2.3) estimate that some 40 per cent of the total stock is pre-1945, with just 17 per cent being built post-1975. Fothergill, Monk and Perry (1987: Table 2.4) estimate that some 44 per cent of firms are still carrying out production on more than one floor of their factory. This is indicative of the aged building stock and the likelihood of this being less than ideal for modern production methods. King & Co. (1989) point out that in 1989 just 22 per cent of all vacant buildings were new.

5   Data for 1986 were collected but not published by the Department of the Environment. However, a summary was compiled by Hillier Parker (1988). Local district valuers continue to hold and collect similar data for rating purposes; some may be prepared to release some data by negotiation. However, it is a poor substitute for the *CIFS*.

6   EE data incorporates that of the (English) Rural Development Commission (RDC). The RDC also produce separate reports. There is also an occasional publication *Rural Focus* that has occasional analyses of property and occupants. Current proposals are for EE to be incorporated into the new Urban Regeneration Agency (Department of the Environment 1992).

7   These figures are clearly related to the balance of new and historic stock in an area (related to its past pattern of industrialization), as well as the particular mix of property provision (public or private). There are likely to be regional variations; for example, Pratt (1993) found that some 49 per cent of properties (63 per cent of floorspace) was rented in Cornwall. There is some recent evidence that this trend towards renting, albeit at lower levels, seems to be being duplicated in Europe as a whole (Wood and Williams 1992: 274).

8   It would not be too difficult to get an estimate of the actual funds dedicated to industrial property by relating the standard portfolio mix of financial institutions to this general figure.

9   Copies can be consulted in the British Library of Political and Economic Science in London (the LSE library).

10 A Scottish Property Market Report, a forerunner of this current publication, was produced in 1990 and 1991 by IPD and James Barr and Sons.

11 The majority of research using establishment level data has only been concerned with the manufacturing and not service sector.

12 See Healey, M. (1991).

13 Despite this wealth of data, researchers do not seem to have integrated any analysis of the differential importance of property in different sectors, or to different sizes (except the importance of an historical legacy of small industrial units; see Lloyd and Mason 1984). While one might expect lack of proximate expansion space to be important for large and medium-size firms, it is less likely to be an issue for smaller firms.

14 Perry draws upon conceptualizations developed in research on residential property, in particular theories of urban managerialism (see Chalkley and Perry 1982).

15 Boddy developed this insight, in a less explicitly theoretical manner, in work on the relationship between local authorities and industrial property development (see Boddy 1979, 1982, and Boddy and Barrett 1980).

16 Strictly, the work by Massey *et al.* (1992) stresses class rather than capital as the site of major cleavage in society. However, the approach does have similar problems to those approaches that stress the centrality of capital.

REFERENCES

Armstrong, H. and Fildes, S. (1989) 'Industrial development initiatives in England and Wales: the role of district councils', *Progress in Planning* 30(2): 91–156.

Ball, M. (1986) 'The built environment and the urban question', *Environment and Planning D, Society and Space* 4: 447–64.

—— (1988) *Rebuilding Construction*, London: Routledge.

Ball, R.M. (1989) 'Vacant industrial premises and local development: a survey, analysis and policy assessment of the problem in Stoke-on-Trent', *Land Development Studies* 6, 105–28.

Boddy, M. (1979) 'Investment by financial institutions in commercial property', in M. Boddy (ed.) *Land, property and finance*, Working Paper No. 2, School for Advanced Urban Studies, University of Bristol: 17–25.

—— (1981) 'The property sector in late capitalism: the case of Britain', in M. Dear and A. Scott (eds) *Urbanisation and Urban Planning in Capitalist Society*, London: Methuen.

—— (1982) 'Local government and industrial development', Occasional Paper No. 7, School for Advanced Urban Studies, University of Bristol.

—— (1983) 'Changing public–private sector relationships in the industrial development process', in K. Young and C. Mason (eds) *Urban Economic Development*, London: Macmillan.

—— and Barrett, S. (1980) 'Local government and the industrial development process', Working Paper No. 6, School for Advanced Urban Studies, University of Bristol.

Bone, R. (1987) 'Warehousing', *The Planner*, September: 20–4.

Burden, W. (1990) 'The use of employment density', *The Planner*, April: 14–15.

Cameron, S., Dabinett, G. and Gillard, A. (1985) 'The supply of new industrial premises by public and private agencies in Tyne and Wear', in S. Barrett, and P. Healey (eds) *Land Policy: Problems and Alternatives*, Aldershot: Gower.

Camina, M. (1974) 'Local authorities and the attraction of industry', *Progress in Planning* 3: 83–182.

60 *Industrial Property*

Chalkley, B. and Perry, M. (1982) 'On using social geographical concepts and approaches in the study of industrial location', Discussion Papers, No. 14, Department of Geography, University of Southampton.

Dale, P. (1991) 'Land and property information systems', in M. Healey (ed.) *Economic Activity and Land-use*, London: Longman.

Department of the Environment (1992) *The Urban Regeneration Agency*, Action for Cities, Consultation Paper, July.

Fothergill, S. and Gudgin, G. (1982) *Unequal Growth*, London: Heinemann.

——, Kitson, M. and Monk, S. (1985) 'Urban Industrial Change', Inner Cities Research Programme Report No. 11, London: Department of the Environment.

——, Monk, S. and Perry, M. (1987) *Property and Industrial Development*, London: Hutchinson.

Geddes, M. (1988) 'Social audits and social accounting in the UK: a review', *Regional Studies* 22(1): 60–5.

Gore, T. and Nicholson, D. (1991) 'Models of the development process: a critical review', *Environment and Planning A* 23: 705–730.

Hayton, K. (1990) 'The future of local economic development', *Regional Studies* 23: 549–57.

Healey and Baker (1991) *Industrial Land Value Survey,* Healey and Baker, 29 St George Street, Hanover Square, London W1A 3BG.

Healey, M. (1984) 'Industrial change in Warwick district 1974–84', Industrial Location Working Paper No. 6, Department of Geography, Coventry Polytechnic.

—— (ed.) (1991) *Economic Activity and Land-use*, London: Longman.

Healey, P. (1991) 'Models of the development process: a review', *Journal of Property Research* 8: 219–38.

—— (1992) 'An institutional model of the development process', *Journal of Property Research* 9: 33–44.

Henneberry, J. (1988) 'Conflict in the industrial property market', *Town Planning Review* 59(3): 241–62.

Hillier Parker (1988) *Commercial and Industrial Floorspace Statistics, England, 1983–1986*, London: Hillier Parker.

HMSO (1973) 'Memorandum of the Department of Trade and Industry minutes of evidence to the select committee on Regional Development Initiatives', House of Commons Papers 85–1, London: HMSO.

Joint Unit for Research on the Urban Environment (JURUE) (1980) 'Industrial Renewal in the Inner City: an Assessment of Potential and Problems', Inner Cities Research Programme, Report No. 2, London: Department of the Environment.

King & Co. (1989) *Industrial floorspace survey*, London: King & Co.

Kivell, P. (1993) *Land and the City*, London: Routledge.

Lloyd, P. (1979) 'The components of industrial change for Merseyside Inner Area: 1966–75', *Urban Studies* 16: 45–60.

—— and Dicken, P. (1981) 'The components of change in metropolitan areas: events in their corporate context', in J. Goddard (ed.) *Urban and Regional Perspectives on Contemporary Economic and Social Trends in Britain*, London: Methuen.

—— and Mason, C. (1984) 'Spatial variations in new firm formation in the United Kingdom: comparative evidence from Merseyside, Greater Manchester, and South Hampshire', *Regional Studies* 18: 207–20.

—— and Shutt, J. (1985) 'Recession and restructuring in the North West region 1975–82', in D. Massey and R. Megan (eds) *Politics and Method*, London: Unwin Hyman.

McIntosh, A. and Keddie, V. (1979) 'Industry and employment in the inner city', Inner Cities Research Programme, Paper No. 1, London: Department of the Environment.

McKinnon, A. and Pratt, A.C. (1984) 'A nation of regional distribution centres', *Town and Country Planning* 53(7): 210–12.

—— and —— (1986) 'Jobs in store: an examination of the employment potential of warehousing', Occasional Paper No. 11, Department of Geography, University of Leicester.

Massey, D. and Catalano, A. (1978) *Capital and Land: Landownership by Capital in Great Britain*, London: Edward Arnold.

—— and Meegan, R. (1982) *The Anatomy of Job Loss*, London: Unwin.

——, Quintas, P. and Wield, D. (1992) *High Tech Fantasies*, London: Routledge.

Mills, L. and Young, K. (1986) 'Local authorities and economic development: a preliminary analysis', in V. Hausner (ed.) *Critical issues in Urban Economic Development*, Vol. 1, Oxford: Clarendon Press.

Newman, R. (1982) *Small Advance Factories in Rural Areas*, Final Report, Buildings Research Team, Department of Architecture, Oxford Polytechnic.

Pattison, D. (1981) 'A review of employment data sources', in G. Shaw and A. Williams (eds) South West Papers in Geography, No. 1, University of Exeter.

Perry, M. (1986) *Small Factories and Economic Development*, Aldershot: Gower.

—— (1991) 'Floorspace and commercial developments', in M. Healey (ed.) *Economic Activity and Land-use*, London: Longman.

Pratt, A.C. (1993) 'Property, finance and industrial location', in E. Schamp and C. Rogerson (eds) *Finance, Markets and Industrial Change*, Berlin: Walter de Gruyter.

—— (1994) *Uneven Reproduction: industry, space and society*, Oxford: Pergamon.

Scottish Enterprise (1992) *Scottish Property Market Report*, Edinburgh: Scottish Office.

Sellgren, J.M. (1989) 'Assisting local economies: an assessment of emerging patterns of local authority economic development initiatives', in D. Gibbs (ed.) *Government Policy and Industrial Change*, London: Routledge.

Tempest, I. (1982) 'Warehousing as an employment source – a study of employment density figures and local authority estimates', *Planning Outlook* 25(3): 105–10.

Thomas, I. and Drudy, P. (1987) 'The impact of factory development on growth town employment in Mid-Wales', *Urban Studies* 24: 361–78.

—— and —— (1988) 'The impact of factory development on growth town employment in Mid-Wales revisited: a reply', *Urban Studies* 25: 532–7.

Thrift, N. (1986) 'The internationalisation of producer services and the integration of the Pacific Basin property market', in P. Taylor and N. Thrift (eds) *Multinationals and the Restructuring of the World Economy*, London: Croom Helm.

—— (1987) 'The fixers: the urban geography of international commercial capital', in J. Henderson and M. Castells (eds) *Global Restructuring and Local Areas*, London: Sage.

Townsend, A. (1991) 'Employment', in M. Healey (ed.) *Economic Activity and Land-use*, London: Longman.

Turok, I. (1990) 'Evaluation and accountability in spatial economic policy: a review of alternative approaches', *Scottish Geographical Magazine* 106: 4–11.

Valente, J. and Leigh, R. (1982) 'Local authority advanced factory units: a framework for evaluation', *Planning Outlook* 24(2): 67–9.

Valuation Office (various) *Property Market Report*, Chief Executives Office, New
Court, Carey Street, London WC2A 2JE.

Willis, K. (1983) 'New jobs in urban areas – an evaluation of advance factory
building', *Local Government Studies* 9(2): 73–85.

—— (1985) 'Estimating the benefits of job creation from local investment subsidies', *Urban Studies* 22: 163–77.

Wood, B. and Williams, R. (1992) 'Some comparisons and contrasts', in B. Wood
and R. Williams (eds) *Industrial Property Markets in Western Europe*, London:
Spon.

Worrall, D. (1991) 'Local and regional information systems', in M. Healey (ed.)
Economic Activity and Land-use, London: Longman.

Official statistical sources

Central Statistical Office (CSO) (1991) *Regional Trends*, (Tables 13.20, 13.21),
London: HMSO.

—— (1993) *Economic Trends*, Annual Supplement (Table 10), London: HMSO.

—— (Various) *Business Monitor MA3 Company Financing*, London: HMSO.

—— (Various) *Business Monitor MQ5 Insurance Companies and Pensions Funds
Investment*, London: HMSO.

—— (Various) *Commercial and Industrial Floorspace Statistics*, London: HMSO.

—— (Various) *Commercial and Industrial Property Statistics*, London: HMSO.

—— (Various) *Housing and Construction Statistics*, London: HMSO.

4 The funding of developments on derelict and contaminated sites

Paul M. Syms

INTRODUCTION

An important aspect of industrial development, particularly in periods of decline or renewal, is the derelict industrial site (see Kivell 1993). This chapter highlights the fact that reclaiming and recovering such land for new uses is a particularly thorny problem. As such, it emphasises the broader environmental questions related to the redevelopment of industrial sites: many of which are polluted as the result of present or former manufacturing activities. Questions of finance are often the most important factors in such cases and a key focus of the chapter is the problem of persuading investors to fund the development of these sites.

Within the United Kingdom there is an increasing pressure for derelict or 'brownfield' sites to be redeveloped in preference to rural or greenfield sites. In the context of this chapter we regard 'brownfield' sites as any areas of land which have previously been the subject of a man-made or non-agricultural use of any type. This would include industrial uses such as chemical works, heavy engineering, shipbuilding and textile processing, together with unfit housing clearance sites and docklands, both inland and coastal, as well as mineral extraction sites and those used for landfill purposes.

The pressure to re-use such sites is at its greatest when it is advocated as the alternative to the development of sites situated in the greenbelts around major cities, as the residents of those cities, both individuals and businesses, seek to escape from the urban environment. For a highly populated island nation, with a very limited land resource, the arguments in favour of re-using previously used sites would seem to make good sense. Yet there are many constraints which seriously limit the potential for such re-developments, of which one of the foremost is the question of funding.

This chapter seeks to examine the constraints affecting the re-development of derelict and contaminated sites, with particular reference to the funding issues. The reclamation of sites to 'soft' after uses, such as landscaping and public open space, is not the concern of this chapter. Rather, it is intended to concentrate on the provision of 'hard' after uses, providing homes and employment.

THE DERELICT LAND PROBLEM

There is comparatively little literature on the subject of reclaiming and redeveloping derelict and contaminated sites. For the most part, published works address the technical issues, for example Cairney (1987) and Fleming (1991), and pay little attention to the financial issues involved. Even where such issues are considered (Haines 1987; Ironside 1989), the authors appear to confine themselves to a discussion of the availability of public sector finance to go towards the cost of site reclamation. It is of course very true that without public sector support in one form or another many site reclamation projects would fail to come to fruition. However, in many cases, the private sector input is of equal or greater importance.

Derelict or contaminated sites have previously been used for a wide range of purposes, often over a period of many centuries, during which time the use may well have changed and quite often buildings may have been constructed over the remains of earlier developments. Fleming (1991) has commented that the state of such land is often so poor as to be unsuitable for continued use or re-use without major land engineering works. The Department of the Environment adopts a similar view in its definition of derelict land as 'land which has been so damaged by industrial and other development that it is incapable of beneficial use without treatment' (Department of the Environment 1986).

Taking the country as a whole, dereliction is not widespread, although the problem of derelict land is by no means insignificant. Kivell (1987) noted that, according to a survey by the Department of the Environment carried out in 1982, the total area of dereliction (in England) had increased from 43,300 hectares (1974 survey) to 45,700 hectares, despite major programmes of reclamation which dealt with 17,000 hectares during the same time period. By 1988, however, the equivalent study indicated a reduction to 41,456 hectares (Department of the Environment, 1991a). Table 4.1 sets out the changes in the amount of derelict land in England between 1974 and 1988, under the different categories used in preparing the study.

Looked at another way, taken as a percentage of the total area of England, this is equal to only 0.32 per cent, but it is still 160 times the area of the City of London, where so many property investment decisions are made. It should also be borne in mind that not all derelict land can justify reclamation. For example, in the 1988 study only 32,010 hectares (77 per cent) were considered to justify reclamation. From Table 4.1 it can be seen

Table 4.1 The composition of derelict land in England

Type of dereliction	Stock (ha)	1974 (%)	Stock (ha)	1982 (%)	Stock (ha)	1988 (%)
Spoil heaps	13,118	30.3	13,340	29.2	12,015	29.0
Excavation and pits	8,717	20.1	8,578	18.8	6,186	14.9
Military	3,777	8.7	3,016	6.6	2,624	6.3
Railway	9,107	21.0	8,210	18.0	6,650	16.0
Other	8,554	19.8	12,539	27.4	13,981	33.7
Total	43,273	100.0	45,685	100.0	41,456	100.0

Source: Kivell 1987; Department of the Environment 1991a
Note: Kivell's 1987 figures transposed two digits in the 'other' category. This has been corrected.

that spoil heaps, arising from mineral extraction and other industrial processes, account for the largest area of dereliction. Many of these sites, especially those of a metalliferous nature, are considered to be so badly contaminated, or in such remote locations, as to not justify reclamation.

The survey of derelict land provides only a small part of the overall picture. There are many other sites which are still in use, or may be semi-derelict, which suffer from the same instability or contamination problems as those sites which are officially classed as derelict. Kivell cites as an example Stoke-on-Trent which, in 1984, identified 332 hectares of derelict land, but added 291 hectares of potential dereliction (where existing industrial activity is (sic) expected to cease shortly, leaving behind land which is unsuitable for use without treatment) and a further 538 hectares of neglected land (at present uncared for, untidy and in a condition detrimental to the environment).

Of the 32,010 hectares of derelict land justifying reclamation, and the industrial land still in use, an unknown but believed to be very significant percentage is undoubtedly contaminated. This contamination, lying in or on the ground, takes many forms: heavy metals, PCBs and coal tars to name but a few. The most recent estimates suggest that 50,000–100,000 sites may be considered to be contaminated, affecting perhaps 50,000 hectares. Only a small proportion of these, however, are likely to pose an immediate threat to public health or the environment (Hobson 1991).

The 1988 survey provides details of the post-reclamation use of almost 12,000 hectares of derelict land which was reclaimed between 1982 and 1988 (see Table 4.2). As can readily be seen, local authorities play a major role in the reclamation of derelict land, accounting for the reclamation of 45

Table 4.2 Derelict land reclaimed and brought back into use, 1982–8: the use of land after reclamation (hectares)

Land use	By local authority with grant	By local authority without grant	By other agencies	Total
Industry	901	44	622	1,567
Commerce	118	11	460	589
Residential	294	79	675	1,048
Sub total (hard end use)	1,313	134	1,757	3,204
Sport and recreation	793	96	251	1,140
Public open space	3,078	251	475	3,804
Agriculture/forestry	1,282	199	1,212	2,693
Sub total (soft end use)	5,153	546	1,938	7,637
Other	289	103	736	1,128
Total	6,755	783	4,431	11,969

Source: Department of the Environment 1991a

per cent of land reclaimed for hard end uses and 75 per cent of land reclaimed for soft end uses. Nevertheless, the area of land reclaimed and brought back into use by other agencies, which includes private sector developers and investors, is of considerable importance, representing many millions of pounds worth of development projects.

THE REDEVELOPMENT OF DERELICT AND CONTAMINATED SITES

The Environmental Protection Act, 1990

Potentially, one of the most important factors affecting the redevelopment of derelict or contaminated sites is the impact of the Environmental Protection Act, 1990. A well intentioned piece of legislation, reaching far beyond land and development issues, it does, however, have the effect of highlighting the environmental responsibilities attaching to the redevelopment of such sites. Section 143 of the Act provides for the setting up of registers of sites which are currently, or have previously been, used for a potentially contaminative purpose. The immediate 'knee jerk' reaction to the setting up of these registers in all local authority areas was the fear that all land listed on the register would be deemed to be contaminated, whether or not any such contamination was in fact present, and therefore land values would be blighted. This view was heightened by the fact that the government did not intend to provide for any appeal procedure against register listing. It was also the intention that once on the register sites could not be removed, even if it was subsequently proved that no contamination was present or that the site had been reclaimed to an acceptable standard.

The reasons given for not making provision for an appeal procedure, and the subsequent removal of sites from the register, were twofold. First, that the register was one of 'potentially contaminative uses', a matter of fact, rather than an absolute register of contaminated land. To have undertaken site investigations so as to identify sites of actual contamination would have taken years and an expenditure running into millions of pounds. Even then there would have been no guarantee that all contaminated sites would have been identified in such a process.

The second reason lay in the fact that there is no single agreed definition of what constitutes contamination and also no single standard of reclamation. All contaminated sites need to be investigated and remedial processes designed on a discrete basis, as no two sites are alike. Consideration also needs to be given to the proposed after use of the site as different standards of reclamation may be applied to different uses, such as industrial or residential, although there are strong arguments in favour of reclaiming contaminated sites to a standard which makes them suitable for any future use. The counter argument to this asks whether it is worth reclaiming a site to a higher standard than that which will exist, post-reclamation, in the general locality of the site. For example, there would seem to be little point in reclaiming a site to the highest possible standard while the adjoining factory continues to emit toxic fumes and other contaminative waste products. Standards need to evolve as uses cease to exist, or new techniques are introduced to control the pollution from manufacturing processes, so as to ensure a continual improvement in environmental quality.

Recognizing the problems involved, therefore, the registers were seen as an attempt to identify sites where problems might exist and the Department of the Environment's consultation paper (Department of the Environment 1991b) noted that the registers could not be expected to contain details of all contaminated sites. It was, however, considered that registers would provide a record of a large proportion of land which may be contaminated (Denner 1991).

The consultation paper also recognized the possibility of blighted land values, but Denner made the point that, of the information proposed to be included on the registers, much 'is likely to be required in any case by planners and/or purchasers, whenever a site is sold or a new use proposed' (Denner 1991: 4.1). A great deal of the information is already available through diligent research and all the registers were intended to do was to bring this information together. In view of this, the Department of the Environment considered that any blighting effect was likely to be short-lived and would reduce once the registers were accepted in daily use.

Nevertheless, it must be said that many of the objections to the setting up of the registers contained a great deal of validity. Implementation of the legislation was to have commenced at a time when the property markets in the UK were in the depths of depression. Initially, it was intended that local authorities would commence work on preparing the register for their administrative area on 1 April 1992, with the register to be completed and available for public inspection from 1 April 1993. Central government envisaged that the average cost to each local authority, for the initial register compilation, would be around £35,000 to £40,000, with the annual cost of maintenance thereafter being around £8,000, although the estimated ongoing cost of maintaining the registers has subsequently been revised in an upwards direction.

The methods used for the register compilation were to be based on desk studies of current and historic information, mainly map based. The sources to be used and the methodology for compiling the registers are all discussed in the consultation paper (Department of the Environment 1991b) and additional guidance was to have been made available to local authorities by the Department of the Environment.

One criticism of the method of register compilation made by landowners and developers was that there appeared to be no standard format for compilation, let alone a standardized computer software and hardware package. Each local authority was to be left to set up and run the register in its own way, an approach which, it was felt, would lead to disparity between authority areas. It was, however, the potentially blighting effect of the registers which attracted the greatest criticism. In March 1992, the government took the decision to postpone, for an indefinite period, the introduction of the register. However, in view of the fact that the measure had been supported by all major Parliamentary parties, abandonment of the proposal was not envisaged. The delay was to be for the purpose of allowing further discussions to take place.

Following these discussions, the draft regulations for the implementation of the Section 143 register provisions were published on 31 July 1992 and contained a number of significant changes to the original proposals. Most important of all was the reduction in specified contamination uses (originally a list of sixteen main categories, divided into forty-two sub-categories, covering

Table 4.3 Specified contaminative uses

---

1 Manufacture of gas, coke or bituminous material from coal.

2 Manufacture or refining of lead or steel or an alloy of lead or steel.

3 Manufacture of asbestos or asbestos products.

4 Manufacture, refining or recovery of petroleum or its derivatives, other than extraction from petroleum-bearing ground.

5 Manufacture, refining or recovery of other chemicals, excluding minerals.

6 Final deposit in or on land of household, commercial or industrial waste (within the meaning of section 75 of the Act) other than waste consisting of ash, slag, clinker, rock, wood, gypsum, railway ballast, peat, bricks, tiles, concrete, glass, other minerals or dredging spoil; or where the waste is used as a fertilizer or in order to condition the land in some other beneficial manner.

7 Treatment at a fixed installation of household, commercial or industrial waste (within the meaning of section 75 of the Act) by chemical or thermal means.

8 Use as a scrap metal store, within the meaning of section 9(2) of the Scrap Metal Dealers Act 1964(a).

Source: The Environmental Protection Act, 1990 (Section 143 Registers), Schedule 1, Regulations 1992 (Draft)

a wide range of activities, see Department of the Environment 1991b) to a list of eight land uses, as set out in Table 4.3. The government did, however, reserve the right to extend the list in the light of experience and this, in itself, caused widespread concern in the property development industry. It was estimated by the Department of the Environment that, on the basis of the reduced list, the area of land covered by the registers would be reduced to some 10–15 per cent of the area previously envisaged.

Provision was to have been made for owners and others to be notified of the intention to include properties on the registers and for them to be able to challenge authorities on the facts of a site's history of contaminative use or other particulars, both of these being changes to the original proposals. Local authorities were to be expected to respond promptly to any such challenge and to make available their documentary evidence. The register was to have been split into two parts, to be called Parts A and B. Part A would record land which has been subjected to a potentially contaminative use but has not been either investigated or treated. Part B would record land which has been investigated and/or treated for any contamination found. Caveat emptor would still apply and local authorities could not be held liable if, for example, a treatment was later found to have been unsuccessful.

The original intention that sites would not be removed from the register, even after decontamination or site investigation, was retained in the draft regulations. Two reasons were given for this. First, the history of the previous uses on the site is a matter of fact and, second, contamination from the site may have migrated to adjacent sites. Subsequently, the timescale given under the draft regulation to local authorities for the compilation of the Section 143 registers was increased from twelve to fifteen months.

Reaction to the Section 143 registers

In spite of the postponement, in March 1992, in the implementation of the Section 143 registers, there were a number of immediate impacts affecting the funding of development on brownfield sites. These impacts were attributable in whole or in part to the Environmental Protection Act proposals and the revised proposals contained in the draft regulations did nothing to diffuse the situation. On the contrary, the author understands that the number of objections to the revised proposals received by the Department of the Environment was even greater than those received in response to the original consultative document.

The nature of these objections was no doubt widespread, but the main thrust is believed to have centred around two issues. First, reduction in the list of specified uses, from more than forty to only eight, focused attention on those few categories. This, by implication, would appear to have indicated that all sites used for those specified purposes would be undoubtedly contaminated. Thus sites used for those purposes may be regarded as having only minimal or even negative value. Second, reserving the right for the Secretary of State to add in other uses in the future left behind an air of uncertainty. At the very least those uses specified in the original consultative document could be seen as targets and therefore very difficult to value without taking some account of the fact that they may be added to the specified categories under Section 143.

In the face of increasing opposition to the proposed registers, the Secretary of State for the Environment announced, on 24 March 1993, that the registers were to be abandoned, stating that:

> There has been substantial criticism of the proposals. The proposed registers would have reduced confidence in the value of sites placed on the register, thereby exacerbating blight without giving any clear indication on how such sites could be brought back into good condition and confidence restored.
>
> (*Estates Gazette* 1993)

At the same time the Secretary of State announced plans for a wide-ranging review into land contamination, to be chaired by the Department of the Environment but seeking views and recommendations from many sources.

One alternative to the Section 143 registers, proposed by this author, is the setting up of a comprehensive register of land use so as to provide full information on land usage throughout the UK. Such a register could not be produced within the timescale of fifteen months envisaged by the Department of the Environment, but could be prepared 'in several phases and a comprehensive register compiled by the year 2000' (Syms 1993: 6).

In spite of the abandonment of the Section 143 registers the government's proposals are likely to have a long-lasting effect on the property industry. Prospective developers are making play upon the fact that even if contaminated sites are adequately reclaimed a stigma may be attached to the site by virtue of its previous use. This is being done so as to drive down land prices even further in what, at the time of writing, is already a depressed market. The author is aware of at least one case where a prospective purchaser has demanded a discount of 40 per cent from open market value for a decontaminated site because the site will be blighted by the fact that it was formerly contaminated.

Solicitors, conscious of their professional responsibilities, are also advising clients to think very carefully before entering into contracts to purchase sites which may be contaminated. Many legal firms are also increasing the scope of their environmentally based pre-contract enquiries and are organizing training seminars so as to ensure that their property lawyers are adequately briefed on environmental matters.

A number of banks, led by National Westminster, have issued environmental guidelines to their managers to warn them of the risks involved in lending to companies which pollute the environment. The banks are being forced to carry out 'environmental audits' of companies before they decide to lend. An internal report of National Westminster Bank is reported as stating that, 'where the risk is too great, prudent financiers will stay away, and neither the national economy nor the environment will benefit' (Bennett 1992).

Within the property development industry, at least one major developer, Mountleigh, is reported to have been severely affected by the implications of the Section 143 register. The company had,

> agreed the sale of the Merry Hill Centre (a large shopping development in the West Midlands) to Hammerson, the UK property company, and the O'Connor Group, a US pension fund adviser. The deal would have brought in £125m, which although less than the property's £160m book value, would have allowed the company to meet its coming obligations. But the deal fell through . . . in part it was because of the likelihood that the shopping centre was built on contaminated land, a risk that had been heightened by the possibility that the government would bring in a register of contaminated land.
>
> (Houlder 1992: 23)

The reference to 'a register of contaminated land' in this report typifies the way in which the proposed register had been reported in the press, thus heightening the concern felt by both the property industry and the public at large.

Although Section 143 of the Environmental Protection Act 1990 is of considerable importance to the property development industry, it is probably less important, in terms of valuation implications, than Sections 61 and 79 of the Act. Under Section 61 the waste regulation authorities are given the power to enter land and carry out tests if they have reason to believe that the site in question, or an adjoining property, contains contaminated material which may be harmful to humans, animals or the environment. Similar powers already exist under the Control of Pollution Act 1974 but the Environmental Protection Act gives the waste regulation authority the power to require the owner to clean up the site or, in default, for the authority to carry out the work and to recover the reasonable cost of the work from the owner.

This action is enforceable against the current owner of the property, even if the contamination has come about as a result of actions which occurred under a previous owner, or indeed if the contamination has migrated from an adjoining site. From the valuer's point of view, therefore, the question must be asked as to the extent that provision should be made to allow for the possible cost of clean-up. It should be mentioned that the margin note for Section 61 refers to closed landfills, but sub-clause (3)(c) appears to extend the scope of the section beyond such sites by reference to '[any land] in which there are, or the [waste regulation] authority has reason to believe there may be, concentrations or accumulations of noxious gases or noxious liquids' (Environmental Protection Act 1990). Taken to its extreme, this sub-clause would appear to give the waste regulation authority power to enter any land where potentially contaminative materials may be stored, buried or otherwise contained and to compel the land owner to clean up the site.

Section 79 of the Act imposes a duty on local authorities to inspect their areas so as to detect any statutory nuisances, and to investigate complaints of such nuisances (this includes deposits on land which may be harmful to health) with a view to obtaining the abatement of the nuisance under Section 80 of the Act. In respect of this Section, it could be argued that a valuer, observing a possible nuisance during the course of a property inspection, should take account of the likely cost of compliance when preparing the valuation.

In terms of future development on such sites the problem is even more serious than that of complying with legislation. Banks are cautious institutions, as evidenced by National Westminster's requirement for environmental audits, and are likely to become even more cautious having had their fingers burnt by the downturn in property values and resultant collapse of many property development companies in the early 1990s. It would not be unreasonable, therefore, to expect them to reject all requests for development finance in respect of contaminated sites unless it can be conclusively demonstrated that all possible contamination has been removed, even if such removal was not absolutely necessary for the proposed end use. Insurance cover may be available in respect of any remaining risks, although that aspect is beyond the scope of this chapter, but any such cover would have to meet with the approval of the banks.

The banks' fear is one of increased exposure. Take for example the proposed redevelopment of a site in a major industrial city where the former uses were railway sidings, goods yard and gas works. The land under the area previously occupied by the gas works is contaminated with coal tars and heavy metals. The railway sidings have been removed and a railway cutting, running diagonally across the site, has been filled with a mix of materials, including demolition rubble from the old gas works, surface material from the railway sidings and household refuse. Since the site was cleared and levelled, uncontrolled fly tipping has taken place, with drums and bags of unidentified contents having burst open on site. Unauthorized burning of waste materials, such as vehicle tyres and insulated cables, has also taken place.

The site therefore illustrates a not untypical local environmental situation – a mixture of contaminants, originating over a long period of time from a variety of different sources. Assuming that the site is to be redeveloped for industrial purposes, with buildings, service yards and car parks covering most of the site area, it may be perfectly acceptable in engineering terms to leave much of the contaminated material *in situ*. But is such a course of action going to be acceptable to the financial institutions?

In considering applications for development finance the banks and other financial institutions, such as insurance companies, must have regard for the possibility that the developer may fail to complete the project and go into liquidation, or indeed the bank itself may have to put in a receiver. Given such circumstances, the decision will have to be taken as to whether the project should be completed, altered or abandoned. If, in the period since agreeing to finance the development, custom and practice, and possibly also legislation, have changed in such a way as to dictate that contaminated material should not be left *in situ*, then there would seem to be little point in continuing with the project as originally intended.

Substantial alterations to the project would then have to be considered and weighed against the cost of abandonment. There is a strong possibility that the latter course of action would not only involve the financial institution in the total loss of its investment to date but may also result in additional expenditure in cleaning up the contamination.

The concern of financial institutions extends far beyond the development process itself, into the provision of long-term finance by way of mortgage or debenture. Loans secured on contaminated sites may, following the failure of the borrower, result in the institution finding itself burdened with a liability which it could not have anticipated at the time the loan was approved. Once again there are valuation implications which may well affect the asset values of many industrial companies and, in a number of cases, banks are reviewing their loan books so as to assess the extent of their possible exposure.

All of a sudden property investment and the use of property as security for loans, especially where industrial property is concerned, is becoming less attractive to financial institutions as the level of risk is seen to be greater than hitherto envisaged. The onus is clearly on the developer to fully investigate site conditions, so as to be able to supply end users, investors and funding institutions with a comprehensive report on the land upon which buildings have been developed.

PUBLIC SECTOR FUNDING FOR REDEVELOPMENT

Central government is prepared to assist in the reclamation and redevelopment of derelict or contaminated land and buildings by making a contribution towards the viability gap. Financial assistance may be obtained through three schemes administered by the Department of the Environment: Derelict Land Grant, referred to earlier in this chapter; City Grant; and the Urban Programme. Responsibility for the first two schemes is to be transferred to the newly created Urban Regeneration Agency (URA), due to commence in late 1993. The URA will have powers of compulsory purchase in order to be able to assemble sites for redevelopment and will also take over responsibility for English Estates, the government-owned industrial development organization sponsored by the Department of Trade and Industry. As an interim measure, administration of the Derelict Land Grant and City Grant schemes has been brought together in the Land Development Grants Division of the Department of the Environment.

Government policies and principles relating to the environment were set out, in 1990, in the White Paper *This Common Inheritance*. One important principle with regard to the responsibility for clearing up pollution was clearly stated: 'those causing contamination should pay for the costs of putting it right' (*This Common Inheritance* 1990: 92). The 'polluter pays' principle adopted by the British government, in common with many others, is seen as an important means of influencing potential polluters.

Nevertheless, the problem remains of what should be done about the pollution and contamination arising out of the activities of previous generations. To compel present-day owners of land to clean up after previous owners would seem to be inequitable, especially as those same owners may well be having to face up to the fact that the property, for which they paid the market price several years ago, now has a nil or even negative value. Even forcing businesses to reclaim land which has been contaminated over earlier years by the industrial processes of the firm may be counterproductive if it has the effect of forcing the company out of business. At the present time there is no provision in the UK for a 'superfund' of the type which exists in the United States, or any means of requiring industries to put into place a financial deposit or bond in respect of any potentially contaminative manufacturing processes. Therefore, financial intervention by government would appear, for the time being at least, to be an essential component in the reclamation and redevelopment of derelict land.

Returning to the former gas works and rail siding site referred to above for the purpose of considering how the public sector grant systems work, it will be seen that the public sector contribution may well be fundamental in ensuring that sites are redeveloped. The site in question is located in one of the fifty-seven local authority areas designated under the Inner Urban Areas Act 1978 as being eligible for Urban Programme money and, as the completed project value exceeds £500,000, it falls into the category which would be considered for City Grant appraisal.

The site contains an area of 3.04 hectares (7.5 acres) on which it is intended to build eighteen industrial units with a gross internal floor area of 11,148 square metres (120,000 square feet). A detailed site investigation has revealed that the site is heavily contaminated with cyanide and heavy metals, including cadmium, mercury and arsenic, as well as toluene extractable matter and high levels of sulphates. Monitoring has also revealed high levels of methane.

Technically, much of the fill material could be consolidated under impervious finishes such as concrete and the foundations piled through the fill to suitable load bearing strata. The recommendation of the structural engineer is, however, that the fill should be removed and replaced with clean granular fill, properly consolidated in layers, so as to provide a good base from which to build. This view is also shared by the investment consultants advising the developer.

The total cost of undertaking the project is estimated as being £5 million excluding professional fees, interest charges and other costs, of which £1.3 million is in respect of site reclamation works. In 1989 the site was valued, for the purpose of the owner's annual accounts, at £1 million and at the time of writing (May 1993) industrial land values in the area, for clean serviced sites, are around £240,000 per hectare (£100,000 per acre), or £750,000 for the site, which is typical of the fall in values over the three year period. If the cost of reclaiming the site is deducted from the serviced site value, a negative value of £550,000 is arrived at.

Clearly, the site owner would be unlikely to pay this sort of money to reclaim the site, unless compelled to by a legal obligation. As the site is located in the inner urban area of the city and has the potential to create a substantial number of jobs, there is a good chance that the scheme will receive favourable consideration from the City Grant appraiser. The amount of City Grant to be allocated to the project would be calculated as shown in Table 4.4.

Table 4.4 Calculating a City Grant allocation

Paul Syms Associates – development appraisal

Client:	Anyclient Limited
Project:	The Roundhouse Site
Scheme:	Industrial B2 units
Sheet title:	City Grant appraisal

Investment value

	Occ. rate	Lettable area	Gross rent	Yield %	Years purchase	Totals
Industrial units	100.00%	120,000	£600,000	10.50	9.52	£5,714,286
		120,000	£600,000			
Rent per square foot	£5.00					

Estimated investment value			£5,714,286
Institutional acquisition costs	2.75% of est. inv. value		£157,143
Net investment value			£5,557,143
Estimated total value of development			£5,557,143

Development costs

	%	Area	Period	Rate	Totals
Existing value		7.50		£33,333	£250,000
Acq. costs	2.75%				£6,875
Buildings		120,000		£24.38	£2,925,000
Infrastructure					
Abnormal and demolition					
Preliminaries					£1,300,000
Prof. fees	11.09%				£468,345
Statutory fees	0.90%				£38,025
Any other costs	4.23%				£235,050
Non-rec. VAT					
Finance charges	12.50%		1.25		£485,434
Contingency	3.50%				£164,267
Total develop- ment costs					£5,872,996
Profit on value	15.00%	Profit on net cost		17.29%	£833,571
Total cost plus profit					£6,706,568
Development surplus (deficit)					(£1,149,425)
Saving on finance costs		(Net finance cost		£386,695)	£98,740
City Grant requirement					(£1,050,685)
City Grant gearing				1 TO	5.44
City Grant cost per job based on		300 jobs			£3,502

(*Notes follow on next page*)

Note: 1 The rental values and yields used to calculate the investment value must be in keeping with those expected to be found in the general area. There must be a market for the completed buildings, albeit with the allowance of a suitable marketing period and grant is not awarded so as to enable one development to compete on a more favourable basis than others in the vicinity.
2 The existing site value has to be one which meets with the approval of the Department of the Environment and may bear no relationship with the price actually paid by the prospective developer. Site values included in grant applications should reflect the argument that, without the grant, the site cannot be used beneficially and cannot be developed. In many cases this value will be negligible (Department of the Environment 1992).
3 Building costs, site reclamation costs and professional fees will all be scrutinized during the appraisal process and must be seen to be reasonable.
4 Finance charges are calculated on the basis of a cash flow which assumes that the grant will be drawn down quarterly in arrears, with the receipt of grant being used to reduce the financing cost of the development.
5 The developer is expected to make a reasonable profit out of the development but not one as high as might be expected in respect of a project which does not involve a public sector partner. The developer is not expected to make a profit on the grant aided element of the expenditure and grant is therefore calculated as a percentage of end value. A profit of 15 per cent on value is usually considered acceptable in respect of a wholly speculative scheme but this may be reduced if the accommodation is partly pre-let.
6 If the value which the developer receives on completion of the project is higher than that anticipated in the agreed City Grant appraisal, then the excess amount may be subject to clawback by the Department of the Environment.

Under the City Grant method of assessing the need for grant aid, which looks at the entire development project, the amount of grant required so as to enable the industrial redevelopment project to proceed is slightly in excess of £1.050 million. This results in a public sector contribution of one pound for every £5.44 of private sector contribution, based on the end value, otherwise referred to as a gearing of 1:5.44. Such a level of gearing would normally be acceptable to the Department of the Environment, which seeks to achieve an average gearing of at least 1:4. The public cost of job creation is also at an acceptable level, being an estimated £3,502 for each expected new job.

If the derelict site were not located in one of the fifty-seven priority areas for City Grant, then it may be suitable for reclamation under the Derelict Land Grant scheme. Its broad aim is to reclaim land which reduces the attractiveness of an area as a place in which to live, work or invest or, because of contamination or other reasons, is a threat to public health and safety or the natural environment. Such land, when reclaimed, should be capable of being used to provide for development, amenity value for the community or to contribute towards nature or historic conservation (Department of the Environment 1991c). In Assisted Areas and Derelict Land Clearance Areas (areas with high levels of dereliction, mostly in the north and Midlands), grant is payable at the rate of 100 per cent for local

Table 4.5 Derelict Land Grant calculation

Site value as existing (7.5 acres at £33,333 per acre)		£250,000
Site value post-reclamation (7.5 acres at £100,000 per acre)		£750,000
Betterment (increase in site value)		£500,000
Cost of site reclamation		
Reclamation contract	£1,300,000	
Site investigation	£25,000	
Professional fees @ 8 per cent	£106,000	
Total reclamation cost		£1,431,000
Deduct betterment		£500,000
Amount eligible for grant aid		£931,000
Rate of grant (Derelict Land Clearance Area)		80 per cent
Amount of grant		£744,000

authorities and English Estates, and 80 per cent for other applicants. Outside these areas the rate is 50 per cent, except in National Parks and Areas of Outstanding Natural Beauty where local authorities can receive 75 per cent grants.

Unlike the City Grant, Derelict Land Grant does not require an appraisal of the entire project to be undertaken for the purpose of assessing the grant requirement. It does, however, take into account the existing use value of the site and the anticipated post-reclamation value. A Derelict Land Grant calculation for the proposed industrial redevelopment would take the form shown in Table 4.5.

The City Grant basis of calculating financial assistance for development projects therefore produces a grant requirement £306,000 greater than the Derelict Land Grant method. Even allowing for the fact that the private sector DLG scheme only contributes 80 per cent towards the excess cost of reclaiming the site, it can be seen that the City Grant basis has the ability to provide an additional subsidy so as to assist the commercial viability of the project.

The size of the development used as a case study in this chapter is such as to make it ineligible for Urban Programme support but, for smaller projects, this can also assist in the reclamation and redevelopment of derelict sites. Within the areas designated under the Inner Urban Areas Act 1978 and subsequent amendments, loans can be made available for the acquisition of land and the carrying out of works on land. Grants and/or loans can also be made available, within Improvement Areas in the designated districts, for environmental improvement and also for the conversion, modification or extension of industrial and commercial buildings. As with both of the other forms of grant aid, it is necessary to demonstrate that the project will not proceed without assistance.

It should be noted that, at the time of writing in May 1993, consideration was being given to the replacement of City Grant and Derelict Land with a unified grant system. This may well come into being under the auspices of the Urban Regeneration Agency, although some observers consider that it may well be necessary to retain the two different methods of appraisal so as to be able to adequately consider the various types of projects needing public sector support.

CONCLUSION

Without doubt, the Environmental Protection Act 1990 has produced a heightened awareness in the minds of property developers and investors, of the problems of developing on contaminated and derelict sites. Initially this has had the effect of making such brownfield sites less attractive for redevelopment and may have increased the pressure for the release of greenfield sites.

It must be borne in mind, however, that the legislation was to have come into effect at a time when property markets generally were depressed and property users could afford to be very selective in deciding upon their new acquisitions. Therefore, they were likely to avoid problem sites, as the possible yield differential had yet to be proven or fully tested. In a buoyant market a different picture may well emerge, with problems tending to be overlooked in the competition to acquire development opportunities.

Banks and other financial institutions are conscious of the fact that the level of their exposure could be increased as the result of contamination of land from former industrial uses. They are therefore tending to play safe and require sites to be fully investigated and, if found, any contamination removed from the property. Such an attitude does little to assist in tackling the problem of contaminated land as it simply removes the contamination to another location, albeit under controlled conditions.

There is no real reason, in engineering terms, why many contaminants should not be safely encapsulated under industrial buildings. Such encapsulation would need to be adequately documented, so as to facilitate future changes to, or even redevelopment of, the building. Other, more esoteric, forms of site remediation, such as soils washing and thermal treatments, have yet to gain much of a foothold in the UK, although they are used quite extensively throughout Europe and North America.

The real problem lies, however, in the question of valuation and potential future liabilities in respect of the encapsulated material and treatment methods other than total removal. There may, therefore, be some need for central government to consider ways in which developers of former industrial sites may be indemnified against such liabilities in return for them making arrangements to contain or treat contaminated material on site rather than disposing of it elsewhere.

Government already plays an important part in the redevelopment of brownfield sites through the provision of grant aid. Without such assistance many sites would not be reclaimed and redeveloped, especially those which are contaminated. Existing legislation should have the effect of minimizing future contamination, although certain manufacturing processes are still bound to cause a degree of contamination. Use of the 'polluter pays' principle should eventually reduce demands on the public purse, provided of course that polluters can be held to account. In the meantime there is still a considerable area of land which is capable of being reclaimed and perhaps consideration should be given to the setting up of a fund to assist in site reclamation works.

From the research point of view there are many topics which could provide an agenda for the future. This could include studies into the impact on land values in countries which have already introduced tighter controls on the redevelopment of contaminated land, such as Germany and the Netherlands. The establishment of a fund for the reclamation of sites, where the polluter is no longer in existence or for some other reason cannot be held to account, should be considered, together with ways in which such a fund may be financed. As a newly-formed government agency, the performance of the Urban Regeneration Agency will need to be monitored. Perhaps most important of all, there is a need for research aimed at producing a set of standards for the reclamation of contaminated and derelict sites. Such standards must be acceptable to occupiers, investors, funding institutions and government alike, without simply transferring the problem from one location to another, leaving the permanent solution to a future generation.

REFERENCES

Bennett, N. (1992) 'Clean-up costs force banks to rethink lending', *The Times*, 14 January.

Cairney, T. (ed.) (1987) *Reclaiming Contaminated Land*, Glasgow: Blackie.

Control of Pollution Act 1974, London: HMSO.

Denner, J. (1991) *Contaminated Land: Policy Development in the UK, a Paper*, London: Department of the Environment, HMSO.

Department of the Environment (1986) *Transforming our Waste Land – The Way Forward*, report by University of Liverpool, Environmental Advisory Unit, London: HMSO.

—— (1991a) *Survey of Derelict Land in England 1988*, London: HMSO.

——/Welsh Office (1991b) *Public Registers of Land Which May be Contaminated, a Consultation Paper*, London: HMSO.

—— (1991c) *Derelict Land Reclamation Grant (DLG)*, information note, London: Department of the Environment.

—— (1992) *City Grant Guidance Notes*, City Grant Team, London: Department of the Environment.

Environmental Protection Act 1990, London: HMSO.

Environmental Protection Act 1990 (Section 143 Registers); Regulations 1992, Draft Statutory Instrument, London: Department of the Environment.

Estates Gazette (1993) 'Contamination registers: formally abandoned', 9312, 27 March: 35.

Fleming, G. (ed.) (1991) *Recycling Derelict Land*, London: Telford.

Haines, R.C. (1987) 'Policy, planning and financial issues', in T. Cairney (ed.), *Reclaiming Contaminated Land*, Glasgow: Blackie.

Hobson, J. (1991) 'Contaminated Land', Paper presented at IBC seminar on Paying for Environmental Improvement, December 1991.

Houlder, V. (1992) 'Why the Receivers have moved into Mountleigh', *Financial Times*, 26 May: 23.

Ironside, C.D. (1989) 'Private sector funding for redevelopment of contaminated land', *Journal of the Institution of Water and Environmental Management* 3(2): 147–53.

Kivell, P.T. (1987) 'Derelict land in England: policy responses to a continuing problem', *Regional Studies* 21(3): 265–9.

—— (1993) *Land and the City*, London: Routledge.

Syms, P. (1993) 'Contaminated land', *The Valuer*, January: 6.

This Common Inheritance: Britain's environmental strategy (1990), London: HMSO.

5 New land uses

The recommodification of land for new uses on the city fringe

Dick Pratt

INTRODUCTION

The aim of this chapter is to explain the redevelopment of previously derelict inner city and city fringe industrial sites. The goal is to consider changes both in the role of the state and the role of capital in this process. The argument developed here highlights the importance both of a consideration of the state and, in particular, of the analysis of changes in the mode of regulation. The chapter is illustrated first, with material on the Use Class Order and change of use – especially with regards to high-tech property that occurred in the late 1980s – and, second, with a case study of an industrial district – the Jewellery Quarter in Birmingham. This latter case is a very rich example as it brings together the themes of de-industrialization, urban regeneration, state and property.

The introduction of new modes of state regulation have accompanied the massive destruction of the manufacturing industry. While many analyses have focused upon de-industrialization, rarely has it been properly analysed in relation to this crisis. An often ignored, but significant, part of the new modes of state regulation is that of state control of land uses. The post-war planning machine was the subject of an onslaught from sections of investment and development interests during the 1970s (Ambrose 1986). This regulation has forced these actors – institutional investors, property companies, construction companies – to modify their activities.

Moving beyond description towards explanation requires the important step of theorization. Theorizing the nature of the relationships between the state and development interests is difficult. In essence, a theory which attempts to relate significant changes in the state regulation of the built environment (for example, but not exclusively, planning) to 'long waves' of capital accumulation would be attractive. It would help to distinguish those pressures resulting from short-term fluctuations from those determined by more profound crises of oversupply and more general loss of value through depreciation and obsolescence.

One attempt to understand the more significant crises of capital accumulation has been outlined by Harvey (1989). He argues that capital is invested and disinvested in different sectors and locations in order to maintain returns on investment and to generate profits more generally. Where profits fall, investments are switched. Birmingham firms have ceased production and replacement production facilities have opened on the other side of the world. Switching between sectors also takes place, but these switches do not necessarily involve such dramatic locational switching. Sometimes existing land uses can be renewed and revalued; this process is termed recommodification.

Put simply, recommodification in this context means that once commercial interests recognize that existing land uses do not match the needs of potential buyers, a new set of legal and administrative arrangements is necessitated before rights to use land can be successfully exploited once more. If this is not enacted then the pre-existing land-use pattern becomes a fetter upon commercial opportunities for the development industry. The Use Classes Order is the principal, although not the only, way in which the state regulates rights to use land.

Fundamental to industrial restructuring has been the growth of high-technology industries and the new professional services. This has produced bottlenecks associated with insufficient availability of land. The rash of business parks, office parks and the science parks that emerged during the 1980s are but the most outward sign of this general phenomenon. The area immediately outside of the central business district (the city fringe) is the next area to become ready for recommodification, just as previously the outer limits of the urban area (the metropolitan fringe) have. Both are areas adjacent to historically well-developed infrastructural provision but where development values are yet to be realized.

This process of recommodification is regionally uneven. But whereas the legal and administrative basis for recommodification must exist nationally if it is to exist anywhere (as codified in legislation), the possibility of it being realized in any single location will be determined by locational advantage and the confidence of property investment fund managers. Yet, providing a new land use in isolation from the development of a market would not achieve the desired result for the property industry. Markets are not 'natural', they must be created and this means that the land with particular permitted uses attached to it must be taken to the market for investment certainty to be achieved. A process similar to this has been observed in the case of 'post-industrial' transformation of loft space previously used for small, artisanal business activities in New York to residential uses (Zukin 1988). Goodchild (1990) has made a link between texts on town planning and the debate on post-modernity. Stoker (1990) has attempted to relate changing patterns in local government management to the so-called period of flexible specialization. This chapter relates land-use regulation to the new period where flexibility and specialization of land uses have become more critical factors.

In the UK investment fund managers who handle funds for insurance and pension funds simply do not have a track record by which potential investment in mixed use and studio offices could be evaluated. Venture capital by which market boundaries are enlarged and redefined and in this sense created has yet to find a development industry equivalent. In this sense the new land uses such as science parks and studio offices have to develop confidence during the process of commodification. In the UK the new B1 use class (see below) was a unique opportunity to widen the range of permitted developments. This means that over time and given greater economic certainty and growth, we might expect to see a new round of investment engendered. Such investment will depend, however, on location and the ensemble of associated land uses in proximity to any given site.

RE-INVIGORATING AND RECREATING LAND USES: NEW LAND USES FOR OLD – SOME EMPIRICAL TENDENCIES

The massive destruction of value embodied in the kind of capital dedicated to Fordist production, as represented by de-industrialization, has brought with it a prolonged crisis in the industrial property market. A number of writers have addressed the changing pattern of land-use investment. What follows is a brief survey of previous studies relevant to a consideration of new land uses such as science parks and studio offices.

Luithlen (1985) has analysed office building which has sustained the lively interest of property developers. He describes how, despite large funds being available for investment, ordinary shares were losing their attraction due to the continuously ailing industrial sector and fixed interest securities were too blunt a weapon against inflation. A number of authors have pointed out how direct investment in property became very attractive, given the right arrangements. Such special arrangements included the 1965 Finance Act and its results, the Corporation Tax and Capital Gains Tax (see Pratt 1994). Nabarro and Cullen (1986) have documented the shift in interest from office to retail developments from 1983 onwards. Subsequently, they calculated the enormous increases in the capital value of industrial property occurring during the last property boom and following the introduction of the new B1 use class (IPD 1988).

By comparison, Fothergill, Monk and Perry (1987) have described the stagnant conditions of the industrial market reflecting the relative decline of the British manufacturing industry. With a reduction of manufacturing jobs from 8 million in the 1960s to 5 million in the mid-1980s, it is hardly surprising that the attendant property market should be so depressed.

At the same time a number of surveys have revealed the existence of profitable niches within this otherwise unpromising market. Nabarro and Cullen (1986) considered that investors might be prepared to include some industrial property in their portfolio on the basis of more adequate information. Lodge (1986) identified some of the property requirements for 'modern industry'.

In the early 1980s, commercial surveys identified the potential market for industrial/office complexes with site cover of between 25–34 per cent and ample car parking as a potentially profitable commodity (see Fuller Peiser 1985; Debenham, Tewson and Chinnocks 1983). But institutional investors remained sceptical; it was not until the 'invention' of the venture capital market that the new market began to form.

A fundamental dilemma existed for all 'high-tech' developers: either speculatively build to a high specification and face the prospect of being left with a fully fitted building which no one wants; or alternatively build speculatively to much lower specification and face the prospect of total disinterest borne of either lack of product identity or inability to assist the client in visualizing the final building.

Investment advisors recommended that a rule of thumb be adopted such that any building with less than 30 per cent office space should not be considered high-tech by the market (Fuller Peiser 1985). However other considerations were: more flexible lease terms; break clauses; gross internal floor area; car parking standards requiring one space per 23–32.5 square metres.

The Use Classes Order is the day to day set of rules established by the state by which the development industry can visualize the realizability of projects at certain locations. We should be reminded that in the case of the new B1 category, the 1987 changes to the Use Classes Order did not produce a class specifically for the knowledge-based industries but merely amalgamated the 1972 classes II (offices which were not in the financial and professional services sector but were research and development, studios or laboratories) and III (light industry) into a new B1 'business' class. Since the change, several science park watchers have suggested that the impact has been far less than was anticipated.

Another dilemma faced planners according to Fuller Peiser (1985) on the one hand hoping to achieve job creation and subsequent stimulation of the local economy; on the other hand a fear of the 'devious developer' who might twist liberal planning permissions (designed for flexibility) to allow uses which force up land values.

In 1985 the issue of planning permissions exercised the would-be developers at some length, firstly in terms of 'existing consents'. The national Development Control Forum found existing Use Class Orders inappropriate for high-tech planning consents since they produced unnecessarily restrictive permissions. At the time of the Fuller Peiser report (1985), high-tech consents were granted specifying a particular Use Class (for example Class III with permitted ancillary uses). But Fuller Peiser argued that a high-tech company would often require greater flexibility of uses than such permission offered. It is also more difficult to market a high-tech building which has restricted uses. Local authority planners in any case became more flexible following the release of Circular 14/85 which placed the importance of generating employment opportunities (however measured) over complying with office floorspace limits laid out in structure plans.

Second, the question of 'bespoke consents' was considered, i.e. those which make no mention of the Use Classes Order. Instead, planning consents are designed to accommodate the flexible requirements of high-tech industry, via the imposition of reasonable planning conditions or if necessary through the use of planning agreements. In some cases the local authority may choose to retain a stake in the scheme in order to ensure that it is developed along the right lines. Fuller Peiser commented that office contents of high-tech developments can be expected to rise above 50 per cent and noted that the Royal Institute of Chartered Surveyors and the Development Control Forum were opposed to the idea of a new Use Classes Order as being potentially more restrictive than *ad hoc* planning conditions designed to meet the particular circumstance of individual cases.

Institutional investment in industrial property has been limited to particularly brief periods and particular geographical regions (Pratt 1983, 1994). The late 1970s saw hopes for rapidly designed and built light industrial units. At the same time the sheer scale of funds was rising. The hopes for this type of investment were dashed as the recession of the early 1980s set in. Chartered Surveyors Debenham, Tewson and Chinnocks (1983) commissioned a report. Its findings revealed that, at the time, two-thirds of pension funds' property holdings were in the south east, and over 40 per cent in London itself. In contrast the whole of the north of England (the north west, Yorkshire and Humberside and northern region) accounted for just 7 per cent.

> Investment funds for industrial property development have been limited to modern properties, built to high standards and let on long leases, to tenants of unquestionable financial standing who take full responsibility for repairs and insurance. They also prefer to fund or acquire general purpose buildings in preference to units designed especially for manufacturing.
>
> (Fothergill, Gudgin, Kitson and Monk 1986: 48)

While financial institutions had increased their involvement with property massively in the early 1980s (investing in excess of £2,000 million in commercial property in 1982), only a minute proportion of this was aimed at the needs of the knowledge-based industries and studio offices. Essentially investment managers had not developed techniques for identifying the sites, firms and technologies which are most likely to sustain rental growth well ahead of inflation, the volume of capital expenditure justified by that rental growth and the capital value capable of being sustained by that investment.

In the 1980s knowledge-based industries were new and studio offices were newer. The institutions had little evidence of how they would perform in relation to their investment criteria. Assessing the rental value of such properties will remain difficult because there are no others of a similar type in the neighbourhood with which comparisons can be made. The institutions have believed so far that property for the knowledge-based industries and studio offices has to be specialized; if the firms tenanting the property fail and no replacements are forthcoming the institutions will be left with a 'white elephant'. Studio offices in particular can be expected to attract interest from those who have experienced the failure of office developments on the metropolitan fringe where supporting services such as shops, restaurants, bars and cafes have failed to develop.

APPROACHES IN CONCEPTUALIZING THE PROCESS OF COMMODIFICATION OF NEW LAND USES

The development of an explanatory framework for these changes in land use is extremely important. It permits at least the possibility of foreseeing where and how leverage for change might occur. A consideration of new land uses demands a re-evaluation of theoretical frameworks used in both the creation of land markets and also in its segmentation into uses and zones.

Neoclassical approaches take for granted the state regulation of land use and the consequent pattern of zoning. In such an approach state regulation and market exchange is separated from the commodity form of land use. State regulation is seen as a sort of valve restricting or enhancing the supply of 'raw land' to a particular use. It is assumed that permission or prohibition to use land in certain ways will follow along behind actual use.

Strands of thought developed in the 1970s and 1980s that drew upon a Marxist analysis of the property sector, and which are critical of the neo-classical tradition, can be woven into a most useful approach. This approach essentially sees state regulation as part of the process by which a land use is brought to the market as an exchangeable asset. State regulation in the context of new land uses is seen as a process of administrative recommodification. In this sense value and the use of land occurs through changing legislation and is exemplified in the 1987 changes to the Use Classes Order.

Massey and Catalano (1978) focused on the changes in rights to use land in certain ways that bear the commodity characteristics. This led to the idea that land itself was the property rather than the rights attached to the parcels. Thus, previously unsaleable or not always saleable rights in things could now become saleable. Massey and Catalano viewed as being significant certain changes in the legal definition of land which have taken place during the dominance of capitalism. These changes took place in the law of entail, crofters rents and tenure, the nationalization of royalties in the coal industry, 'planning' measures to limit use, density and character of new housing developments and, finally, the nationalization of development rights during the Second World War.

However, when we come to survey how the precise form of the commodity is analysed in relationship to the development industry we do not see such clarity of thought being maintained in the literature of the last two decades (see Hooper 1984; Roweis and Scott 1981). What matters in determining whether things are commodities is not so much that they are produced as that they are produced and exchanged. For land to be exchanged it must be commodified in certain appropriate ways.

Roweis and Scott (1981) argued that historically the state has played a role in developing the pre-floorspace stage of land development through the provision of major infrastructural facilities. This they term subject to democratic accountability. Once land has been serviced in this way it is, they say, exchanged through a series of private market transactions which decisively determine the geographical pattern and intensity of urban land uses. They focus solutions in terms of the sphere of distribution rather than production. The state is ascribed a role as a producer of 'non-commodities'. In their approach it cannot be made clear what interests capital in general has in state regulation of the development process.

It would make much more sense to view the state as playing a vital role in almost every aspect of the reproduction of capital. It may be argued that the objective of state intervention is to stabilize accumulation in the face of all kinds of contradictions, only to find that faced with the prospect of choosing when and where the measures of devalorization will take place, it may be challenged with crises of a political kind. The state is not external to the means of production, it may even only be partially external to the relations of production as in large-scale nationalization. But to intervene to regulate the conditions of production and reproduction means that the state internalizes these contradictions.

David Harvey has suggested a useful approach to the commodity aspects of land. For Harvey the value of the built environment derives from its 'ensemble setting' in that 'the built environment, then, has to be regarded as a geographically ordered, complex, composite commodity. The production, ordering, maintenance, renewal and transformation of such a commodity poses serious dilemmas' (Harvey 1982: 233).

The capitalist logic of these tendencies, according to Harvey, is that control over the production of space is passed to the interior of the credit system – as he terms it – land as fictitious capital. However, this line of argument fudges the issue of the state as an object of the analysis, although it does avoid dumping the state completely outside the means of production (as in Roweis and Scott). To identify the state as a regulator of land-use values it is necessary to place law much more at the centre of the analysis, a concept hardly developed in Harvey's work.

The work of Eugeni Pashukanis (1978) has seldom been if ever referred to in this context. Yet his approach to 'Commodity and Subject' is relevant to an understanding of the state regulation of land use. In particular he argues that the commodity form does not exist 'naturally' but that it is legally, or juridically, constituted. What this means is that the commodity form includes the creation of rights of disposal in respect of the general circulation of commodities. The legal ownership of land is an entitlement to use it in certain ways. These certain ways are governed by the relations of production. Crucially then, from this point of view capital is not outside the juridical law of society and the state is not outside the economic laws of capitalism.

While the historical development of capitalism brought with it the commodification of labour power, it also brought about the commodification of the rights to use land. Commodities cannot take themselves to market and perform exchange in their own right. They are taken to market by actors in the context of a set of legal rules – the legal form. In other words the market is a creation. The establishment of the complex legal and administrative structures within which markets operate are a case in point.

Stability of expectations is a fundamental prerequisite for the emergence of mature market conditions. Long-term accumulation strategies by those in the market is not possible without performance appraisal being put on an objective basis. Harvey (1985: 27) has already recognized the role of 'cadastral surveys and chorological nets' in the bourgeois development of the productive relations, of generalized commodity production. Such quantifications by the state and by groups of capitalists can be seen as bundles of 'abstract wills of their legal owners' (following Pashukanis). Capitalist economic and legal relations should be understood not only as relations between things (commodities) but also as relations between 'wills of legal subjects'. As Pashukanis (1978: 117) notes, 'legal fetishism complements commodity fetishism'.

Just as a particular commodity form can become obsolete under conditions of the new system, so too can the legal form become inappropriate.

Successive rounds of significant restructuring of the economy require a shadowing juridical process of commodification, ossification of commodity forms, followed by recommodification. In the built environment this produces the 'palimpsest of landscapes' to which Harvey (1982: 233) refers. State regulation will crucially determine the basis for the next period of accumulation; it will do so in the context of the social formation.

McMahon has made two indicative studies of such circumstances (1985a and 1985b). His method could be fruitfully applied to the process now clearly underway for the redefinition of land uses, the general revision of the Use Class Order and of greenbelt policies to allow new rounds of capital accumulation at relatively lower prices of production.

New routes in the circuit of productive capital are opened only after the most fundamental crises have been endured. The 'switching' crisis experienced as a restructuring of British industry was such an event. The office building booms of the early 1970s and the mid-1980s represent a diversion of capital away from production. It was a sign, following Harvey, of 'over accumulation' and 'immanent crisis' (Harvey 1981). But following on from the massive devalorization, capital can be expected to search for new areas and new sectors for profitable investment. The caution evinced by the fund managers (see above) personifies the dilemma of capitalists confronted with the necessity of locking up assets in fixed capital. Once fixed it cannot be easily switched, or converted, to a more advantageous source of rent or interest. Capitalist investment in high-tech land development has the character of both productive and non-productive credit money. It is an advance against both anticipated surplus value and the potential of assisting the creation of future surplus value. The risks attached to the speculative investment of the science park-type lies both in the performance of the high-tech sector and in the future surplus value-creating capacity of the whole of social capital.

In summary then, the property professionals and those that advise them started to identify the emergence of a new property market. From the very beginning they viewed the role of the state with a keen sense. The project of some far-sighted sections of interest-bearing capital can perhaps be viewed as the requirement upon government for the construction of administrative foundations to, and defences around, a mechanism for pumping out a steady rental flow based upon more and more favourable yields. In some instances the demands from developers' advisors were too fussy and unnecessary, the case for instance with the demand for a new Use Classes Order for specifically high-tech land uses. B1 came to the rescue, creating new opportunities for developers and new headaches as well as opportunities for planners.

The 1985 White Paper, *Lifting the Burden* (Department of the Environment 1985) gave formal recognition by the state to the development industry's need for a streamlined route to the market place for a variety of new land uses. The argument was made on behalf of 'high-tech'. Other land uses could arrive in its slipstream.

DOES 'HARVESTING THE CITY FRINGE' JEOPARDIZE INDUSTRIAL COMMUNITIES?

The 'city fringe' has excited developers and planners for some time. Both in London and in the provincial centres the expansion of the personal and financial services sector has raised possibilities for its transformation. For developers, the opportunity to 'bolt' developments on to pre-existing central business districts rather than building in peripheral locations reduces the uncertainty, yields and risks. For planning authorities, development industry interest in the city fringe raises the possibility of increasing land values in locations which have often stagnated for years. Town cramming also becomes an option.

Yet for the institutional investor the land use must usually be comprehensively redeveloped. A clean sweep of existing buildings is preferred. This approach, while acceptable in the past, has been increasingly challenged in celebrated cases: in London at Coin Street, Kings Cross, Bishopsgate Goods yard, Spitalfields Market; in Birmingham at the Bull Ring and Brindley Place.

The continuing existence of industrial communities in close proximity to the CBD can be jeopardized by such city fringe developments. Groups who are concerned with protecting 'heritage' streets, squares, courtyards and so on have sprung up (for the classic case of Tolmers Square, see Wates 1976). Planning has become concerned that comprehensive redevelopment has led to a net loss of jobs from the city and to the ultimate destruction of heritage townscapes. Such developments threaten urban vitality, turning the city fringe into a mere extension of the CBD with its deadening effect upon the locality outside office hours. Local strategies have been developed in, for example, Bradford's Little Germany, Nottingham's Lace Market and the Birmingham Jewellery Quarter to partially offset these tendencies.

In such areas development potential rested on opportunistic change in land use from low value to high (Forman 1989; Ravetz 1986). In these areas, rents may rise subject to overcoming certain impediments, not least of which are pedestrian accessibility to the rest of the CBD, good traffic flows and convenient parking for commuting to the city fringe which cannot be expected to be readily equipped with rapid public transport radially to suburban locations. This process of 'harvesting the city fringe' also depends on a level of local community acceptability to the incoming development and perceived displacement threats. Inevitably such developments may change the character of certain areas of cities as occurred, for example, in Spitalfields, Covent Garden, Cecil Court, Savile Row (all in London), which have been the subject of these changes (Dodd 1989; Games 1990; Forman 1989).

Although there are major potential benefits to these fringe locations, homogenization of city centres has also led to the death of the evening economy (Montgomery 1990; Bianchini 1990: especially 38–41). City centres may appear dead and without interest to visitors. Attempts to compensate for this by sustaining evening activities in certain locations – theatres, cinemas, restaurants, new/refurbished public houses and wine bars – have been made (Comedia 1989).

The pace of change in city fringe areas was quickened following the introduction of 'B1' in 1987. However, large-scale conversion of previously industrial property to office uses has resulted in the removal in some areas of the mixed land-use vitality which contributed to their original attractiveness.

The effect of the 1987 changes to the Town and Country Planning (Use Classes) Order has been much discussed with respect to distinctive manufacturing quarters on the 'city fringe'. The examples of Savile Row in the City of Westminster, the Lace Market area of Nottingham and the Jewellery Quarter in Birmingham are mentioned frequently in this connection. The West Midlands Planning and Transportation Sub-Committee report (undated) on the subject noted that 'it seems likely . . . given the demand and pressure for office floorspace in Birmingham City Centre that this could ultimately lead to a shortage of jewellery workshops in the City.'

Are these 'quarter' policies successful in creating any more jobs? As yet, little evidence exists, but they may serve to assist in the retention of the industry even if it is substantially restructured. Inevitably more service jobs are created in the heritage museum and other facilities which spring up around the area. The change in the area may be such that in the long term the more traditional uses are pushed out, leaving empty refurbished buildings with heritage interpretive plaques. As elsewhere, the machinery is replaced by 'studios' in a traditional process of urban succession.

We turn now to look at a particular example of development pressure on the industrial community – the Birmingham Jewellery Quarter – to illustrate some of the complexities before concluding with some remarks concerning the recommodification of the city fringe.

THE BIRMINGHAM JEWELLERY QUARTER – A CASE STUDY

The Jewellery Quarter (JQ) (Figure 5.1) is located on the north-west edge of the city fringe. Birmingham's CBD has a distinctive business and financial character which emerged in the last quarter of the nineteenth century.

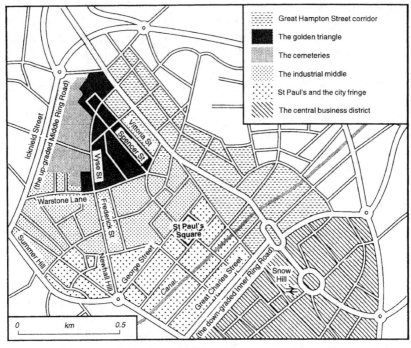

Figure 5.1 Birmingham's Jewellery Quarter

The JQ is separated from the CBD by a four lane multi-level and strongly undulating dual carriageway road. A narrow-gauge canal runs along the JQ's southern perimeter, through a zone which is called St Paul's after a Georgian square at its heart. St Paul's moved 'up-market' in the mid to late 1980s. The JQ's northern boundary is sharply limited by the middle ring road which has been significantly upgraded to compensate for the down-grading of the inner ring traffic circulation (from October 1992).

The Birmingham JQ pre-dated the existence of the modern city centre itself by about fifty years. The employment in the jewellery industry peaked in 1914 with large manufacturers coexisting with small-scale petit bourgeois and artisanal production (see Figure 5.2).

In the immediate post-war era there were found to be 923 works in a single square kilometre in the quarter. The resulting conditions are described:

> The low overheads of these small firms have often hidden poor practices, lack of machinery and power, and poor working conditions, which have discouraged recruitment to the industry. Associated with this has been the increasing division of labour between firms with these

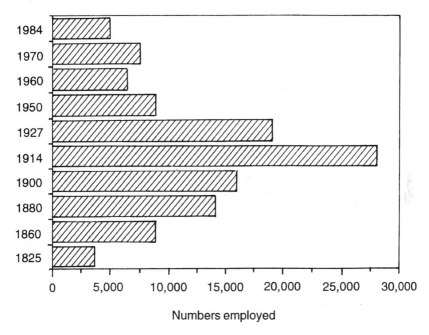

Figure 5.2 Employment levels in the Jewellery Quarter, 1825 to 1984
Source: Gilbert 1972 (quoted in Smith 1989: 96)

effectively linked by a human conveyor belt which carried small but valuable articles from workshop to workshop around nearby streets and within factories.

(Smith 1989: 96)

The area has survived the collapse of major elements of the motor manufacturing industry, albeit in a much reduced form. Within the JQ, the City Economic Development Department has current records of over 400 jewellery firms operating from within the 40.5 hectares quarter. The area has no significant residential population, although many of the workshops have been converted from previous residential use. Few have lived in the quarter since the 1930s, although this has begun to change as a number of rehabilitation and new developments have included apartment accommodation in response to the market in this city fringe area.

Businesses and business space: an historical perspective

An industrial community of jewellery manufacturers has existed at this location since the early nineteenth century (Wise 1949; Rogers 1983). It continues in the face of challenges to its dominant land use within the 'golden triangle'. In this context it is worth prioritizing the issue of leadership. Historically, the area exhibits strong characteristics of both individualist and collectivist strands within the manufacturing community. Facilities such as the Assay Office, the School of Jewellery, the established traditions of outworking as well as the basic physical infrastructures and public amenities are shared. But other resources used by the firms are jealously guarded, in particular designs, processes and so on – 'the tricks of the trade'. These are concealed from each other and from outsiders. Marshalling a commitment to collective outcome seemed to Smith (1987) to be rather difficult, given the traditional attitudes to design secrecy and security.

The cost of working space for all categories of jewellery workers and firms has become a significant issue with regard to redevelopment. 'Renting a peg' in the Jewellery Quarter in the period up until the mid-1950s was a system used by jewellery jobbers, outworkers or subcontractors and typically gave them about 4.6 square metres. Smith (1989) remarks that when the Hockley Centre (the flatted factory designed to take jewellers from the slum clearance programme) opened in 1968 with units of 22 square metres upwards, rents were of the order of £5.06–£8.29 per square metre. Our survey (1990) was only able to establish rent comparisons for a proportion of the total firms surveyed. Nevertheless, it showed that change was already taking place fairly quickly. Of the firms responding 4 per cent were paying in excess of £96.88 per square metre, 17 per cent paid between £43.06 and £64.58, 43 per cent paid between £10.76 and £43.06 and 31 per cent paid less than £21.53. A useful comparison can be made with the rents being asked on Aston Science Park, located on the eastern edge of the city fringe. They are calculated at the median between inner city industrial and city centre office rents. The March 1990 figures for the new lets were £118.40 per square metre.

The St Paul's area contains Birmingham's only Georgian square and it separates the Jewellery Quarter from the central business district. Property developers with an interest in this district in 1990 were expressing a hope for £247.57 per square metre for JQ office developments when they could be realized (Pratt 1990). These kinds of development might be observed along the transect from Highgate Hill, around the perimeter of St Paul's Square to Caroline Street and George Street.

The survey: premises, employment and business activity

The area is dominated by four major landowners, one of which is the City of Birmingham. The City was landlord to 48 per cent of the tenants in our firms survey. Eighty-seven vacant plots were identified in the survey. Ten plots were awaiting development (estimated at 21,160 square metres of which two-thirds was committed to a large jewellery manufacturer who was relocating from the Leeds area). Seventy-seven plots were void buildings, of which twenty-one were awaiting refurbishment, eighteen were undergoing refurbishment and thirty-eight were available for sale or to let. In all, it was calculated that there were 83, 982 square metres of B1 poised to be released on to the market (of which 40,494 square metres was information given by estate agents signs and 43,488 square metres was estimated).

The availability of sites was far from equally distributed through the Quarter. The JQ can be easily subdivided into five zones (see Figure 5.1 above):

1 the cemeteries;
2 the golden triangle containing most of the retail and the smallest manu- facturing workshops;
3 the Great Hampton Street corridor where larger engineering concerns were traditionally found and where a new clothing wholesale presence is found;
4 the industrial middle with a range of larger jewellery-related firms;
5 St Paul's and the city fringe where the greatest commercial changes are being experienced and which is the only part of the Quarter that currently sustains an evening economy.

The least voids/vacant sites were found in the corridor and at the city fringe reflecting the development pressures from the city and vehicle access opportunities to the corridor.

Of the eighty-seven plots, thirty-eight were to be for rent, fifteen for sale, seven for sale or rent, while the future tenure of seventeen was not known. In terms of the concentration of the handling of the marketing of future land uses, one firm had control of no less than fourteen of the plots, eleven firms controlled between two and four plots and twenty-two firms had control of one plot. The control of a remaining twenty-three was unknown.

In terms of employment, the 112 firms surveyed employed 1,163 workers (not including outworkers). The use of jobbers/outworkers/ subcontractors was recorded 485 times within the firms survey but indivi- duals could obviously be working for more than one of the firms being surveyed and therefore might have been counted more than once. The average size of firms surveyed was thus 10.4 employees.

The size and pattern of employment of the firms in the JQ is distinctive. Currently the JQ has single person firms operating on their own account or as subcontracting 'outworkers'. It also has firms which employ up to 150 people on the shopfloor and up to another 110 in offices. There is a range of firms between these magnitudes with a significant bias toward firms employing less than five persons. Smith (1987) found that the process firms were the smallest (averaging 3.7 in her survey), while the product firms tended to be larger employers (averaging sixteen). The average for combined retail manufacturers/retailers was 7.8; for retailing it was 5.2. Our survey of firms did not seek to make a distinction between product firms and process firms.

From the responses of the firms it appeared that 23 per cent of the jobbers operated from within the JQ, while 29 per cent of the self-employed contractors encountered through the firms' interviews actually worked from the survey firm's premises. Of the firms themselves 90 per cent were independent producers, 77 per cent were leaseholders, 23 per cent were freeholders. Only 5 per cent had been on site since 1900, 88 per cent had been established since 1945, while 62 per cent had been established since 1980. Eleven per cent operated from more than one property within the locality.

From the more limited responses to the question on turnover it appeared that there was both a high birth rate and, at least potentially, a high death rate. Many firms could attain a turnover of £50,000 but to get to £250,000 was much harder. Firms which had a turnover of over £1 million appeared currently to be extremely stable. But the turnover figures may have reflected historic rates of capital accumulation; the history of the area shows that larger firms have vanished. More generally a significant restructuring of the jewellery sector has taken place nationally, resulting in concentration in the hands of the retail chains (see Smith 1987).

The locality has outstanding attractions in terms of being a business community. Fifty-two per cent of the survey firms perceived their location as very good while 23 per cent thought it was good. The advantages and the disadvantages of the location were prompted from a list. Proximity of suppliers, the advantage of the JQ address, knowledge of trade buyers of where to come, the character of the workforce, the proximity of the Assay Office, the quality of the motorway network, all scored as being significant in over 10 per cent of firms surveyed. Parking was mentioned as being a significant problem in just under 70 per cent of firms surveyed, despite 41 per cent of the total workforce of the firms surveyed bringing cars into the Quarter.

Our firms survey did not cover the issue of wholesaling. Smith (1987) has implied that the relative decline of the wholesale market for jewellery manufacturers has removed an important advantage of locational concentration. Wholesalers would arrive from London by train and be able to shop throughout the Quarter. The disappearance of independent high street jewellery retailers and the recession in the industry in the 1970s removed the requirement for such wholesalers, so few continue to exist.

Tensions within improvement strategies for the Jewellery Quarter

The visible signs of an area-based improvement strategy beginning to work are evident in the JQ. Such schemes are often expected to fulfil many different and frequently conflicting objectives. Evaluation of these strategies can therefore be very difficult (Montgomery 1990).

The idea for 'quarterizing' the city fringe of Birmingham came together in its first coherent form in the Highbury Initiative which described the JQ as 'a craft/creative quarter'. This idea was further developed (Pratt and Morphet 1990) into a critique of existing strategies for creating 'cultural quarters'. The jewellery industry is not strictly a cultural industry in the sense of the arts and entertainment industries, yet it does at least share some of their characteristics. These could be listed as promoting a sense of occasion and of celebration, an association with awards and ceremonies, and of cultural activities in the wider sociological sense. In terms of urban design and the vitality of the streets and pavements there are obvious parallels with the development of established arts and entertainments quarters of cities. But whereas entertainment quarters tend to spring to life in the evening, producing a nocturnal economy, the JQ is currently most notable for its urban vitality during the day. It shares with the central business district the unenviable characteristic of becoming virtually deserted after 6.00 p.m.

A variety of different interests may coincide, overlap and conflict in such situations – those of property owners, firm owners, employees, professionals, visitors, existing residents etc. For property owners, the intervention of the local authority in promoting the area and giving it some marketing support will inevitably lead to an improvement in property prices and in the value of property assets. Properties in such areas may have been demonstrating high vacancy rates, while the local authorities' involvement is designed to reduce these vacancy rates. However, such strategies may give rise – as in the JQ – to contradictory processes. For example, an increase in property prices, even of hope value, may serve to undermine the firms which are already located in these areas. Longer-term expectations on the part of property owners or managers may lead to an increase in rents or to the non-renewal of short-term leases. Often firms were attracted to these areas for traditional reasons which would include the availability of property at the levels which firms could afford.

Existing firms may also view the recognition of the area as a means of attracting unwelcome competition from other firms, while the official attentions of council officers may reveal the difficulties in complying with fire regulations or planning requirements.

Employees may find that the enhancement of such areas provides a more agreeable place to work. The introduction of other similar firms may also mean that there are more jobs to choose from, or that wage rates are increased. The council's involvement may also increase the level of training available or give individuals the support required to establish their own businesses.

These quarters are often set in very mixed areas of the inner city, where residential and industrial uses have always co-existed. The people who live with these firms often accept them as part of their lives. In many areas they may be pleased to see that others have come to regard their way of life as interesting, although they may not appreciate the incursion of wandering tourists. New residents are likely to be people who wish to live closer to their work and who have the resources to pay rents for the improved buildings. Such areas are particularly attractive to single people or childless couples who do not wish to use local inner city schools or other support services. For this group, the character of the area is often one of the key features of its attractiveness, while the property improvement serves to enhance their capital investment.

Thus, in conclusion, the JQ case study provides one of the first opportunities to examine the fate of such an area while it is moving through this process. It will provide considerable evidence which may enable those who follow to pursue such initiatives with more sensitivity and success in meeting their proposed objectives.

So far as the Birmingham Jewellery Quarter is concerned the biggest impacts are yet to be felt. They will be the continuing demand for city fringe office space as opposed to more standardized office space, the development of business tourism within the city, and the continued restructuring of jewellery retailing and jewellery manufacturing with the introduction of new technology. At the time of the survey, there appeared to be an ample supply of B1 space with over 90,000 square metres already in the development process. But the balance between light industrial/workshop use and office use may have a significant long-term effect on the current amount of space utilized by the jewellery industry. The effect of the implementation of the uniform business rate was not addressed in the firms survey.

The jewellery firms undoubtedly were very clear about the advantages of a JQ location for themselves. However, without a detailed financial analysis of the ability of the firms to respond to upwards pressure on rent levels, it is difficult to be sure how robust they will be in their present locations. It seems likely that those most vulnerable would be the process firms which are both smaller and have far more specific locational requirements. Future research could usefully identify and specifically monitor these firms.

The effect of rising rents could be at least partially offset by the availability of other advantages of geographical concentration within the JQ, namely the sharing of costs of design development, marketing and promotion as well as training. General physical environment and infrastructural improvement would attract and hold quality workers within the area and contribute to the area's prosperity. Similarly, the commitment of key personnel and local decision makers to the area would be underwritten.

Currently, Birmingham City Planning Department do not monitor specific types of office use within B1. So very detailed data is not available on the extent of studio office use. However, a number of local firms of estate agents are actively involved in marketing studio office space. They actively utilize various features of the locality, whether it be the proximity of the Georgian St Paul's Square, the waterside of the Birmingham Canal or the remarkable factory architecture evident in some locations. As the effects of the recession were felt in 1992 there was strong evidence of competition between different sectors of the city fringe to attract users in a shrinking market. This has been exacerbated by the release of more sites and buildings from the city core as department stores have closed. Efforts by Jewellery Quarter Action to promote the jewellery trades via a trade centre, better car parking, more stylish architecture for the Light Rail halts, and gateway features to mark the principal access points seem likely to enhance the appeal of the Quarter to studio office developments. But Birmingham City Council has scaled down its commitment to public infrastructural investment in the Quarter.

City fringe studio offices, particularly those in 'heritage' locations, are a relatively scarce commodity. Like many other B1 uses, the incidence of studio offices is concealed by the existing planning regulatory mechanisms. The degree to which the planning authority can monitor the expansion of the CBD and its incursion into light industrial land uses and others is therefore limited.

CONCLUSIONS

We have looked at the relationship between the development sector and the state in terms of the judicial and administrative methods of facilitating new ensembles of uses. We have compared the process by which high-tech emerged with what was happening on one city fringe – the Birmingham Jewellery Quarter. Other instances, such as the creation of Enterprise Zones, present themselves as candidates for similar analysis.

This work emphasises the need to consider from a theoretical perspective the relationships between the state and the property development sector. It helps us to understand the processes that areas such as the JQ are going through. This analysis provides us with an insight into the impact of recommodification in one locality.

Juridical recommodification of many types of land uses is possible with revision of the Use Classes Order. A new general development order would have an impact of a similar scale. An even more radical version of current liberalization would be the abolition of the Use Classes Order and its replacement by stronger environmental control. Since studio offices would not normally expect to have significant environmental impacts, apart from generating significant amounts of private car use, further liberalization in this direction would not generate additional activities by the planning authority. However, parking would be a major issue on the city fringe should further studio office developments take place.

A degree of administrative recommodification took place under the previous more restrictive Use Classes Order. This took the form of the more liberal granting of consents and in relation to high-tech offices we saw the argument for 'bespoke' consents. Additionally there is the possibility of establishing regulated development under Section 106 of the 1990 Town and Country Planning Act; the relaxation of restrictions on office space in Structure Plans and Article 4 Direction Orders.

The law is being given a period of stability in respect of B1. The Department of the Environment appear to be content with the operation of the B1 use class. Recent appeal cases where local authorities have attempted to use Article 4 Direction Orders to prevent change from 'light industrial' to 'offices' have been unsuccessful (Planning 1992: 7). This is precisely in keeping with the notion of juridical recommodification. Administrative amendments would introduce uncertainty into the process of revaluing city fringe locations so far as the market is concerned.

Current attempts to lobby for a 'mixed use' zoning designation, be it by developers, conservationists or others, seem in the light of this to be as doomed as a 'social housing' use class order is under the present regime of regulation. Both would give more power to administrators than the market would consider appropriate. However, planners could still hope to give preferential consent to applications for mixed use within the curtilage of a plot if the application met with the requirements of local statutory plans. The grant regime can be used to assist the economics of plot assembly and mixed use development – a form of administrative recommodification more acceptable to the market.

The JQ survey provided a considerable amount of information on the locality, which allows some analysis of current pressures together with some assessment of the extent of change over the last forty-five years. At present, the JQ still seems to function in a traditional way. That is, it is used by those from the region who have some knowledge of it. As yet there seems to be little evidence that it is attracting new visitors, although it does seem to have a role in drawing people to Birmingham.

The 'quarter' approach to promoting the development of cultural indus-tries now carries with it considerable risk, particularly where it is built upon an existing industry. Promoting the coherence and identity of these areas attracts developers to them. Further, their run down character, together with their physical proximity to the city centre can offer far greater potential for asset value improvement for owners. Until 1987, British planning controls were able to ensure that the mix of light industrial and other land uses remained; but as indicated above this is no longer the case.

However, it would also be wrong to assume that those who work within these quarters do not welcome the prospect of change. It is clear in many of these areas that existing firms are often very anxious to offload their businesses to developers. Those who work in those localities also welcome the improvement in facilities that such 'packaging' promotes. Although, as with all 'heritage' activity it may be the romantic notions of the policy makers which are actually being pursued rather than those of the indigenous firms. Also, the 'real' conditions of these industries, by tradition, may be very different from those promoted in the 'quarterization' of an area, and existing firms may have considerable difficulties in surviving in these new circumstances. The enhanced environment may be little more than a theatre for activities against a facade which has little reality. The firms may be displaced to other areas of the city where they can continue their activities in much the same way as before, or they might go out of business altogether.

ACKNOWLEDGEMENT

Thanks to Jane Pugh, Cartography Office, Department of Geography, LSE for redrawing Figure 5.1.

REFERENCES

Ambrose, P. (1986) *Whatever Happened to Planning?*, London: Methuen.
Bianchini, F. (1989) 'Urban renaissance?: the arts and the urban regeneration process in the 1980s Britain', Working Paper No. 7, University of Liverpool, Centre for Urban Studies.
—— (1990) 'Out of hours: the evening economy and town centre live- ability', paper presented at conference on Quality Environments, Civics, Culture and Public Space, Bristol Polytechnic, 10–11 May.
Comedia (1989) *The Cultural Industries*, London: Comedia.
Debenham, Tewson and Chinnocks (1983) *High-Tech: Myths and Realities: a Review of Developments for Knowledge-Based Industries*, Chartered Surveyors Information Services Department, July.
Department of the Environment (1985) *Lifting the Burden*, Cmnd 9571.
Dodd, J. (1989) 'Hanging by a thread: are the tailors about to be squeezed out of Savile Row?', *Sunday Times Magazine*, 22 October: 12–15.
Forman, C. (1989) *Spitalfields: a Battle for Land*, London: Hilary Shipman.
Fothergill, S., Gudgin, G., Kitson, M. and Monk, S. (1986) 'The deindustrialisation

of the city', in R. Martin and B. Rowthorn *The Geography of Deindustrial-
isation*, London: Macmillan.
——, Monk, S. and Perry, M. (1987) *Property and Industrial Development*,
London: Hutchinson.
Fuller Peiser Partners (1985) *High-tech '85*, London: Fuller Peiser.
Games, S. (1990) 'Court out; Charing Cross Road second-hand bookshops', *Even-
ing Standard Magazine*, March: 27–9.
Gilbert, C. (1972) *The Evolution of an Urban Craft: The Gold Silver and Allied
Trades of the West Midlands*, unpublished M.Soc.Sc. thesis, University of
Birmingham.
Goodchild, B. (1990) 'Planning and the modern/post-modern debate', *Town Plan-
ning Review* 61(2): 119–38.
Harvey, D. (1981) 'The urban process under capitalism: a framework for analysis',
in M. Dear and A.J. Scott (eds) *Urbanisation and Urban Planning in Capitalist
Society*, London: Methuen.
—— (1982) *The Limits to Capital*, Oxford: Basil Blackwell.
—— (1985) *The Urbanisation of Capital*, Oxford: Basil Blackwell.
—— (1989) *The Urban Experience*, Oxford: Basil Blackwell.
Hooper, A. (1984) 'The role of landed property in the production of the built
environment', proceedings of the 6th Bartlett International Summer School,
Venice, September.
Investment Property Data Bank (1988) *Annual Review*.
Lodge, M. (1986) *Accommodation Needs of Modern Industry*, unpublished report
to Department of the Environment: Drivers Jonas, Chartered Surveyors.
Deposited at the Department of the Environment Library, 2 Marsham St, London
SW1P 3EB.
Luithlen, L. (1985) 'Interest bearing capital and commercial property investment in
the United Kingdom', proceedings of the 7th Bartlett International Summer
School, Vaux-En-Velin, September.
McMahon, M. (1985a) 'The law of the land: property rights and town planning in
modern Britain', in M. Ball (ed.) *Land Rent, Housing and Urban Planning: a
European Perspective*, London: Croom Helm.
—— (1985b) 'A contradictory form of regulation', proceedings of the 7th Bartlett
International Summer School, Vaux-En-Velin, September.
Massey, D. and Catalano, A. (1978) *Capital and Land: Landownership by Capital
in Great Britain*, London: Edward Arnold.
Montgomery, J. (1990) 'Cities and the art of cultural planning', *Planning, Practice
and Research* 5(3): 17–24.
Nabarro, R. and Cullen, I.G. (1986) *The Investment Property Databank Review*.
Pashukanis, E. (1978) *Law and Marxism: a General Theory*, London: Ink Links.
Planning (1992), No. 981, 14 August: 7.
Pratt, A.C. (1983) 'Finance for industry', *Town and Country Planning* 52(1):
110–12.
—— (1994) *Uneven Reproduction: Industry. Space and Society*, Oxford: Pergamon.
Pratt, D. (1990) 'Indirect Monitoring Report to Jewellery Quarter Action Steering
Group', May, Working Paper No. 42, Department of Planning and Landscape,
Birmingham Polytechnic
—— and Morphet, J. (1990) 'Cultural quarters in local economic development: the
case of Birmingham', paper presented to the 6th International Conference on
Cultural Economics, Umea, June.

Ravetz, A. (1986) *The Government of Space: Town Planning in Modern Society*, London: Faber & Faber.

Rogers, N. (1983) 'Industrial decline, restructuring and relocation: Aston and the Great Victorian depression', in J. Anderson, S. Duncan and R. Hudson (eds) *Redundant Spaces in Cities and Regions?*, London: Academic Press.

Roweis, S.T. and Scott, A.J. (1981) 'The urban land question', in M. Dear and A.J. Scott (eds) *Urbanization and Urban Planning in Capitalist Society*, London: Methuen.

Smith, B.M.D. (1987) 'Report of an interview-based survey in the Birmingham Jewellery Quarter relating to the jewellery industry', University of Birmingham, Centre for Urban and Regional Studies, Research Memorandum No. 107.

—— (1989) 'The Birmingham Jewellery Quarter', in B. Tilson *Made In Birmingham: Design and Industry 1889–1989*, Studley, Warwickshire: Brewin Books.

Stoker, G. (1990) 'Regulation theory, local government and the transition from Fordism', in D.S. King and J. Pierre, *Challenges to Local Government*, London: Sage.

Wates, N. (1976) *The Battle for Tolmers Square*, London: Routledge and Kegan Paul.

West Midlands Planning and Transportation Sub-Committee (undated) 'Report of the Chief Engineer's and Planning Officers' Group; The Implications of the B1 Business Class'.

Wise, M. (1949) 'On the evolution of the jewellery and gun quarters in Birmingham', *Transactions of the Institute of British Geographers*, 15: 57–72.

Zukin, S. (1988) *Loft Living: Culture and Capital in Urban Change*, London: Radius.

6 High technology firms and the property market

John Henneberry

Property is important for firm performance because 'the premises in which the firm operates impose constraints on the nature of its operations and may limit its growth and efficiency' (Fothergill, Monk and Perry 1987). Manufacturing firms incur considerable additional operating costs when they occupy old, substandard premises (Bozeat and Williams 1979). A move to modern, well-designed accommodation can be expected to reduce maintenance and energy costs significantly and to result in dramatic improvements in efficiency via better plant layouts and the proper utilization of floorspace. Empirical evidence of efficiency gains is hard to come by. However, there are case studies which describe moves resulting in increases in floorspace productivity (output value per square metre) of 227 per cent (Building Employers' Confederation, 1985) and 191 per cent (Strachan 1986) over that in an older unit. This being the case, it is clearly important for firm performance, and for the performance of the local and wider economies of which they are a part, that premises meeting their needs are available. However, the property market is not homogeneous. Different types of firm, depending on their size, organizational status, the product with which they are involved and the activities which they pursue will require a similarly differentiated range of buildings. Furthermore, structural economic and industrial change will alter the balance of demand for different building types both between sectors – for example the dramatic growth of the service sector relative to manufacturing resulting in a similarly large increase in demand for retail and office premises – and within a sector – for example the increase in expenditure on DIY and bulky goods leading to the development of the retail warehouse.

To understand the behaviour of the property market one must necessarily consider both the demand and supply sides of that market. One important feature of the property market is its split between owner occupied and rented sectors. In the former sector, by definition, the occupiers finance the provision of their own premises. In these circumstances, particularly in the case of newly-built premises, the size, design and location of the premises should match the occupier's requirements reasonably closely. However, in the rented sector the owner and the occupier are different entities, each with an interest in the same property but using that property to satisfy different objectives. The owner views the property as an investment producing rental and capital returns. To the occupier the property is a factor of production.

The investor is primarily concerned with long-term growth and security of returns from property investments and, within these constraints, with maximizing such returns. Interpretation and application of such aims within the property market result in the development of buildings which, *inter alia*, are appropriate to as wide a market as possible. Designing for a wide market enhances the chance of quick lettings and re-lettings, minimizes voids and ensures the availability of extensive comparable evidence for rent assessment at letting and review. General building types to service various market sectors have been informally derived (the 'institutional specification') and, to maximize letting and rental growth prospects, development activity focuses on those locations and property types where demand exceeds supply. Thus, property for rent forms a significant proportion of accommodation in the office, shop, light industrial and warehousing sectors of the property market and property investments are geographically concentrated in the south east.

Occupiers derive considerable benefits from renting rather than owning premises. Many small firms cannot afford to acquire freeholds, others prefer to invest in business development rather than in property. Others do not have the expertise to handle the design, planning and construction of purpose-built accommodation. If, as is often the case, the property has been speculatively developed and is available for immediate occupation, additional advantages arise. Changing market demands may produce a need to move into a building quickly. However, in order for an occupier to derive the benefits of renting, premises for renting must be available. Such premises are only provided in circumstances which meet investors' financial criteria. If these criteria are not met in the property market, investors have the choice of putting their money into alternative, non-property investments which better meet their aims. As a consequence, through the medium of the growth of the rented sector of the property market, the property supply industry has had an increasing influence over the availability and type of premises that firms occupy and hence over firm and economic performance.

A good example of demand/supply side interaction is provided by the evolution of the retail warehouse sector. Initial examples of the development of this property type took the form of conversions of former industrial buildings. Such development was funded by retailers themselves because the property market was not yet aware of this new property type. With increasing experience, retailers were better able to define their property needs which included large single storey units of a fairly low specification coupled with extensive adjacent car parking, preferably with frontage to a main road. Owners were still the main providers of space, developers/ investors who entered the market did so on a test basis which involved minimal exposure. High yields were required to compensate for the additional risk of entering an untried market. Further refinement and enhancement of building requirements by occupiers accompanied by continuing modest activities by developers/investors resulted in the establishment of the market subsector and the steady accumulation of rental data. Once sufficient evidence of the physical requirements and financial performance of retail warehouses existed, they became an accepted medium for property investment and the sector expanded rapidly; far more rapidly than if the development of retail warehouses had been dependent solely on the financial resources of retailers.

Retail warehouses are not the only new property type to have emerged in recent times. High technology firms have been perceived as a high growth sector of the economy and, as such, might be expected to be a new source of demand for a particular type of property. The reaction of the property supply industry to high technology firms' accommodation requirements is the main focus of this chapter.

CONCEPTUALIZING THE RELATIONSHIP BETWEEN HIGH TECHNOLOGY FIRMS AND THEIR PROPERTY

In a 1977 study, Drury (1978) showed how the nature of different industries' accommodation requirements was determined by the characteristics of their production processes. Four main factors which influence the demands made by firms on their buildings were identified. The first factor is the intensity of production plant, defined as the density of production equipment in the area exclusively used for manufacture and associated materials handling. The rate of change of production plant was the second factor. The level of adaptability demanded of a building structure is affected by the frequency of significant alterations to production machinery and services. The third factor, the intensity of use of mechanical handling equipment in production areas, is also a guide to the demands made by the manufacturer upon accommodation. The final factor considered by Drury was the range and intensity of services required to be provided in the building.

Next, Drury considered the inter-relationship of these four characteristics of the production process in different industries. The combinations of characteristics existing in each industry were then placed in similar groups and a taxonomy of industrial building purpose types derived. The types were:

1a light production and assembly – high technology;
1b light production and assembly – low technology;
2   batch production and assembly;
3   mass production and assembly;
4a process based production: centralized facility;
4b process based production: dispersed facility;
5   heavy engineering.

This type of industry-based analysis is useful because it provides a categorization of the subsectors of the industrial property market. It also provided, for the first time, a definition of a high technology building. Drury saw high technology light production as 'less common' than low technology light production with the former combining dense building services with a need for rapid process change. Industries typically accommodated in high technology light production buildings were seen to include producers of electronic components and scientific instruments, surgical equipment manufacture and prototype engineering. However, Drury gave little consideration either to the underlying economic and industrial trends which give rise to the pattern of industry he analysed or to the behaviour of firms over time and the implications this has for their use of accommodation. It is to these matters that we now turn.

The growth in demand for high technology property arises from changes in the structure of the British economy and the characteristics and behaviour of the firms which make up that economy. As Pavitt (1979) comments, many of the manufacturing sectors which grew rapidly in the OECD (Organisation of Economic Cooperation and Development) area during the 1950s and 1960s were involved in the volume production of relatively standard goods with price competition crucial to market share. The continued growth of such industries in the 1970s and 1980s was constrained by saturated markets and the spread of process technologies to regions outside the OECD which had more favourable cost structures and demand elasticities. OECD countries increasingly concentrated 'their production and trade in sectors dominated by product and systems innovations produced by organised research, development and design' (Pavitt 1979: 460). Additionally, exploitation of markets where non-price factors were critically important was enhanced by 'shifts of emphasis within sectors: towards product novelty, quality and reliability' (1979: 460). Competitive advantage was seen to derive from the 'ability to respond to . . . threats and opportunities emerging from changing tastes, technology, relative prices and competition. Essential features of this ability are capabilities in R&D and design, and the ability to couple them to developments in . . . markets'

(1979: 461). This shift in industrial orientation affected firms' organization and means of production. For the conventional firm, preoccupied with volume of output and cost competition, activities (research and development, manufacturing, storage and distribution, administration and marketing) tend to be clearly defined and are frequently pursued in separate buildings, often in separate locations. In contrast, firms in some industries brought together their production activities to respond better to changing customer requirements in the demanding markets they served. Production could be switched from one good to another with relative ease via the use of the latest production technologies. The proportion of the workforce undertaking technical, professional, scientific and managerial tasks increased as the proportion of the value embodied in firms' products attributable to research, design, marketing, etc. grew. Firms exhibiting the new characteristics grew relatively faster than conventional firms. The former were concentrated in high technology industries.

The property supply industry perceived these trends as giving rise to the need for a new type of building to accommodate a fast growing group of high technology firms. Drury had already suggested some of the characteristics which such buildings might display. Property advisors stressed other features: flexibility and quality. In order to attract and retain the well qualified employees high technology firms need, their premises, both building and setting, must be of high quality (Debenham, Tewson and Chinnocks 1983; Herring Son and Daw 1982). The building must also be sufficiently flexible to accommodate a mix of different activities (Debenham, Tewson and Chinnocks 1983; Herring Son and Daw 1982; Morton-Smith 1984; Property Advisory Group 1986). Additionally, significant shifts in the proportion of floorspace given over to each activity may occur and need to be accommodated in the building. Theoretical bases for the preceding deductions concerning firm–premises inter-relationships are to be found in behavioural analysis and life-cycle theory.

Behavioural analysis focuses on firm–environment interaction (Wood 1987). The firm is characterized as a complex entity of individuals and groupings with differing objectives, such as management, employees and shareholders, who manipulate the firm's resources. Decisions are the outcome of interactions between these parties and the resources which they control. Internal structure and external environment condition such decisions. Suppliers, customers, competitors, government and other bodies constitute the firm's external environment and affect its behaviour. Firms differentiated by size, industry, product or service, location, etc. operate in a range of environments which may be stable or turbulent, fast or slow growing, highly competitive or uncompetitive. They exhibit a range of organizational and behavioural characteristics to match. An equally wide range of property requirements is, therefore, displayed by such firms. Property requirements, like the other resource requirements of a firm, are subject to continual pressure for change from external and internal sources. Fothergill, Monk and Perry (1987) identified three main external pressures: technical and other advances in the organization and means of production; changes in the nature and design of products; and changes in demand for products. All firms in an industry are affected by such pressures to some degree, although their relative importance varies by type of industry and over time. The three main sources of internal pressure are changes in the function of the establishment within the wider organization of the firm; changes in the products or product mix of the firm; and the competitive success or failure of the firm within its industry. Thus, in the face of internal and external pressures, the firm is continually re-appraising the efficiency and effectiveness with which its existing resources, including its accommodation, meet its current operational needs.

If high technology firms are considered within this behavioural framework certain inferences can be drawn. Following Pavitt's (1979) analysis, the operational units of such firms would tend to be small to medium sized and to operate in turbulent, highly competitive, demanding and high growth markets. In addition, product design and process technology, particularly the former, change rapidly with consequent fluctuations in the level of demand for the firm's output. In comparison with the operational units of conventional firms, those in high technology firms might, therefore, be expected to exhibit much more rapid and significant changes in their property-using behaviour. What must also be considered, however, is the degree to which any one building might be expected to cope with such change. Firms adopt a wide range of spatially differentiated policies to resolve externally and internally generated pressures upon them (Edwards 1983; Hamilton 1978; North 1974; Townroe 1969; and Wood 1978). These include:

1 intensification or decline in the use of existing buildings or some other change in the way they are used;
2 physical expansion or contraction on existing sites, via extension/new building or disposal/demolition;
3 other tactics which avoid moves and are alternatives to 1 and 2: for example sub-contracting activity or licensing agreements;
4 takeovers, amalgamations or mergers with other companies;
5 rationalization programmes involving the closure of older operating units;
6 the establishment of new units;
7 company births and deaths;
8 relocations of part or the whole of a firm.

It can be seen that, of the above policies, it is only the first which requires existing buildings to meet the changes in firms' requirements.

Life-cycle theory has been used to analyse the distinctive way in which high technology firms use their premises. The basis of the product cycle is that sales and profits from a product begin at a low level when a product is an innovation, then grow rapidly, and finally become stable or decline as a product becomes standardized and no innovation takes place. At higher levels of aggregation, firms or industries can be considered to be in similar phases of a firm or industry life cycle. Firm characteristics other than sales and profits have also been posited to display cyclical behaviour including innovation levels and organizational structures (and, consequently, property using behaviour). All these factors vary depending upon the stage reached in the cycle.

Oakey (1984) used the life-cycle concept to examine the pattern of activities pursued by small high technology firms. The products of such firms tend to have a relatively short life cycle: five years is a common duration. To ensure the continued survival of the firm existing products must be improved or replaced sooner rather than later. Oakey suggests that the emphasis will be on research and development activity prior to a new product launch. Subsequently, however, priority will be given to production (see Figure 6.1). Research and development will again peak before the introduction of the second product and so on. Such variations in the pattern of activities pursued by the firm have implications for the way the firm uses its premises. If floorspace usage is assumed to mirror activity levels, the proportion of floorspace given over to research and development and to production will vary over time (see Figure 6.2). It was on this basis that the property industry at the time maintained that high technology buildings needed to be capable of accommodating a mix of activities whose pattern might change significantly over time (see for example Fuller Peiser 1985; Organ 1986; Eul 1984; and Morton-Smith 1984).

This position is open to question on a number of grounds. First, Figures 6.1 and 6.2 describe the activities and property using behaviour of a single product firm. However, firms tend to develop multiple product lines in order to avoid cyclical fluctuations in revenue arising from differing balances between expenditure on R&D and income from product sales. Figure 6.3 describes a firm with two product lines and two associated activity patterns. Even in this simple example, a marked smoothing of overall activity patterns is evident (see Figure 6.4). The implications for the firm's pattern of floorspace use are clear. As one electronics company commented in a survey by Freer (1986);

> although individual products do in fact normally follow the suggested product cycle, activity levels and as such, space needs do not fluctuate

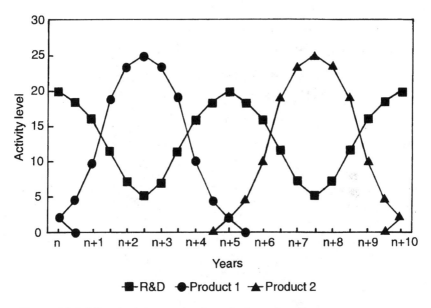

Figure 6.1 R&D and product cycles for a single product firm

substantially in any area. This is a result of products in our business being grouped into like commodities and as old products are phased out new products are substituted. This maintains a flat or slow growth activity level through research and development, manufacture/ assembly, storage and office areas.

(Freer 1986: 62–3)

In a study of innovating and non-innovating firms, Meyer-Krahmer (1985) found that firms conducting R&D regularly had a greater tendency to have multiple product lines than those conducting R&D occasionally. One might conclude that innovative firms are less likely to experience fluctuations in the amount of floorspace given over to different activities than conventional firms.

Second, life-cycle theory is an attempt to produce a descriptive generalization of certain patterns of behaviour which provide a framework for the consideration of that behaviour rather than a model or stereotype. Sayer (1985) stresses how circumscribed the logic of life-cycle theory is. The evolution of many products does not conform to the generalized model. A product may be 'rejuvenated' to increase its life via design refinements and the upgrading of specifications. Stages in the life-cycle can also be passed through very quickly or even omitted altogether. A large multi-plant firm which has developed a new product as part of a long-term research

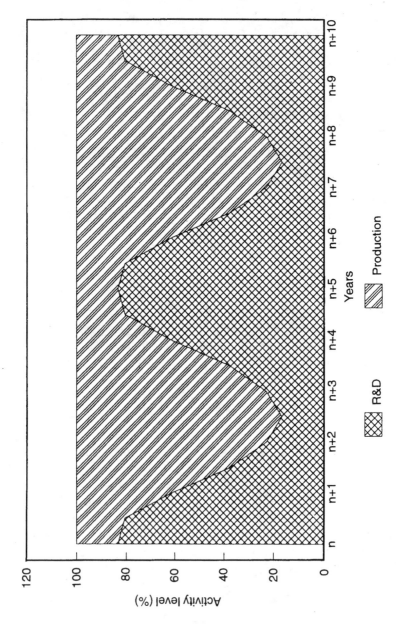

Figure 6.2 Activity levels for a single product firm

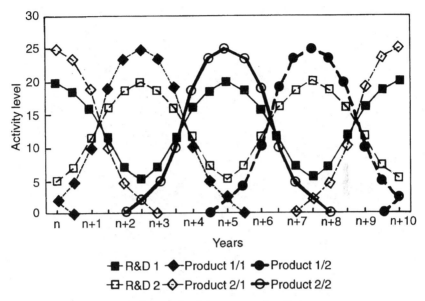

Figure 6.3 R&D and product cycles for a two-product firm

programme may put it into volume production almost immediately. This example highlights the problem of conflation of product and firm life cycles. This is the assumption that new products are more likely to be developed by young small firms than large old firms. Relaxation of this assumption allows the influence of a firm's locational and organizational structure to be considered.

Massey (1984) identifies three organizational structures within a spatial division of labour. In the locationally concentrated spatial structure all activities occur in the same location. Small, independent, single site firms typify this structure. Such firms generally display a relatively simple internal structure with no well-developed technical division of labour, implying a lack of major economies of scale. Next is the cloning branch-plant spatial structure. This is characterized by multi-site firms constituted of branch plants which undertake the same productive activities as the parent plant, with the exception of overall company administration. In this form, spatial division of labour is achieved without any significant altera-tion to the technical division of labour. Finally, there is the part-process spatial structure represented by firms which have expanded geographically and have restructured their technical division of labour. The result is that different production activities are pursued by different types of labour in different locations, all within a single production process. Only firms with

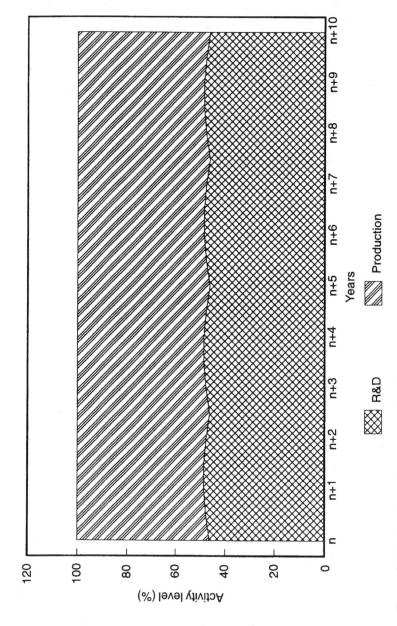

Figure 6.4 Activity levels for a two-product firm

a locationally concentrated spatial structure will fully exhibit the patterns of floorspace use described in Figures 6.1 to 6.4. In operational units within firms with a cloning branch plant spatial structure, a more restricted range of activity patterns will be evident. At the other extreme, firms with a part-process spatial structure will pursue R&D and production in different buildings in different locations.

The final objection to the use of life-cycle theory to relate production activities to floorspace use is the assumption that the only reaction to changes in the former is changes to the latter. The wide range of spatially differentiated policies adopted by firms to cope with change has been noted. Even for the single-site firm unable to move or to alter its premises, many strategies are available to cope with rapid fluctuations in demand which require the organization and output of the production process to be altered. The production line can be speeded up or slowed down; overtime/ extra shifts can be introduced or working hours reduced; sub-contractors can be engaged or dispensed with; the balance of floorspace given over to different activities can be changed. It is not clear why high technology firms, in contrast to any other group of firms, should suddenly put increased emphasis on the last option.

Thus, significant theoretically based objections can be made to the contention that high technology firms are a substantial and growing source of demand for a new type of property. This is not to say that small to medium-sized, single site, high technology firms requiring high quality mixed use, flexible accommodation do not exist. Rather, it suggests that the high technology sector of the property market, like any other sector, is heterogeneous rather than homogeneous and that the firm type described constitutes a relatively small part of this wider sector.

HIGH TECHNOLOGY FIRMS AND THEIR USE OF ACCOMMODATION

Empirical evidence concerning the way high technology firms use their accommodation is sparse. One of the main exceptions is the work under-taken by the author in the mid-1980s (Henneberry 1984a, 1984b, 1987a, 1987b). Surveys of eighty-three schemes – science parks, high-tech developments and conventional industrial estates – were conducted. Infor-mation relating to the characteristics and property using behaviour of 148 occupiers of these schemes was obtained in 1983. Similar data relating to 226 occupiers was obtained in 1986. Eighty-one occupiers responded to both surveys. Figure 6.5 describes the differences between occupiers by industrial sector and technology level for the different types of scheme in 1986. In science parks, high technology occupiers are evenly balanced

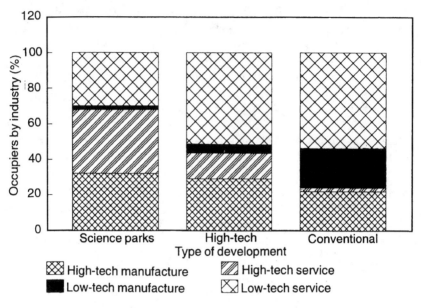

Figure 6.5 Property developments by occupiers' industrial sector

between the manufacturing and service sectors; for high-tech schemes high technology manufacturing industries are the larger group and predominate in conventional industrial estates. Examples of high technology firms encountered during the surveys include, for manufacturing, those involved in the production of electronic data processing equipment and electrical instruments and control systems; and for those in the service sector, firms involved in research and development and those providing professional and technical services not elsewhere specified. In science parks and high-tech schemes, low technology occupiers are overwhelmingly in service industries such as business services not elsewhere specified and in central offices not allocatable elsewhere. Conventional industrial estates have a similar proportion of their occupiers in low technology services but the majority of such firms are involved in wholesale distribution and storage. In addition, a sizeable group of occupiers in low technology manufacturing industries such as finished metal products not elsewhere specified are present on conventional industrial estates.

The varying characteristics of the occupiers of different types of scheme result in patterns of floorspace use differing significantly between schemes (see Figure 6.6). Occupiers on science parks and high technology developments use a much higher proportion of their floorspace for offices than do occupiers on conventional industrial estates. Much more space is given over to laboratories

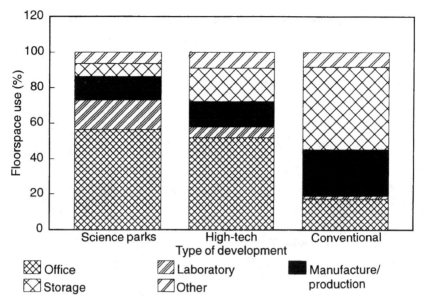

Figure 6.6 Floorspace use by type of development

on science parks than on the other schemes. Conversely, manufacturing/production occupies a much greater proportion of floorspace on conventional industrial estates than on science parks and high-tech schemes. The link between occupier characteristics and patterns of floorspace use by scheme is clear. Thus, high levels of office and laboratory floorspace on science parks is a reflection of the high proportion of occupiers of such schemes falling within high technology service industries, while the high level of storage floorspace on conventional industrial estates attests to the large number of their occupiers engaged in distribution. However, the patterns of floorspace use described in Figure 6.6 are the averages for all the occupiers in the different types of scheme. The floorspace use of individual occupiers within any group may diverge markedly from such an average. For example, three occupiers with an average pattern of floorspace use of 33 per cent offices, 33 per cent manufacturing/production and 33 per cent storage may be made up of one occupier with 100 per cent office floorspace, one with 100 per cent manufacturing/production floorspace and one with 100 per cent storage floorspace.

A firm-by-firm analysis of patterns of floorspace use is illuminating. Figure 6.7 describes the proportion of occupiers on the different types of scheme with more than half their floorspace in a single use. For example, 87 per cent of all occupiers of high-tech developments put more than half

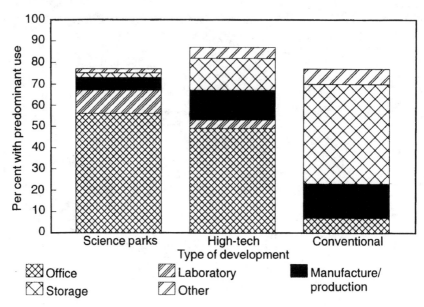

Figure 6.7 Occupiers and their predominant uses by type of development

their floorspace to a single use; for 49 per cent of these occupiers the predominant use was offices, for 4 per cent it was laboratories, and so on. Two points can be made concerning this data. First, high technology firms are no less likely to have premises with a predominant use than are low technology firms. Second, the similarity between the distribution of dominant uses described in Figure 6.7 and the pattern of average uses described in Figure 6.6 supports the conclusion that it is variations in the characteristics of groups of occupiers rather than variations in the characteristics of individual occupiers that produce differences in patterns of floorspace use across schemes. Consequently, buildings on any type of scheme need to be able to accommodate a range of activities, not so much because individual occupiers pursue such a range of activities simultaneously as because successive occupiers may pursue them.

The analysis of floorspace use can be taken further by considering the experience of the group of occupiers who responded to both surveys. The total proportion of floorspace which changed from any one use to any other was calculated for each occupier. Occupiers were classified by type of scheme occupied, corporate status, size (of premises and of workforce), industrial sector and technology level. Floorspace change rates were analysed by these occupier characteristics. A single factor, technology level, was found to be pervasive in its influence on floorspace change rates.

That is, whatever its other characteristics, a high technology firm was likely to change a significantly higher proportion of its floorspace from one use to another than was a low technology firm (21.3 per cent of floorspace over the three year period between surveys for the former and 12.1 per cent for the latter).

At first sight the findings relating to predominant use and floorspace change rates may appear paradoxical. However,

> high technology firms may experience much higher levels of change in the pattern of floorspace use, but this is across a narrow range of different uses. Thus, for high technology service industries, floorspace typically changed from offices to laboratories, or vice-versa with storage coming a poor second. High technology manufacturing industries have manufacturing as the focus of activity with the main changes being to or from offices and storage. One does not encounter firms which have a wide and even spread of activities (although high technology manufacturing industries come nearest to this) and which experience dramatic shifts in the pattern of that floorspace use between, say, office and manufacturing activities.
>
> (Henneberry 1988: 258)

Massey's spatial division of labour offers a useful explanation for the pattern of property using behaviour encountered in these surveys. Many high technology service operational units occupying space on science parks and high technology developments comply with the part-process spatial structure, whether as individual firms specializing in that part of the wider production process or as parts of multi-plant/multi-site larger firms focusing thereon. By their nature, such establishments pursue a narrow range of activities. High technology manufacturing firms are more likely to exhibit a locationally concentrated or cloning branch-plant spatial structure where a wider range of activities is pursued in a single location. However, such firms are in a minority on any type of scheme (see Figure 6.5). The implications of this empirical evidence (and of the earlier theoretical considerations) for property market behaviour and for policy which aims to control that behaviour will be considered in the following sections.

HIGH TECHNOLOGY FIRMS AND THE PROPERTY MARKET

The property supply industry's interest in the property using behaviour of high technology firms is not unconnected with its perception that such firms represent a new and growing source of demand for accommodation. In the mid-1980s the growth in the number of high technology developments which were constructed was explosive. Such schemes became a recognizable and distinct subsector of the industrial property market. Significant differentials in rents and yields between conventional and high technology industrial developments became evident. At the time, prime sites in the south east suitable for high technology development changed hands for sums in excess of £1 million per acre (£2.47 million per hectare). These land prices were a reflection of the level of rents achieved upon development, commonly in excess of £9 per square foot (Richard Ellis 1986). Indeed, some commentators expressed concern that high technology schemes were 'crowding out' the development of standard industrial and warehouse units, to the long-term detriment of the affected areas' property markets and local economies (Pearson Williams and L.S. Vale 1985). While the new market subsector was developing, the property industry was subjecting the 1972 Town and Country Planning (Use Classes) Order to a growing barrage of criticism.

Effectively, the Use Classes Order (UCO) divides the property market into separate categories in planning terms. Under the 1972 Order such categories included: offices – class II; light industry – class III; laboratories or R&D uses were 'sui generis'; general industry – class IV; warehousing – class X. The property industry maintained that this Order was in certain respects obsolete. It divided industry into categories relating to manufacturing (and other) activities which had existed for decades. Consequently, it was contended, high technology firms whose property-using behaviour departed significantly from that of conventional firms, might find – because of the mix of activities pursued by the firm – that its premises did not fall neatly within any one use class and a specific planning permission might be required. Even where premises did fall within a use class, two difficulties might arise. First, were the pattern of floorspace use to change, the firm's property might be taken outside the original use class (or the terms of the original specific permission), necessitating a fresh application for planning permission with all the consequent delays and uncertainty. Second, specific permissions or difficulties in complying with the UCO drastically reduce the potential range of occupiers of a property. Developers wishing to obtain external funding for a scheme must demonstrate to the investor that, should the initial occupier leave, the building could be marketed to a reasonable range of alternative tenants. Inability to do this significantly reduces the chances of obtaining finance. The 1972 UCO was, therefore, characterized as inhibiting the supply of multi-use accommodation suitable for high technology firms and, therefore, hampering the development of the economy.

These claims did not go unchallenged. The National Development Control Forum (1983) noted that there were other, opposing views of high technology development. For example, 'with certain notable exceptions involving complex purpose-designed structures, there is simply no general demand for specialised (multi-use) buildings of this kind' (Grant & Partners 1982, quoted in NDCF 1983: 3). Department of the Environment officials also were of the view that,

> high technology occupiers . . . will not normally be involved in activities on the same site whose general or overall purposes are substantially different . . . the principal use on most sites is likely to be industrial, and storage, warehouse, office or research uses, no matter what proportion of the building they occupy, are likely to be subservient in function to this industrial use, and therefore ancillary uses which will not need to be specifically permitted . . . although developers may represent their needs as being for a mixture of uses the permission appropriate will normally be expressed in terms of a single use of the use classes order (often class 3 or class 4).
>
> (Quoted in NDCF 1983: 9)

Before considering these opposing views it is important to identify clearly the two arguments which were being advanced by the property supply industry. The first was that, in its failure to evolve in line with changes in the organization and means of production, the 1972 UCO was imposing constraints upon the operational efficiency of high technology firms. The second argument was that, by restricting the market within which high technology developments could be let, the Order was restricting the supply of rented accommodation of this type. While this might be to the ultimate detriment of high technology firms, the cause of under-supply was the constraint imposed by the Order on the marketability of schemes and hence on their profitability to developers/investors. In the first case, the Order represented a functional constraint on the profitability of high technology firms (the demand side of the property market). In the second case, the Order was characterized as a regulatory constraint on the pursuit of profit by property developers (the supply side of the property market). Finally, the whole of this discussion focused implicitly on the property requirements of high technology manufacturing firms.

In 1987 the government introduced a new Use Classes Order, followed by a revised General Development Order in 1988. The UCO 1987 introduced a business use class, B1, bringing together the former office and light industrial classes and including also use for the research and development of products or processes (previously *sui generis*). The new GDO made provision for changes from use classes B8 (storage and distribution), or B2 (general industry) to use class B1, and to use class B8 from use classes B1 or B2, to be permitted development, providing the total floorspace involving B8 uses did not exceed 235 square metres. The changes were enacted with the specific intention of removing restrictions within the planning system and allowing the free market to determine the nature and pattern of land and building uses to a greater extent. Such an intent has been clearly supported by subsequent decisions on applications for planning permission of secretaries of state for the environment and their inspectors on appeal.

If the arguments of the property industry regarding the impact of the 1972 UCO are accepted, one of the main outcomes of the deregulation of the property market would have been an increase (both relative and absolute) in the output of accommodation suitable for high technology firms. However, significant theoretical and empirical reservations have already been raised over such a position. These suggest that the generality of high technology firms do not display any greater tendency than conventional firms either to put their accommodation to other than a single predominant use or to change significantly the pattern of their floorspace use any more frequently. Outcomes of processes differ from those expected if the premise upon which analysis is based is false. Essential to an understanding of the market's reaction to deregulation is a knowledge of both the behaviour of the building supply industry and the dynamics of the wider demand side of the property market.

Property developers seek to maximize their profits, *inter alia*, by constructing buildings which can be used by as wide a range of occupiers as possible. The result, in the industrial sector of the property market, has been the erection of light industrial/warehouse units. Such buildings are designed to accommodate more than one use not because any individual occupier might switch from one use to another, but because successive occupiers might wish to pursue different activities; hence the building can be offered to a wide market. The type of occupier is not constrained by the building's structure. However, the statutory planning system might act as such a constraint. Under the 1972 UCO developers relied upon (and normally received) either dual class III/class X planning permissions or the ready granting of subsequent applications for changes between those uses. The refusal to grant such permissions would affect the value of a building to its owner but would not alter its functional utility to the occupier.

The parallel to the case of high technology developments is clear. Continuing industrial and economic change produced both high technology firms requiring high quality premises and decentralizing office users, both of whom could be accommodated in peripheral business parks. However, local planning authorities were much less willing to contemplate changes between office and light industrial uses than between light industrial and warehouse uses. Consequently, the application of planning policy acted as a barrier to the pursuit of profit maximization by the property development industry (but did not impair the functional efficiency of buildings for the occupiers). In these circumstances, the major outcome of the introduction of the new UCO/GDO would be a market restructuring produced by the activities of the building supply industry. Property developers and investors focus their attention on the development and ownership of accommodation whose design, size and location maximizes financial returns and minimizes risk. Given the choice, the private sector will develop office space in preference to high technology schemes and the latter in preference to light industrial/warehouse space. The main result would be a significant expansion of out-of-town office developments. This is exactly what happened.

An examination of the effects of the revisions to the UCO and the GDO was commissioned by the Department of the Environment (Wootton Jeffreys Consultants Ltd and Bernard Thorpe 1991). The report highlighted the predictable market reaction to deregulation.

> every site with a light or general industrial use or allocation is potentially an office location. The choice between these uses is no longer something that planning can seek to determine, but is entirely a market decision, to be made on the usual criteria of location and demand. With the return from office space significantly greater than from other types of business space, then if the location is right it is office space that will be built.
>
> (Wootton Jeffreys Consultants Ltd and Bernard Thorpe 1991: 21)

Developers and users of office space were not slow to respond to the opportunity presented. A substantial majority of B1 development was carried out to full office specification (King & Co. 1989), resulting in the proportion of total completed floorspace provided in office buildings on business parks increasing from 22.9 per cent in 1987 to an estimated 57 per cent in 1991 (Applied Property Research 1990). The impact of these dramatic changes for occupiers in different sectors varied considerably.

> For companies requiring office space in previously restricted areas, the revision to the UCO has brought the benefit of greatly increased choice with more floorspace on the market, and a greater range of locations . . . the direct result of the change has been to lessen the proportion of mixed space in new out-of-town developments, in favour of office development . . . (and) has been to the almost total exclusion of shed space, suitable for B1 (C), B2 and B8 use, despite long-term persistent shortages of such accommodation.
>
> (Wootton Jeffreys Consultants Ltd and Bernard Thorpe 1991: 25–9)

The report concluded that:

> a principal purpose of the introduction of the business use class and hence a freer planning context, was to increase the supply of mixed use or high tech buildings for flexible occupation and to assist emerging new

technology industries . . . such space was being provided and such industries were being accommodated prior to the UCO. . . . Since the UCO this type of space has increasingly been overtaken by higher order space – pure offices – . . . (consequently) the introduction of the business use class has been neither a necessary nor an appropriate mechanism for increasing the supply of flexible business space and it is now acting contrary to the interests of this objective.

(Wootton Jeffreys Consultants Ltd and Bernard Thorpe 1991: 30)

CONCLUSIONS

An increasing proportion of the country's building stock is rented. Property developers and investors will only supply property which satisfies their financial objectives of maximizing profits and returns. Buildings for rent are, therefore, concentrated in sectors, both geographical and industrial, where demand exceeds supply and where, by a combination of building design and relatively undifferentiated occupier requirements, premises can be marketed to a wide range of potential tenants. Because property is only one of a range of possible investments, the suppliers' needs must be met for development to proceed. If buildings are produced which meet such criteria, occupiers derive considerable advantages from them via increases in operational efficiency and flexibility, and by investing scarce capital in products and processes rather than buildings. In these circumstances, the property supply industry can underpin the development and growth of local economies and particular industrial sectors (e.g. retail warehousing).

In the emergence of high technology firms, the property supply industry perceived a potential new source of demand for its product: buildings. However, this did not distract the industry from its overall objective of profit accumulation in the wider property market. This involved shifts in activity between sub-markets according to their relative financial perform-ance, as well as seizing opportunities presented by change within sub-markets. These two points influenced fundamentally the experience of high technology firms in the property market.

Historically, organizations within the property market such as property agents, the Royal Institution of Chartered Surveyors and the British Property Federation, have acted more in the interests of property suppliers than of occupiers. Analysis of occupiers' behaviour and property require-ments has been relatively unsophisticated (Harris 1989). This is well illus-trated by the inadequacies of the property industry's consideration of the property needs of high technology firms. Consciously or otherwise, atten-tion was focused on those aspects of high technology firms which suggested the need for a new building type. The extent of the application of these characteristics was not considered, leading to an overstatement of the scale of the need for such buildings; and this served the purpose of the industry in its wider attempts to remove regulatory barriers to profit accumulation in the property market at a time of strong economic growth.

It should have come as no surprise, therefore, that the introduction of the new UCO/GDO ultimately acted to the detriment of high technology firms. The freedom for occupiers to shift the pattern of their floorspace use from R&D to industry, to offices (even if the need to exercise it is rare) is also the freedom for developers to construct pure offices instead of high technology, mixed-use buildings or light industrial/warehouse 'sheds'. Developers built offices to the exclusion of other types of property because they could make more money doing so. The lesson for (central) government policy makers is clear. Supply-side deregulation pursued in any sector of the economy, including the property sector, which ignores both the balance of power between consumers and producers and their characteristics and behaviour, will be exploited by the dominant party to the ultimate cost of the weaker.

REFERENCES

Applied Property Research (1990) *Living with B1*, London: Allied Property Research.

Bozeat, N. and Williams, H. (1979) 'Property investment decisions by manufacturing and distributive industry', Working Paper 23, Birmingham, Joint Unit for Research on the Urban Environment, University of Aston.

Building Employers' Confederation (1985) *Building – The Nation's Needs: Spotlight on Industrial Buildings*, London: Building Employers' Confederation.

Debenham, Tewson and Chinnocks (1983) *Hi-Tech: Myths and Realities. A Review of Developments for Knowledge Based Industries*, London: Debenham, Tewson and Chinnocks.

Drury, J. (1978) *A. J. Handbook of Factory Design*, London: Architects Journal.

Edwards, L. (1983) 'Towards a process model of office location decision making', *Environment and Planning A* 15: 1327–42.

Eul, F. (1984) 'Matching development with demand', in CALUS, *Development for High Technology*, Reading: College of Estate Management.

Fothergill, S., Monk, S. and Perry, M. (1987) *Property and Industrial Development*, London: Hutchinson.

Freer, D. (1986) *The Use Classes Order and the High Technology Industries*, unpublished BSc. (Hons) dissertation, Sheffield City Polytechnic.

Fuller Peiser (1985) *High Technology '85*, London: Fuller Peiser.

Grant & Partners (1982) *The Industrial Property Market*, London: Grant & Partners.

Hamilton, F.E.I. (1978) 'Aspects of industrial mobility in the British economy', *Regional Studies*, 12: 153–65.

Harris, R. (1989) *The Central London Office Market: a Study in the Structure of Demand*, unpublished PhD thesis, University of Bristol.

Henneberry, J.M. (1984a) *A Survey of British Science Parks and High Technology Developments*, Sheffield: PAVIC.

—— (1984b) 'Property for high technology industry', *Land Development Studies* 1(3): 145–68.

—— (1987a) *British Science Parks and High Technology Developments: Progress and Change, 1983–1986*, Sheffield: PAVIC.

—— (1987b) 'Occupiers and their use of accommodation on science parks and high technology developments', *Land Development Studies* 4: 109–44.

—— (1988) 'Conflict in the industrial property market', *Town Planning Review* 59(3): 241–62.

Herring Son and Daw (1982) *Property and Technology – the Needs of Modern Industry*, London: Herring Son and Daw.

King & Co. (1989) *Hi-tech Survey*, London: King & Co.

Massey, D. (1984) *Spatial Divisions of Labour: Social Structures and the Geography of Production*, London: Macmillan.

Meyer-Krahmer, F. (1985) 'Innovation behaviour and regional indigenous potential', *Regional Studies* 19(6): 523–34.

Morton-Smith, G. (1984) 'The requirements of high technology industry', in CALUS, *Development for High Technology*, Reading: College of Estate Management.

National Development Control Forum (NDCF) (1983) *High Technology Development: The Planning Control Considerations*, London: NDCF.

North, D.J. (1974) 'The process of locational change in different manufacturing organisations', in F.E.I. Hamilton (ed.) *Spatial Perspectives in Industrial Organisation and Decision Making*, London: Wiley.

Oakey, R.P. (1984) 'Innovation and regional growth in small high technology firms: evidence from Britain and the USA', *Regional Studies* 18(3): 237–51.

Organ, J.D. (1986) 'Developing space for growth industries', in Healey and Baker, *The Workplace Revolution*, London: Healey and Baker.

Pavitt, K. (1979) 'Technical innovation and industrial development: the new causality', *Futures* 11: 458–70.

Pearson Williams and L. S. Vail and Son (1985) *Standard Industrial Warehouse Units*, Reading and Southampton: Pearson Williams and L.S. Vail and Son.

Property Advisory Group (1986) *Town and Country Planning (Use Classes) Order, 1972*, London: Department of the Environment.

Richard Ellis (1986) *Property Investment Quarterly Bulletin: the Industrial Sector*, London: Richard Ellis.

Sayer, R.A. (1985) 'Industry and space: a sympathetic critique of radical research', *Environment and Planning D* 3: 3–29.

Strachan, B.S. (1986) *The Design of Industrial Buildings and the Needs of the Occupier: Speculatively Built Units or Purpose Built Units*, unpublished BSc. Dissertation, Sheffield City Polytechnic.

Townroe, P.M. (1969) 'Locational choice and the individual firm', *Regional Studies* 3: 15–24.

Wood, P.A. (1978) 'Industrial organisation, location and planning', *Regional Studies* 12: 143–52.

—— (1987) 'Behavioural approaches to industrial location studies', in W.F. Lever (ed.) *Industrial Change in the United Kingdom*, Harlow: Longman.

Wootton Jeffreys Consultants Ltd and Bernard Thorpe (1991) *An Examination of the Effects of the Use Classes Order 1987 and the General Development Order 1988*, London: HMSO.

7 The new partnership
The local state and the property development industry

Rob Imrie and Huw Thomas

This chapter considers the changing nature of the local state's support for land and property development, and, through the use of case studies, explores some of the main continuities and differences in state–property development relations between the 1970s and late 1980s. We divide the chapter into three. First, we outline the main changes that have occurred in state–property development relations since the mid-1970s, and we develop the argument that the activities of property developers are highly dependent on their evolving relationships with the state. We then illustrate this general point by comparing two episodes of property development in Cardiff – the city centre redevelopment in the 1970s and the redevelopment of the docks in the 1980s to illustrate the changing face of state–property industry relations. We conclude the chapter by discussing the need for more sophisticated analyses of the 'context' of property development, while outlining some of the research resources required to investigate the influence of state actors and agencies on the property development industry.

INTRODUCTION

An emergent literature describes the dynamic flux in contemporary property development, characterized by new forms and flows of finance, the emergence of new development opportunities created by government policy, and the flow of overseas capital and development intermediaries into the UK property market (Rydin 1986; Healey and Barrett 1990; Imrie and Thomas 1993a). In particular, the last ten years have witnessed the significant involvement of both the central and local state in property development, with the former encouraging inner city policies of market-led property regeneration, while the latter has increased its support of levering the private development industry into areas adversely affected by economic decline. Indeed, Harding (1991) and others refer to a new organizational and procedural paradigm involved in property development, characterized by coalitions between public and private sectors which, as Healey and Barrett (1990) suggest, are involving a re-orientation of interests, strategies, working methods and relationships between the various actors and agencies involved in property development (Bennett and Krebs 1991; Lawless 1991).

These trends are reflected in a growing body of research on the relations between development processes and the state as one way of understanding how the actions of property developers are mediated, influenced and constrained by other actors and agencies (Adams 1987; Leitner 1991; Imrie and Thomas 1992). The state influences property development in quite complex and diverse ways, as a developer itself, by setting development parameters in planning documents, through its utilization of statutory tools to acquire and assemble land for development and by providing developers with investment opportunities. Indeed, throughout the 1980s, property-led urban regeneration came to symbolize an important part of the state's facilitation of private sector property development. A whole range of initiatives – Enterprise Zones Urban Development Corporations, City Grants, Garden Festivals, Simplified Planning Zones, and Inner City Task Forces – were added to an already expanded programme at both central and local levels, programmes which were encouraged as the most visible and viable way of reconstructing some of Britain's older industrial areas.

All of this suggests that an understanding of the inter-relationships between developers and the state is crucial both to assist in the practical activities of urban management and planning, but also, as Healey and Barrett (1990) suggest, to develop a critical capacity to evaluate such practices (1990: 90). In particular, the 1980s witnessed significant changes in the organizational nature of central–local state relations, including the centralization of local government expenditures, the utilization of the poll tax as a form of centralization of power under the guise of democracy and a significant curtailment of local state involvement in activities like property management. Yet, while authors like Ambrose (1986) and Thornley (1991) suggest the virtual demise of the local state and the subjugation of communities to the dictates of the market, others note the development of new state practices, policies, and frameworks, forms of local state entrepreneurship which continue to mediate and shape private property investment strategies (Brindley *et al.* 1989; Healey 1992b; Imrie and Thomas 1993a).

In particular, it is useful to characterize the transformation in state–property development relations between the 1970s and 1980s as a shift from state direction of property development, or a form of corporatism, to one more readily characterized by, specifically, the local state's adoption of a subordinate or facilitative role. Indeed, the period has witnessed a marked transformation in the nature of local state autonomy, characterized by the emergence of a hostile central state with a political agenda aimed at eroding the fiscal, functional and administrative bases of the local level while strengthening its own capacities. The reformation of central–local state relations has been well documented, yet underpinning the project of successive Conservative governments has been the propogation of a right-wing, neo-liberal revolution, overtly set against any form of corporatism, with the net result that decision making has been shifted from quasi-democratic forums to 'the market' (Gyford 1985; Duncan and Goodwin 1988). Yet, as Brindley *et al.* (1989) and others note, despite a decade of centralist measures, the local state still retains particular forms of autonomy and discretion, and remains an influential player in land and development processes (Clavel and Kleniewski 1990).

THE CHANGING NATURE OF STATE–PROPERTY DEVELOPMENT RELATIONS

A wide range of authors concur that western societies are undergoing a significant transformation in socio-political and economic organization (Urry 1981; Jessop *et al.* 1987; Lash 1990; Sassen 1991). Familiar facets of the transformation are the dismantling of once powerful industrial centres like the United States, the rapid internationalization of the financial services industry, and the development of new global and regional trade blocs (Drache and Gertler 1991; Budd and Whimster 1990). Moreover, the decline of staple manufacturing industries, coupled with the development of new industrial sectors, has been paralleled by significant spatial shifts in employment. Sassen (1991) and Harloe, Marcuse and Smith (1992) refer to the emergence of new class alignments in the cities, characterized by polarities between high and low income populations, while Urry (1990) refers to a 'disorganized' capitalism as one of the features of contemporary society, characterized by the economic fragmentation of previously coherent regional economies.

These social and economic processes have been linked to what Harvey (1987) refers to as the evolution of a 'seemingly new and quite different regime of capital accumulation' (1987: 2). While there is a huge debate over the detail of this transformation, there is a consensus that an era of flexible accumulation is a characteristic of contemporary political economy, involving a shift from previous periods of state-dominated employment, politics, and policy, to fiscal retrenchment, the demise of the social wage and the high (social and private) costs of Keynesian demand management. These shifts have coincided with the resurgence of neo-liberalism and a retrenchment of social consumption spending, the depression of real wages, and the demise of spatial, redistributive, policies.

Moreover, the importance of the local state, in formulating, controlling and delivering a wide range of social and economic policies, has been challenged by central government controls on fiscal policy and legislation to encourage deregulated government and public–private partnerships in policy formulation and implementation (Moore and Richardson 1989; Stoker 1991).

In turn, public policy has increasingly reflected the diminution in the dominance of public sector decision making and donor-recipient, redistributive policies towards increasing levels of local state reliance on private sector-led efforts in developing competitive, entrepreneurial capacities. As Amin and Malmberg (1992) note, the new strategies are aimed at turning localities into self-promoting islands of entrepreneurship, generating inter-regional and urban competitiveness aimed at linking localities into wider global trajectories (Cooke and Imrie 1989; Amin and Robbins 1991). Indeed, a number of authors concur that the new urban entrepreneurialism is concerned with the state relinquishing control of the development process to a multitude of private sector agencies. In particular, Amin and Malmberg (1992) consider the entrepreneurial approach as 'novel' in drawing upon locally (private) based resources to improve the competitive potential of weaker cities, in contrast to previous periods of urban policy which were geared more towards the provision of collective consumption goods and services.

Throughout the 1980s, the emphasis on private decision making, the deregulation of public control and the centrality of property development in urban regeneration were crystallized in the main urban policy initiatives introduced by successive Conservative governments. As Turok (1992) notes, the property boom years of the mid-1980s were encouraged by the government's assumption that physical (property) development was a panacea in overturning the social and economic problems of the inner cities. In particular, policy encouraged local authorities to utilize subsidies and grants to lever private sector finance, while central government initiatives, like the Urban Development Corporations and City Grants, were instigated to create the conditions for private property investment and development in the British cities (Healey 1991; Turok 1992; Imrie and Thomas 1993). This placed property development at the fulcrum of urban policy initiatives, or, as Colenutt (1993) notes, commercial criteria were replacing social and community goals in urban regeneration.

Moreover, as Turok suggests, the utilization of property-led regeneration, as part of government urban policy, has been based on the simplistic assumption that property development will encourage economic development or that there is an 'inevitable one-way process leading from physical to economic and community development' (1992: 363). Yet, such causal links, between physical development and socio-economic change also underpinned local authority policies in the post-war period where the emphasis was placed on 'sites, services, and infrastructure' policies as a means of city revitalization. As Boddy (1984) notes, in writing of local economic development in the 1970s, local authority economic development activity was property-led, the emphasis was on bringing forward land and sites for physical development, premised on the assumption that benefits would 'trickle-through' to the labour market (Imrie and Thomas 1993a). In this sense, there is a form of temporal continuity as regards property development.

Yet, the period also comprised a number of different 'development' features from those which emerged in the 1980s, not the least of which was the local authority as initiator and implementor of development projects (a role now much diminished). Indeed, the 1972 Local Government Act, and other legislation, enabled local authorities to have a higher profile in development than was evident by the late 1980s. The local authority as land owner, developer, and property manager – a holistic approach to urban regeneration – was not uncommon. Of course, the period was underpinned by both greater fiscal freedoms for local government and the ability to transfer receipts between budgets. As Healey notes, much of this was pursued with vigour by spatial alliances led by key figures in political and public life. In particular, while the objective was economic development for many localities, especially in the peripheral regions, 'the vision was a wider one of bringing the conurbations forward to achieve a modern vision of the civilized social city' (Healey 1992a: 2).

Indeed, a number of authors concur that the pre-1979 period was characterized by particular forms of corporatism (Pahl 1977; Saunders 1980). Pahl (1977) and Winckler (1976, 1977) describe functions, like land-use planning, as developing an autonomy in the 1970s where its power to control investment, knowledge and the allocation of services and facilities placed it beyond the control of private capital. Yet corporatism was, if anything, indicative of a closer relationship between the central and local state, and the 1974 reorganization of local government, coupled with the development of new 'corporate planning techniques', undoubtedly helped to insulate local powers from popular control while tying them in more closely with centralized policy making. As Saunders (1980) and Veblen (1964) note, the point about the development of corporatism is not that it limited the freedom of private capital, but rather that it denied it through the prescription of use. As Saunders (1980) concludes, perhaps the epitome of corporatism in state–property development relations was the Community Land Act (1976) which, theoretically, gave the local state controls over the utilization (if not ownership) of private land.

However, corporatism and the relative autonomy of the local state was sharply curtailed in the 1980s, led by an urban policy which emphasised the primacy of local authority support for property supply, in distinction to the 1960s and 1970s where the utilization of regional assistance, and other subsidies, had supported the private sectors demand for land and property. Moreover, the 1980s witnessed the diminution in strategic and other planning controls and guidance, with social and community goals being subordinated to economic objectives (Brindley *et al.*,1989; Thornley 1991; Healey 1992a; Imrie and Thomas 1992a). Indeed, as Healey (1992a) notes, the absence of strategic locational policy in the 1980s, coupled with the liberalization of planning controls, opened up new forms of spatial development: the fragmented city structure characterized by the peripheral office schemes, the giant retail complexes and the business parks. These processes were also fuelled by institutional fragmentation, the devolvement of regeneration powers to the UDCs, Enterprise Zones, City Grants and Garden Festivals, with local authority roles, like property provider and developer, severely curtailed. Clearly, by the end of the 1980s, the public sector's ability to provide a coherent support framework to 'stabilize' land and property values, and to give confidence to developers and investors, had diminished (see Healey 1992a: 4–5).

Indeed, the evolving frameworks are partly evident in the 1989 Local Government and Housing Act which empowered local authorities to develop local economic plans and strategies, yet placed restrictions on their activities where central government identified the private sector as the preferable (best) provider. In particular, the Act introduced what was termed 'a new balance' of business needs with the social and political questions which tend to dominate local councils, while restricting the scope of local authority involvement in a range of activities, like estate agency, investment businesses and the management of land and buildings. As Mayer (1989) notes, the Act signalled an active co-option of public policy instruments with the private sector and a shift in local economic policies, from utilizing activities like property development as a mechanism for ensuring the provision of public utilities to all citizens, towards the objective of initiating and stimulating private capital accumulation.

In particular, the 1989 legislation signalled a complete break with state forms characteristic of an earlier, corporatist era. The onset of institutional fragmentation, and a simultaneous shift in the state towards subordinating its intervention to the differentiated interests of private capital, are evident. The power of the local state has been significantly reduced by fiscal controls: from the introduction of expenditure targets for specific local authorities, with sanctions for overspending, to the utilization of local tax capping with limits placed on the level of local taxes which local government may levy. Stoker (1991) has argued that local government has lost powers in policy formulation and service delivery to a range of sectional interests, including parents, voluntary groups and, significantly, businesses. The strategy of privatization has involved the withdrawal of key activities from local government, the contracting out of services and an increase in legal forms of control over local authorities. Moreover, the focus on business élites, quangos and other localized forums for policy delivery has led to a proliferation of non-elected bodies dealing with the socio-economic poblems of British cities.

However, the general thesis that 'planning is dead' reflects, as Brindley *et al.* (1989) point out, a certain loss of perspective. Indeed, far from the 'withering away' of the local state, we concur with Healey (1992a) that the public sector remains, *de facto*, a dominant player in property development. In particular, the little research on local authority–property industry relations of the last decade suggests that developers, far from undercutting (or wanting to undercut) the 'bureaucracies' of the local state, are dependent on local authorities to tackle a range of legal and administrative tasks, to 'create the conditions' conducive to private sector involvement in property development, whether through legal processes of land assembly (using compulsory purchase powers) or sponsoring developers for City Grants. Indeed, all of this supports the general contention that, while the form (and objectives) of local state support for property development has changed, its substance remains closely aligned with previous periods.

PROPERTY DEVELOPMENT, THE STATE AND URBAN REGENERATION: A COMPARATIVE STUDY

While a range of authors concur that the role of the local state has significantly diminished in regulating and controlling property development, illustrative material from Cardiff, South Wales, clearly indicates that while local state–property industry relations have clearly changed over the last twenty years, they have done so in such a way as to maintain the proactive role of local government agencies, institutions and community organizations (also, see Clavel and Kleniewski 1990). In particular, one of the dominant contrasts in local state–property industry relations in the city, since the late 1960s, concerns the enlarged role of the central state, particularly in its control of subsidies, grants and other fiscal levers of regeneration. Moreover, the Cardiff cases also illustrate a more general shift in the diversity of interests involved in property development, from the strategic objectives of city modernization, comprising a wide range of social and

community goals, to the more narrowly focused, instrumental developments of the 1980s property development as an expression of both the
speculator and the market (Ball 1983).

In illustrating these and other themes, we present two distinctive, yet
related, episodes of property development in Cardiff. First, we outline a
scheme for the redevelopment of the city centre, Centre Plan (CP), a
scheme which had its origins in the 1950s and, according to the Welsh
Office at the time, was 'the biggest scheme of urban renewal proposed in
Britain' (1972: 1). We then compare and contrast the mid-1970s renewal of
the city centre with a mid-1980s public–private partnership which was
utilized to redevelop a portion of the docklands in the south of the city. Our
analysis broadly illustrates the contention that property-led urban regeneration was, and still is, highly dependent on the organizational capacities of
the public sector.

Partnerships in crisis: the Centre Plan scheme

The redevelopment of Cardiff city centre has preoccupied the local
statutory authorities since the late 1950s when the first plan for a comprehensive solution was mooted. By the late 1960s the basic plan for the
central area had been broadly defined by the Welsh Office, as a redevelopment 'to make a better city centre for Cardiffians and South Walians'. In
particular, the Welsh Office was propagating a particular political line
which held a consensus between local political parties, the idea of civic
pride and a need to restore Cardiff to its capital city status by modernizing
its redundant physical and economic fabric. This idea was clearly outlined
in a Welsh Office memorandum, in that,

> changes in the region from coal and steel production . . . require more
> commercial, professional, and technical services. . . . If Cardiff does not
> grow to fulfil this function, Bristol would . . . (and) the whole of South
> Wales west of Cardiff would have its peripheral character emphasised
> and its economic development handicapped.
>   (Welsh Office 1972: para. 21; quoted in Cooke 1980: 224)

The idea of economic peripherality, coupled with the exhortations of the
Welsh Office, provided the basis for the publication of the Comprehensive
Development Area Plan (CDA) or Centre Plan (CP) in 1973, a document
which envisaged the redevelopment of a 300 acre city centre site, to be
carried out in partnership with a single developer. The core of the proposal
was 36 acres of land adjacent to the main city shopping street, comprising
plans for 93,000 square metres of offices, 70,000 square metres of shopping
and nearly 46,000 square metres for leisure, culture and entertainment.

Yet, the original scheme for the city centre redevelopment, which pre-dated the CDA plan, was a victim of the early 1970s property crash and, in 1975, a joint agreement between the City Council and Ravenseft Properties Ltd, a national property developer, collapsed. In 1968, when the original agreement was signed, the City Council had stood to make a financial windfall from the development by an equity share agreement which guaranteed the City a 50 per cent share of the profits after Ravenseft had received an average 9.25 per cent return on its capital investment. But, by 1975, Ravenseft had terminated the partnership with interest rates of 17 per cent more than absorbing their rental income. Furthermore, while taxation charges were progressively depreciating the profitability of property companies, the scheme was also becoming increasingly untenable for the local authority on economic grounds in that it was estimated that 10 per cent of the city's annual capital programme would have been swallowed up, a situation which would have led to a fiscal deficit and probably higher rate charges for the community.

When the City re-advertised the scheme under the CDA plan, and with the possibilities of a development partnership, a more cautious approach was adopted. It was stated that there should be no financial involvement by the City in the shopping redevelopment, while the developer, in being permitted to develop prime office space, was also required to commit themselves to redeveloping the shopping centre. These conditions were placed as safeguards to prevent a fiscal crisis in the City, while guaranteeing the political objectives of the redevelopment, the modernization of the city centre. Yet as the episode unfolded, the City was forced to concede both conditions by entering into a range of concessionary agreements with Heron, the chosen developer for some key sites. In particular, the City had no time to negotiate legal assurances regarding the shopping development, due to Heron's insistence on drawing up a quick (and incomplete) agreement to permit them to start development before the introduction of Development Land Tax legislation in 1976 (Cooke 1980).

Moreover, while Heron and the City entered into an equity sharing scheme, the terms were more favourably weighted to the private sector compared with the aborted City–Ravenseft proposal. Indeed, the negotiated equity reflected the less than buoyant property market, with the City guaranteed only 20 per cent of the residual ground rent surplus. It also reflected the times, an era of prolonged national industrial stagnation, characterized by austere government policies and massive outflows of capital overseas (Thrift 1988). Moreover, while efforts to promote the national economy, through various financial measures, had stimulated the switch of capital into property, the so-called 'Barber boom' of the early 1970s and the subsequent interest rate hike from 1974 onwards really diminished the leverage of local authorities in extracting anything other than minimal shares in developers' profits (Ball 1983).

These realities reflected the proactive, and supportive, role of local government in Cardiff where a number of facilitative measures were evident. In particular, a key element in securing the development of the shopping centre related to the congenial lease and leaseback arrangements entered into between the City and a consortium of developers (including Debenham and Marks and Spencer) assembled by Heron. The crucial feature was the City's willingness to release land parcels it owned in the city centre, finance the purchase of key sites, and to negotiate flexible lease arrangements with members of the consortia, with the approval of the Welsh Office. Indeed, this interplay, between central and local government, was particularly important in overcoming the strictures of the Community Land Act (1976), which restricted the scope of local authorities to sell freehold land, while stating that only short-term leases should be granted to private developers on any public-owned land and property.

Moreover, the crucial part of the process was undoubtedly the City Council's willingness to invest public funds in the scheme. Indeed, the City showed its entrepreneurial capacity in utilizing receipts from the sales of freehold land as a means of securing Heron's commitment to the shopping development. This resulted from Heron's insistence that they were £4 million short of the estimated £20 million cost of the proposed shopping centre redevelopment, claiming that 'without the council's financial support, we're unable to proceed' (Hamilton 1988). Faced with the developer pulling out of the crucial element of the redevelopment, the City approved a £4 million package, with finance drawn from two sources: £2.8 million obtained from land purchases, coupled with the £1.05 million received from the sale of leases to members of the Heron consortia.

Underpinned by City finances, Heron engineered, and instigated, the 'jewel in the crown' of Cardiff's modern day shopping complex, the St David's Centre, a development which proceeded on a site-by-site basis, with agreements being made between individual members of the consortia and the City. Between 1976 and the early 1980s, the City negotiated a range of further developments which secured new public buildings, with the strategic planning principles, as originally laid out in the CDA plan, providing a clear focus for the negotiating partners. Indeed, the development of the new library in Cardiff is illustrative of the general approach, whereby the City negotiated an agreement with the developers to build shop units and offices and provide the library shell out of the ensuing profits. As Hamilton (1988) notes, there was a high degree of reciprocity involved in the rebuilding of Cardiff, with developers quite happy to fall in line with the wider strategic goals of the City.

Yet the reciprocity was certainly underpinned by the evolving entre-preneurial capacities of the local authority which were evident in the variety of flexible development packages it put together, primarily as a means of securing both commercial and wider community gains. As well as the library development, the City Council relaxed shopping policy for a 'Toys R Us' development in order to reap a higher price for the sale of the site. In turn, receipts from the sale were used to offset some of the costs of the subsequent ice rink development. Moreover, by declaring Conservation and Improvement Areas in other parts of the city centre, the Council were also able to placate the established retailers in them by providing them with grants and subsidies for the refurbishment and renovation of their buildings. This was an important political move in maintaining a clear consensus in the establishment of the 'new' city centre.

The close working relationships, between the local authority and the development consortia really benefited the larger, multinational develop-ment companies, yet they comprised what Healey (1992a) and Ball (1983) characterize as a growth-oriented spatial alliance. Indeed, in generalizing the CP case, the example is illustrative of UK-wide local government–property industry relations of the period, with the emphasis primarily focused on social and community goals (sometimes called 'use values') providing places with a modern property infrastructure. In particular, the key to city centre redevelopment was the provision of a planning frame-work, a framework which specified the community gains as an integral feature, the financial involvement and commitments of the public sector and the specific financial remunerations to be gained by the City Council. In its fullest sense, the CP project was treated as an investment by the City, underpinned by commercial objectives, agreements and targets, not the least of which was the Council's equity share.

Yet as Ball (1983) notes, the growth dynamic was underpinned by public sector flexibilities in utilizing imaginative fiscal packages, sales and infra-structure projects. Indeed, the cross-subsidization programmes were crucial to the emergent form of the city, while the support of central government was important in underpinning the discretionary behaviour of the City Council. The equity arrangements also provided a close alignment between the commercial and social objectives of the modernization programme and, as the City argued at the time, each was integral to the other. Moreover, the role and expertise of the local authority in assembling land, programming acquisitions and supporting public investment all served to underpin the private investments which were crucial to the redevelopment of the city. As Healey comments more generally about property development at this time, within this highly managed environment, real estate development actively flourished and expanded (1992a: 3).

The redevelopment of the city centre reinforces some of the more general points outlined in the previous section concerning the role of corporatist state–property industry relations. In particular, the local state operated with a high degree of discretion and had a more-or-less free hand in negotiating the financial basis of land deals with the private sector consortia, albeit with the consent of the Welsh Office. What was also indicative of the period was the willingness of all the parties to bend rules, make financial deals and even to undercut the Community Land legislation in order to facilitate mutually shared objectives. Moreover, underlying the partnership was an active commitment to the values and principles of private enterprise, yet values which were simultaneously directed towards social and community, as much as commercial, goals. In particular, a political consensus, between central and local states and the private sector, of the reconcilability, indeed, desirability, of a genuine, community-wide, strategic planning framework, was evident. It was part of a long-held legacy of local politics in the city, a legacy which, as we shall see, began to dissolve in the 1980s in the wake of new national political and economic imperatives.

Organizational networks and partnership: the new specificities of property development?

Cardiff City Council's involvement in the redevelopment of the city centre reflected the evolving entrepreneurial abilities and capacities of the local state. In particular, throughout the 1970s and 1980s, the City Council developed a great sensitivity to redevelopment potential and deal making with the property industry, utilizing both public and private funds, underpinned by considerable political support. The redevelopment of a portion of the docks in the mid-1980s, an area known as Atlantic Wharf (AW), was a continuation of this process and, while the form of local state–property industry relations differed in certain respects in AW compared to the CP case, what we see is the evolution of specific social and economic relations between the local state and the property industry.

Yet there is a significant sense in which the docklands' redevelopment differed from the CP case. The difference, as we argue below, was the increasing strength and capacities of central government, and local quangos, in dictating and determining the form and content of property development in the city. Indeed, at the outset, the role of the central state in the redevelopment of AW was crucial, especially in placing pressures on Cardiff City Council to acquiesce to the idea of office and retail growth extending beyond the city centre. In a debate in the House of Commons on Welsh affairs, the Secretary of State, Nicholas Edwards, publicly stated the reorientation of planning policy in Cardiff, noting that 'in my view the time is now ripe . . . to initiate measures which could lead to the rebirth and rapid growth of South Cardiff' (1983: 1176–8).

This statement was the beginning of a four month period which was critical in establishing the institutional mechanisms by which the redevelopment of AW was to take place. It was during this period that the various agencies which were to play a part defined their roles. In particular, the Welsh Office hinted at the financial windfalls to be gained by the City, with Edwards commenting in the Commons that,

> While I can at this stage make no specific developing commitment, I have made it clear that I will consider sympathetically for inclusion in any future performance any project which commands the support of the local planning authorities, and which attracts investment by the private sector, and which offers a good prospect of viability.
>
> (quoted in Imrie and Thomas 1993a: 93)

The significance of this statement, and its allied political underpinnings, is difficult to underestimate. Welsh Office support, in confirming compulsory purchase powers, in grant-aiding development and in making appropriate planning decisions, was clearly signalling the content and direction of renewal in South Cardiff. The specificity of Edwards' February statement indicated that the Welsh Office saw AW as an opportunity to promote leverage planning, but only if a consensus was forged between the component elements of the local state and some kind of broader understanding developed, a 'coalition' of a kind, with private investors.

The instigation, from a central government minister, of the redevelopment of AW reinforces Harding's (1991) more general point about the nature of spatial coalitions in the British context, where clearly the push factor, for a public–private partnership, came from the outside. Yet, while the Welsh Office could be seen to be encouraging wider (national government) directives towards a regional autarky, it was also acting as a mechanism for promoting the interests of local business people, financiers, real estate and local politicians. As the Cardiff Chamber of Commerce (1985) noted at the time, 'the redevelopment of the docks is a potential windfall for the City', while the local press were convinced that the scheme could do nothing but good for the whole community (see Thomas 1992).

The initial development of a 'coalition of interests' was fraught with difficulties, especially between the two lead local state agencies: South Glamorgan County Council and Cardiff City Council. The City appeared more concerned with maintaining and developing the existing industrial base of south Cardiff, an idea which the County discarded as impractical. In particular, the return of the County to Labour control in 1981 prompted a change in the content of the Structure Plan, with a number of influential local politicians from south Cardiff lobbying for provisions supporting the dissolution of the 'industrial' enclave by opening up the docklands to new forms of inward investment. In 1983 the County jointly produced (with a local architect/ developer) a report and proposal for the Welsh Office which marked a major departure from the area's local plans, indicating their desire to see a mixed development in the docks comprising housing, retailing and offices.

The County continued in this proactive role and, along with the Welsh Office, was the key player in facilitating the development. For instance, the County made an early application for planning permission in its own name in order to set a formal policy review process in motion. The County also invited developers to put forward proposals for the area and sponsored the successful candidate, Tarmac, one of the major construction firms in the UK, for an Urban Development Grant application. Moreover, the County also contributed £2 million in grant aid and presented plans for its new headquarters to be built at the northern end of AW, while contributing to the costs of a new ring road being built around the site. In all these senses, the County had firmly committed itself to the new vision for south Cardiff. In contrast, the City remained ambivalent although it gave planning permission to the County's application. In doing so, the City revised the local plan for the area which, while finally endorsing a mixed use redevelopment, was ambivalent enough in its discussion of details for them to be excluded from giving evidence at the public enquiry into the compulsory purchase order served on AW.

This point highlights significant differentiation, or cleavages, within local government and the possibilities of conflict between different constituent elements of the local state. Whereas the City and County Councils forged a political consensus in the redevelopment of the city centre, the AW proposal was anathema to the City precisely because it threatened the social and economic integrity of the commercial core of Cardiff, representing an alternative location for mobile investment to move to. Yet political pressure from local MPs and the Welsh Office forced the City to publicly accede to the County and to participate in a public–private partnership which, while espousing the sentiments, and noises, of consensus was devoid of the strategic guidance and objectives which the City had identified as 'the future of Cardiff'. Indeed, the AW partnership was clearly linking into wider, global, financial and service sectors as a mechanism for developing the local economy, yet in doing so the strategy did not seem to be addressing the city's status as a long standing maritime and manufacturing centre (see Imrie and Thomas 1993a).

With the developer chosen, the implementation of the project took on the appearance of the 'coalition' of public–private interests adumbrated by the Secretary of State, with regular meetings involving the local authorities, the developer, Associated British Ports (ABP, the major landowner in the locality) and representatives of central government and the major industrial employer in the area, Allied Steel and Wire. Securing the support of the public sector agencies was to be more difficult than attaining private sector acquiescence, and ABP eventually fell in behind the scheme after its privatization in 1983. The site also contained thirty-two small and medium-sized businesses which the coalition branded as 'low grade users', out of touch with the new conceptions of urban space being proffered. Their acquiescence was harder to come by and the coalition was dependent on the involvement of a specifically Welsh state-sponsored organization, a quango, the Land Authority for Wales (LAW), who had powers of compulsory purchase vested in them. The utilization of a compulsory purchase order (CPO) was crucial in assembling, quickly, the fragmented land parcels (Thomas and Imrie 1989).

This episode differs from the city centre redevelopment, discussed above, in that, whereas the commercial opportunity offered by city centre redevelopment was generally recognized from the 1950s onwards (though the precise mix of uses needed to secure profitability might differ at the margins over time), the potential of AW remained unacknowledged until the early 1980s, immediately before its redevelopment. In local plans, AW was regarded as a long-term redevelopment prospect and there was no suggestion that it might be redeveloped for high value uses. As a result, the original idea for a mixed use redevelopment (in 1982) came from a local property developer, in contrast to the CP scheme which was initiated by an amalgam of the local authority and national property development companies. In addition, the lack of any relevant planning framework meant that one important state function performed in respect of CP, namely providing a planning framework within which investment decisions could be made, was not undertaken in AW. The planning framework there was largely derived from the private sector, though public sector endorsement (through the review of the local plan and the utilization of a CPO) was crucial.

While many aspects of the AW redevelopment were dictated by the market, the 'success' of the scheme depended on a realignment of the local state organizational and political apparatus and on the utilization of key strategic players in the locality by the development industry. In particular, the AW case questions the rhetoric of the right, that the successes of redevelopment are best propagated by the market independently of public controls or planning. As Batley (1989) notes, property developers were, in the late 1980s, having to slot into a corporatist tradition which argues a case for public sector intervention as the basis of private investment, although one which has tended to evolve as a form of central corporatism operated locally. In the AW case, quangos, such as the LAW, were instrumental in facilitating the docks' redevelopment, yet the compliance of the local planning authority in changing long-held strategic planning objectives was of vital importance to the scheme.

There are also senses in which local authority support for property development in AW has connections with the past, particularly in the deployment and utilization of statutory powers and instruments in guiding and facilitating property development. Indeed, the basic contours of land-use planning have changed little over the last twenty years, and the AW episode evokes previous rounds of property development, of large-scale site clearances, the problems of site assembly, the utilization of key statutory instrument (i.e. the CPO) and the importance of a supportive planning framework in legitimizing urban regeneration. Indeed, the local authority as a 'lever' in regeneration is one sense in which little has changed in property-led regeneration. In particular, the public sector agencies in AW were, in certain respects, fulfilling the traditional local authority role of land acquisition, assembly and disposal to the private sector.

Yet in other senses, the AW case supports the general argument that local authorities are occupying a more residual, background role in property development than was evident in the 1970s. For instance, equity, or profit, share schemes are less evident in local government–property industry deals today than they were in the mid-1970s which, in part, reflects the interplay between central government concerns to reward private sector entrepreneurship and to diminish local government involvement in specific aspects of public policy. Correspondingly, the Cardiff cases also seem to indicate the diminution in public–private partnership formation in property development, in distinction to the rhetoric which proclaims the public–private partnership as a peculiarly 1980s' phenomenon. Yet, one of the key differences between CP and AW was the close involvement of public and private in the former, in distinction to the marginalization of local government in the latter with a shift in the balance of power between central and local government towards the former.

The cases also highlight distributional issues and, whereas community benefits were extracted from developers' profits in the CP episode as part of a wider strategic framework, the very absence of the latter in the AW case underpinned the relative absence of community gains. In this sense, one of the key differences between the two periods is the redistributive effects of property development and, as Imrie and Thomas (1992) and Lawless (1991) note, a feature of contemporary property-led urban policy is the way it seems to have extended socio-economic divisions in the British cities. Indeed, the CP redevelopment was viewed, politically, as part of a modernization programme which, for good or ill, included the creation of a range of social and civic facilities, not just development for its own sake. Even the shopping developments were intended to provide better facilities, worthy of a capital city, for all. While one can argue about the actual beneficiaries of the CP scheme, there is no denying that the strategic planning with civic ideals was very different from AW where the mix of uses was largely determined by profit criteria. And, as research on the AW scheme has shown, the distributive effects of the development were highly uneven and inequitable (Thomas and Imrie 1989; Imrie and Thomas 1993a).

CONCLUSIONS

The analysis in this chapter reaffirms Healey and Barrett's (1990) observation that contextual study of property development, including how the activities of the property industry are influenced and mediated by other actors and agencies, is crucial to a fuller understanding of the evolving nature of the built environment. As Healey and Barrett have observed, until recently a host of contextual factors, like the role of landownership, the nature of development finance and the significance of intermediaries in property development were hidden or only given passing reference. Indeed, the state, as a development intermediary or a mechanism for supporting land and property markets, has been underresearched and, as Healey and Barrett note, 'the processes by which the production of the built environment is accomplished have been given little attention in the social science literature on urbanization and urban development' (1990: 89).

Significantly, many of the frameworks utilized in the analysis of property development lack the capacity to address how the development industry is influenced by a range of external forces, tending to reduce the 'processes of production' of the built environment to a series of unproblematical, functional stages. For instance, one of the more popular conceptions of property development, the 'property pipeline', describes the production of the built environment as comprising a series of sequential stages – evaluation, preparation, implementation, disposal – carried out primarily by the private sector. In particular, the model tends to assume static, fixed roles for the agencies involved and assumes that the public sector does little more than 'regulate' the process. Yet as the specificities of the Cardiff cases clearly illustrate, the dynamics of property development are fashioned by a wide range of political values and complex inter-institutional dynamics, not the least of which are the 'organizational capacities' of the state and the particular forms of both central–local and state–capital relations, all of which are much more crucial than in a purely 'regulatory' sense.

Moreover, Healey's (1992b) institutional approach to the analysis of property development (one which emphasises the crucial, determinate role of the resources, rules and ideas or values of actors and agencies and their inter-relationships with wider structural dynamics in 'processes of production' of the built environment), while a novel departure in conceptual development, seems ambitious given the assertion that the framework 'must be capable of application to all circumstances in which development projects are accomplished' (1992b: 41). As Hooper (1992) notes, this seems to signal a commitment to a totalizing theory which transcends context, whereas Healey seems concerned to develop a 'situated theory'. As Hooper rightly comments, this contradiction never seems to be resolved in Healey's writings, while the theoretical eclecticism associated with her institutional approach surely contains irreconcilable conceptual elements (e.g. placing neo-Marxist structural theory alongside neoclassical theories of land supply!). While Healey's institutional approach requires clarification, we concur with Hooper that the historical development of institutions, and the dynamics which underpin their transformative capacities, form the basis of empirical investigation.

In particular, the Cardiff cases are revealing in illustrating a number of dimensions of the transformative nature of the state through its support for property development over a period which has seen significant changes in the institutional organization of property development. Indeed, crucial facets of contemporary property development, as exemplified by the AW case, concern the organizational capacities of the private sector in a context where, increasingly, political emphasis is being placed on their role in 'building the city' (see Healey 1992a: 1). As Healey (1991) and Ball (1983) note, there are real dangers for localities in wholly privatizing property development, given the significant (local) variations in the degrees of robustness of the property industry. As Healey (1992a) shows in the Newcastle-upon-Tyne context, the local property industry remains highly dependent on a stable public sector framework. It does too in both CP and AW, where particular functions, the assembly and release of land and the identification of development opportunities, were crucial in the facilitation of development. Yet, at a national level the subjugation of the public sector, the diminution in strategic planning and ministerial support for flexible, deregulated, property processes are challenging the involvement of the local state in property development.

The Cardiff cases are also illustrative of particular transformations in the wider socio-economic and political structures of British cities. While the CP case was underpinned by a broad, local political consensus, the need to revitalize the city centre, the AW episode reflected a tension between new economic imperatives and a local political system which was still hanging on to the vestiges of the city's manufacturing status. Indeed, while national politics was attempting to assert the primacy of a regional autarky, creating new competitive potentials by linking localities to the 'sunrise' industries, part of the local political system (i.e. the City Council) was resistant. This resistance reflected the legacy of modernization embodied in the CP development, a programme which, at its heart, was a strategy for maintaining Cardiff city centre as the financial and retail core. Yet, the AW proposals directly challenged the modernization project, espousing a new financial and service locale and the possibility of the spatial fragmentation of the city, a position not dissimilar to those faced by many of the industrial British cities in the 1980s (see Boddy, Lovering, and Bassett 1986).

The research resources required in analysing some of the contextual complexities of property development, outlined above, are wide and varied and, as Healey and Barrett point out, such research 'involves arenas where many powerful actors operate, where secretive strategies are part of the battle for competitive success, where data is scarce, and produced in ways which are often difficult to produce' (1990: 99). In particular, empirical advances are hindered by the contrasting scales at which explanatory propositions can be made about state–property industry dynamics and the difficulties in actually identifying the appropriate scale at which to do empirical analysis (Taylor and Thrift 1982). For instance, while some researchers consider transformations in the built environment to be, in part, the outcome of changes in the structure of monopoly capital, arguing for empirical analysis to be located at the level of macroeconomies, others consider the actions of individual agents and institutions to be as significant in structuring the actions of property developers. While both scales of empirical analysis warrant investigation, too little attention has been paid to the methods by which the contrasting scales of analysis might be linked. This surely requires some intellectual input and attention by researchers of property development dynamics.

In addition, analysis of the institutional specificities of property development requires a greater level of differentiation to be made between the key actors and agencies in that there is no 'typical' property company or developer, while there are significant variations between and within the local state in their approaches to property development. Yet the literature does little to convey the complexity of local state–property industry relations, although, as the Cardiff cases suggested, the partial resolution of internal tensions, between the City and County Councils, was important in providing a legitimate political framework for developers to undertake the redevelopment of the docks. While such specificities require more attentiveness by researchers, a further issue is the relative absence of longitudinal research on the state and property industry, an omission which hinders charting the shifts in local property relations. For instance, how do changes in the legal and fiscal powers of the local state (the central–local dimension) transform the operational, legal and institutional context of the property development industry? Questions like this are more easily researched as a piece of 'action research', part of an on-going project, rather than a retrospective where data is, potentially, much harder to come by.

These points suggest a number of potential elements of a research strategy investigating state–property industry relations. One element is institutional interviews, the identification of the key actors, planning officials, politicians, community group leaders, property managers, etc., locally and nationally, who are involved in providing the parameters for property development. In particular, the study of the state and the property industry is likely to involve the researcher in a web of quite complex relations which can only be unravelled by case study research and the utilization of lengthy survey schedules designed to illicit responses from the key actors on the crucial aspects of their relationships and activities within the 'development nexus'. In addition, interviews must be supplemented with a range of other, complementary data, often specific to the institutions, to provide as full a picture of their actions, motives and rationales. These can variously comprise company accounts, reports, minutes from planning committee meetings, land registry inserts and other sources, many of which are already well documented in the literature (Adams 1987; Rydin 1986).

While no single research agenda or, indeed, method can unravel the full complexities of state–property industry relations, we concur with Healey and Barrett (1990) that what is important is the perspective which underpins any specific research approach. This chapter has argued that any understanding of the nature of property development, its investment strategies, forms of land dealing, building targets and mix of proposed development uses, must recognize the necessary involvement of both the local and central state in mediating and influencing the activities of the private property industry, whatever neo-liberal commentators may have predicted about the demise of the (local) state. Indeed, as the Cardiff cases illustrate, whatever the rhetoric of central government concerning the deregulation of local state powers and controls, local state involvement in the property industry, despite the restructuring of central–local relations, is still of paramount significance in setting the context for processes of production and consumption of the built environment.

REFERENCES

Adams, C. (1987) 'Industrial property: the nature of demand for small premises', *Estates Gazette* 283: 533–5.
Ambrose, P. (1986) *Whatever Happened to Planning?*, London: Methuen.

Amin, A. and Malmberg, B. (1992) 'Competing structural and institutional influences on the geography of production', *Environment and Planning A* 24(3): 401–16.

—— and Robbins, K. (1991) 'The re-emergence of regional economies? The mythical geography of flexible accumulation', *Environment and Planning D: Society and Space* 8(1): 7–34.

Ball, M. (1983) *Housing Policy and Economic Power*, London: Methuen.

Batley, R. (1989) 'London Docklands: an analysis of power relations between UDCs and Local Government', *Public Administration* 67: 167–87.

Bennett, R. and Krebs, G. (1991) *Local Economic Development: Public–Private Partnership Initiation in Britain and Germany*, London: Belhaven.

Boddy, M. (1984) 'Local Economic and Employment Strategies', in M. Boddy and C. Fudge (eds) *Local Socialism: Labour Councils and New Left Alternatives*, London: Macmillan.

——, Lovering, J. and Bassett, K. (1986) *Sunbelt City*, Oxford: Methuen.

Brindley, T., Rydin, Y. and Stoker, G. (1989) *Remaking Planning*, London: Unwin Hyman.

Budd, L. and Whimster, S. (eds) (1992) *Global Finance and Urban Living*, London: Routledge.

Cardiff Chamber of Commerce (1985) *Annual Report*, Cardiff: Cardiff Chamber of Commerce.

Clavel, P. and Kleniewski, N. (1990) 'Space for progressive local policy: examples from the US and the UK', in J. Logan and T. Swanstrom (eds) *Beyond the City Limits*, New York: Temple University Press.

Colenutt, B. (1993) 'Development-led elites', in R. Imrie and H. Thomas (eds) *British Urban Policy and the Urban Development Corporations*, London: Paul Chapman.

Cooke, P. (1980) 'Capital relations and state dependency', in G. Rees and T. Rees (eds) *Poverty and Social Equality in Wales*, London: Croom Helm.

—— and Imrie, R. (1989) 'Little victories: local economic development in three European countries', *Journal of Entrepreneurship and Regional Develop- ment* 1: 313–27.

Drache, R. and Gertler, M. (1991) *The New Era of Global Competition: State Policy and Market Power*, Montreal: McGill-Queen's.

Duncan, S. and Goodwin, M. (1988) *The Local State and Uneven Development*, London: Polity.

Edwards, N. (1983) 'Speech to House of Commons', *Hansard*, 10 February: columns 1176–8.

Gyford, J. (1985) *The Politics of Local Socialism*, London: Allen and Unwin.

Hamilton, N. (1988) 'The city centre, in Cardiff: Capital Development', produced by Cardiff City Planning and Development Department with the Royal Town Planning Institute: 20–32.

Harding, A. (1991) 'The rise of urban growth coalitions, UK-style?', *Environment and Planning C: Government and Policy* 9: 295–317.

Harloe, M., Marcuse, P. and Smith, N. (1992) 'Housing for people, housing for profits', in S. Fainstein, I. Gordon and M. Harloe (eds) *Divided Cities: New York and London in the Contemporary World*, Oxford: Basil Blackwell.

Harvey, D. (1987) 'Flexible accumulation through urbanization: reflections on post modernism in the American city', paper presented at the 6th Urban Change and Conflict Conference, University of Kent, Canterbury, 20–23 September.

Healey, P. (1991) 'Urban regeneration and the development industry', *Regional Studies* 25(2): 97–110.

—— (1992a) 'Urban policy and property development', paper presented to the 6th AESOP Congress, 3–6 June, Stockholm, Sweden.

—— (1992b) 'An institutional model of the development process', *Journal of Property Research* 9(1): 33–44.

—— and Barrett, S. (1990) 'Structure and agency in land and property development processes: some ideas for research', *Urban Studies* 27(1): 89–104.

Hooper, A. (1992) 'The construction of theory: a comment', *Journal of Property Research* 9(1): 45–8.

Imrie, R. and Thomas, H. (1992) 'The wrong side of the tracks: a case study of local economic regeneration in Britain', *Policy and Politics* 20(3): 213–26.

—— and —— (1993a) 'The limits to property-led regeneration', *Environment and Planning C: Government and Policy* 11(1): 87–102.

—— and —— (eds) (1993b) *British Urban Policy and the Urban Development Corporations*, London: Paul Chapman.

Jessop, B., Bonnett, K., Bromley, S. and Ling, T. (1987) 'Popular capitalism, flexible accumulation, and Left strategy', *New Left Review* 165: 104–22.

Lash, S. (1990) *Sociology of Postmodernism*, London: Routledge.

Lawless, P. (1991) 'Urban policy in the Thatcher decade: English inner-city policy, 1979–90', *Environment and Planning C: Government and Policy* 9: 15–30.

Leitner, H. (1991) 'Pro-growth coalitions, the local state, and downtown development: the case of six cities', in M. Fischer and M. Sauberer (eds) *Society, Economy, Space*, Vienna.

Logan, J. and Swanstrom, T. (eds) (1990) *Beyond the City Limits*, New York: Temple University Press.

Mayer, M. (1989) 'Local politics: from administration to management', paper presented at the Cardiff Symposium on Regulation, Innovation, and Spatial Development, University of Wales, 13–15 September.

Moore, C. and Richardson, J. (1989) *Local Partnership and the Unemployment Crisis in Britain*, London: Unwin Hyman.

Pahl, R. (1977) 'Collective consumption and the State in capitalist and State socialist societies', in R. Scase (ed.) *Industrial Society: Class, Cleavage, and Control*, London: Allen and Unwin.

Rydin, Y. (1986) *Housing Land Policy*, Aldershot: Gower.

Sassen, S. (1991) *The Global Cities: London: New York, Tokyo*, New York: Princeton University Press.

Saunders, P. (1980) *Urban Politics*, London: Penguin.

Solesbury, W. (1990) 'Property development and urban regeneration', in P. Healey and R. Nabarro (eds) *Land and Property Development in a Changing Context*, Aldershot: Gower.

Stoker, G. (1991) *The Politics of Local Government*, London: Macmillan.

Taylor, M. and Thrift, N. (1982) 'Industrial linkage and the segmented economy 1: some theoretical proposals', *Environment and Planning A* 14: 1601–13.

Thomas, H. (1992) 'State intervention and the managing of consent: redevelopment in South Cardiff', *Contemporary Wales*, 5: 81–98.

—— and Imrie, R. (1989) 'Urban development, compulsory purchase, and the regeneration of local economies: the case of Cardiff docklands', *Planning Practice and Research* 4(3): 18–27.

Thornley, A. (1991) *Urban Planning under Thatcherism*, London: Routledge.

Thrift, N. (1988) 'The geography of international economic disorder', in D. Massey and J. Allen (eds) *Uneven Redevelopment: Cities and Regions in Transition*, Hodder and Stoughton: Sevenoaks.

Turok, I. (1992) 'Property-led urban regeneration: panacea or placebo?', *Environment and Planning A* 24(3): 361–80.

Urry, J. (1981) *The Anatomy of Capitalist Societies*, London: Macmillan.

—— (1990) 'Places and politics', in M. Harloe, C. Pickvance and J. Urry (eds) *Place, Policy, and Politics*, London: Macmillan.

Valler, D. (1989) 'Economic development strategy formulation: the case of Norwich City Council', *Planning Practice and Research* 4(3): 32–3.

—— (1991) 'Strategy and partnership in local economic development: a case study in local economic strategy making', *Policy Studies Review* 10(2/3): 109–16.

Veblen, T. (1964) *Absentee Ownership and Business Enterprise in Recent Times*, New York: Sentry Press.

Welsh Office (1972) *Inspector's Report of Centre Plan Public Inquiry*, Cardiff: HMSO.

Winckler, J. (1976) 'Corporatism', *European Journal of Sociology* 17: 100–36.

—— (1977) 'The Corporate Economy: Theory and Administration', in R. Scase (ed.) *Industrial Society: Class, Cleavage, and Control*, London: Allen and Unwin.

8   Charting the uncharted

Vacant industrial premises and the local industrial property arena

Rick Ball

INTRODUCTION

One of the least researched and evaluated aspects of the industrial property scene is the problem of vacant industrial premises (VIPs) (Perry 1991). Such industrial spaces are often hard to identify, to explain and to assess. Yet they are an extremely important part of the industrial property scene. VIPs tend to be prominent in the so-called 'old industrial areas'. These core urban manufacturing areas of the mid- to late-nineteenth century have suffered from the vagaries of time and from the decentralization and rationalization decisions of industrialists. Typified by ageing industrial stock that is in need of refurbishment, congested locations and unattractive environments, they have borne the brunt of manufacturing relocation and closure (see for example, Fothergill, Kitson and Monk 1987; Champion and Townsend 1991; London Borough of Ealing 1992; City of Wakefield Metropolitan District Council/Kirklees Metropolitan Council 1992)

From the perspective of the built environment, VIPs are generally viewed by local authorities and other agencies in these areas as important and intractable problems (see for example, Grant Thornton 1989; Civic Trust Regeneration Unit 1989; Burnley Borough Council 1992). They are seen as representing unused potential and projecting a negative image. In reflecting the twin problems of surplus, perhaps limited quality, property supply and inadequate demand to utilize the buildings involved, they are inevitably used as an indicator of area status or performance. The level of VIPs may indicate structural mismatch where available buildings do not meet the needs of local industry (Fothergill, Monk and Perry 1987a). This may result from a physical or an information deficiency where such buildings are not matched to the existing demand for industrial property, if indeed sufficient demand exists. Whatever the explanation, they are problems for the localities involved.

More generally, VIPs connect with wider aspects of the property market. For example, the amount of new building coming on to the market each year is very small in relation to the total stock. As a result, the inherited stock of old, existing buildings is the dominant influence on the market as a whole (Fothergill, Monk and Perry 1987b). At the local level, the incidence of VIPs may have a particularly important impact. For example, such premises are often old and of limited operational quality so that they generally command low rental income relative to new premises. As a consequence, if there are sizeable numbers of them in a locality, they may well influence the local property supply structure, acting as a depressant on the willingness of developers to enter into new building. In this way, VIPs give signals to potential developers in a locality.

There is a general assumption that the floorspace involved in VIPs is often beyond productive use, obsolete and congested. However, it is equally clear that these premises may be reoccupied if they are in some way attractive to alternative users and, of course, if they can be released for reoccupation. Indeed, where they are in reasonable condition such premises are useful, often cheap, locations. As a number of researchers have discovered, they reduce start-up costs for new small businesses by either avoiding initial capital costs for potential owner-occupiers or by offering modest rents (Firn and Swales 1978; Lloyd and Mason 1984; Green and Foley 1986). In this sense, VIPs have some positive effects in the local economy. Such is the complex legacy of the built environment.

Of course, not all VIPs are 'old' and 'old' factories do not always fall vacant. To some extent at least, it is the local circumstances of industrial production – organizational structure, locational attributes, and so on – that are at the root of the VIPs issue. Added to this, successful refurbishment and re-use of vacant industrial buildings is more likely to occur in some localities than in others (Finn 1986). Given this finding, it is important to focus on the local scale in assessing the VIPs issue.

This chapter focuses on VIPs in one local industrial property market – the Stoke-on-Trent locality. It draws on some original, unpublished VIPs survey work conducted in this classic 'old industrial area' during the late 1980s (Ball 1989a). The aim is to both chart the level and nature of vacant industrial premises and to explore some related issues. The discussion is developed around a number of sub-themes. These are largely connected to the approach adopted in tackling such an underresearched and barely documented area and to the policy implications that emerge. As such, it offers an important insight into both the local dynamics of vacant property markets and their relationships to economic development. Such an insight is not permitted with the widely cited regional scale information on property published by firms such as King & Co. (see Chapter 2). Moreover, in contrast with much of the current research and debate on the restructuring of industrial property supply towards new uses, the chapter covers another, less documented, dimension of supply structure. It investigates standard, conventional industrial buildings. However, it also focuses on the more marginal premises that tend to be drawn into the inventory of local industrial property and to be used as a base for production activities in mature industrial places. In these various ways, it provides material on an area of industrial activity that is virtually uncharted in the literature (see Perry 1991; Fothergill, Monk and Perry 1987b).

In addition to the detailed documentation of VIPs, the chapter analyses three major components of VIPs' change occurring over time. This allows us to identify and assess reoccupations, persistent vacancies and redevelopments and to draw out some important perspectives on the dynamics of the industrial property scene. These components are assessed at two spatial scales: first from an aggregate locality perspective; and second by documenting and evaluating the micro-geography of VIPs dynamics.

Finally, the discussion develops some of the policy issues and implications that are apparent in the area of VIPs. It is important to discover the extent of vacant floorspace because local policy may be able to alleviate the problem and, in many cases, make productive use of the VIPs stock. For example, some pressuring for national or European Community resources may be attempted in order to realize local economic potential (see Grant Thornton 1989; Stoke-on-Trent City Council 1992). The potential of disused, but useable, industrial premises reveals itself in various ways. In fact, some of the success stories of economic restructuring are linked to the re-use of previously derelict premises (see Department of the Environment 1987). For example, redundant buildings may be used to fuel the drive for industrial heritage-based tourism – an example would be the Gladstone Pottery Museum in Stoke-on-Trent – or to enhance local leisure provision while alleviating the intrusiveness with which VIPs are often associated (see Ball and Metcalfe 1992).

Against a background of policy constraints, the chapter discusses the actual VIPs policy initiatives developed and pursued by the local authority in the area. The wider implications and applicability of these locality-specific findings are evaluated with a view to the production of an embryo VIPs action plan for old industrial areas.

In all these terms then, the VIPs research reported in this chapter followed from a need, clearly identified in the Stoke-on-Trent Economic Development Strategy (SEDS) (Stoke-on-Trent City Council 1991), to address the issue in an endeavour to tackle both the constraints in the local economy and the potential for development that such VIPs reflect.

THE LACK OF DATA ON THE LOCAL INDUSTRIAL PROPERTY SCENE

Earlier contributions in this book have highlighted the lack of available data on the local industrial property scene in the UK. This inadequacy extends to both quantity/availability and quality. In the former case, and with only a few exceptions (Cameron and Fleming 1990; Adams, Russell and Taylor-Russell 1992), we basically know little about local industrial property. Within the constraints of available resources, local authorities normally monitor marketed properties, at least those being marketed through the local network of industrial estate agencies. Unfortunately, this means that properties being marketed by non-local agents, perhaps in provincial centres, are sometimes omitted from even the superior analyses and that properties not publicized or overtly available in the market are virtually always missed. In addition, of course, many properties never appear on the market, yet are an important part of the local industrial property scene in terms of potentially available floorspace, environmental impacts, etc. As a consequence, much local authority analysis and knowledge reflects only a segment of the local industrial property spectrum of occupancy types. Of course, in addition to this question of quantity there is the even thornier issue of data quality. There is little available secondary data on the subject of industrial property and the sub-topic of vacant industrial premises is no exception. Especially where vacant and sometimes derelict and non-marketed factories and warehouses are concerned, planners and industrial development analysts are forced to rely on very ephemeral sources of information. What data is available must be gleaned from general sources such as King and Co.'s estimates of the marketed floorspace of larger units (over 465 square metres (5,000 square feet)), from brief surveys of local estate agents, or from more detailed and expensive survey work (see Chapters 2 and 3). The first is useful but limited in detail and is essentially focused on the aggregate rather than the local property market. The second is possible and valuable as an indicator but is restricted to the data available from estate agents. The third is clearly the most valuable.

CHARTING THE LEVEL OF VIPs IN STOKE-ON-TRENT: PRODUCING AN INFORMATION BASE

Probably the major reason behind the lack of VIPs research in the UK is the combination of problems that confront the researcher. It is rarely explored because it not only requires detailed and expensive survey work but also because it is a difficult domain of the industrial environment in which to conduct such research activity. Empty premises do not readily give forth their circumstances and owners are difficult if not impossible to locate in many cases. Nevertheless, it is essential to collect information on the subject, and direct survey is the only realistic vehicle.

Questionnaires

Detailed surveys of VIPs were conducted in Stoke-on-Trent in 1985, 1987 and 1989. In the remainder of this chapter we focus on the 1989 data base (for the earlier analysis see Ball 1989b). In addition to basic information on the name, address and precise location of the premises, this questionnaire sought data on ownership, date of construction, original use, whether purpose-built, site and floorspace area, number of storeys, the condition of various aspects of the building (brickwork, roof, etc.), access, parking and available services, activity of most recent user, reasons for vacation and destination of previous business (i.e. closure, relocation, etc.), rental, price (if for sale) and future intentions for the site. Most information could be gleaned from visual survey backed up by available records. However, in a few cases material was, understandably, difficult to elucidate from visual survey (for example, reasons for vacation).

In addition to the core survey, three re-survey questionnaires were designed to collect updated data on premises previously found vacant and involved reoccupations, persistent vacancies, and redevelopments/demolitions.

Sampling frame assembly and other limitations

The survey was based on a sampling frame built up from not only local estate agents' lists, but also from both lists of premises classified as 'void' for local rating/valuation purposes and from careful visual survey.

A number of major difficulties were encountered in completing the surveys. The derivation of a sampling frame proved difficult in itself. Material produced by estate agents or other marketing publicity was not available in all cases, especially, of course, when premises were not being actively marketed. As such, it was necessary to attempt to identify VIPs from visual survey. This proved difficult, not least of all because premises which, at first sight, appear to be disused may in reality be fully operational. To some degree the problem of the exclusion of non-marketed premises was again surmounted by using rating/valuation records. Premises recorded as void for rating purposes are, by definition, officially out of productive use and such information for Stoke-on-Trent proved very useful indeed in identifying non-marketed premises. However, it was not possible to derive much data on ownership from the rating/valuation records.

There were, of course, quite a number of problems associated with using the rating/valuation records. Although only premises rated as void were built into the sample, many proved, when visited, to be either in use or in the process of redevelopment. Notwithstanding that potential confusion, in many cases it was very difficult indeed to precisely locate the buildings using the information provided and in several cases premises turned out to be non-relevant (e.g. with no access or of a building type that could not lend itself to industrial use).

It was also important to arrive at an appropriate definition of industrial premises. In terms of this it was difficult to decide which premises to include in the survey and which to exclude. For example, buildings originally constructed as petrol stations or assembly halls could, with only minimal refurbishment, be used for industrial production or warehousing. Indeed, in an area that has a shortage of industrial land and premises (Staffordshire County Council 1991) these could be of enormous value. In effect, it was decided to include all premises that could potentially be used for such economic activity but to exclude all buildings originally constructed as dwellings, even though these could sometimes be adapted for use as small workshops. No examples were found of the latter and, as such, this was not thought to constitute an omission of any serious consequence.

Given the initial finding of a substantial curtailing of total vacant industrial floorspace between 1987 and 1989 in the Stoke-on-Trent area, an impression confirmed by discussions with local industrial property agents, it was decided to extend the survey to include VIPs that might be described for one or more reasons as marginal. In other words, in the knowledge of a general problem of industrial floorspace shortage, and in the expectation that there would be relatively few VIPs emerging (certainly of medium size or larger), it was decided to make a somewhat broader sweep to pick up the more marginal VIPs. These involved premises that were either very small and/or not initially constructed or recently used for industrial production or warehouse functions as well as small workshops or storage blocks within the perimeter of other businesses or even within residential areas. Buildings with a marginal industrial potential included: cinemas; churches and church halls; bingo halls; pubs and clubs; and some shop/office type premises. With sometimes very little modification, these buildings could often be converted into useful industrial production or warehouse units.

In addition to building type, location was also a consideration in deciding the degree of marginality (or not) and hence many buildings with potential, but located in residential areas with very poor access, could not realistically be classed as having even a marginal industrial potential. On occasions, small garage-type accommodation in mixed areas was ascribed marginal potential. In general terms, and particularly at present, when there is a shortage of industrial units in a city such as Stoke-on-Trent, marginal buildings are clearly of some importance. To illustrate, former schools in Tunstall and Burslem had, until just prior to the survey, been used as pottery factories. Church buildings in Tunstall and Hanley had also been brought into industrial or warehousing usage.

A problem linked to that of establishing usage involved the question of partial vacancy. It is virtually impossible from an external (visual) survey to identify partial vacancy of a building or a section of floorspace within an enterprise. As such, the survey did not attempt to monitor partial vacancy, except where unused floorspace occurred in a readily definable and separate (actual or potential) area. Even then, it was difficult to identify such partial use and this is, in effect, accepted as a necessary limitation of the research methodology.

In more general terms, the volume of resources and the time available for the survey work to be completed, and the time-consuming nature of the survey, meant that each of the 560 or more site visits in the 1989 surveys were of brief duration. An additional survey problem was, of course, the requirement to establish contacts with the occupants of reoccupied premises in order to elucidate information on the factors involved in the re-use of the premises, the degree of refurbishment work carried out, the employment involved and so on. This work involved the questionning of key managerial staff. In most cases it was necessary to deal with the most appropriate member of staff available at the time of the site visit. Clearly, there may well be problems with the data obtained although, in all cases, we can be confident that the small amount of basic data required was accurate. No refusals were encountered and a virtually complete set of data on reoccupying firms was secured.

Finally, there were obvious operational difficulties in measuring and recording VIPs and the floorspace involved. Where there was no marketing documentation, the floorspace volume was carefully but, where access could not be achieved, fairly crudely estimated. This was seen as a pitfall confronting any attempt to research this kind of subject with finite resources of time and finance.

THE OCCURRENCE OF VIPs IN STOKE-ON-TRENT: AN EVALUATION

The VIPs problem in Stoke-on-Trent is the natural corollary of the rationalization and decline of an old industrial area that has traditionally specialized in a narrowly-defined group of pressured activities. These have tended to develop, inhabit and ultimately abandon sets of premises that have gradually become unsuitable for production in the 1980s and 1990s.

Table 8.1 Vacant industrial premises in Stoke-on-Trent, July 1989: size, structure and source of information

Size of premises (square metres)*	Source of information Survey	Agent	Total Number	%
<93	95 (41)†	14 (2)	109 (43)	39
93–465	89 (27)	48 (6)	137 (33)	48
466–1,393	12 (3)	10 (1)	22 (4)	8
1,394–4,645	2 (–)	5 (–)	7 (–)	3
>4,645	3 (–)	2 (–)	5 (–)	2
Total	201 (71)	79 (9)	280 (80)	100

Notes: *The research reported here was completed using non-metric measurements. For purposes of uniformity with other chapters, figures have been recalculated in square metres.
†Figures in brackets refer to the proportion that were classified as 'marginal' premises. These are premises that were either very small and/or not initially constructed or recently used for industrial production or warehouse functions as well as small workshops or storage blocks within the perimeter of other businesses or even within residential areas.

As shown in Table 8.1, some 280 VIPs were recorded in Stoke-on-Trent in July 1989. The majority – around 70 per cent of these units, involving 54,547 square metres of floorspace – were picked up through local survey. The remainder – 53,487 square metres – were on the books of either local estate agents or developers. The vast majority of premises were of modest size with over 87 per cent below 465 square metres and with only five particularly large premises. The group of 'marginal' premises mainly involved small units that were not being actively marketed as industrial premises (Table 8.1).

In terms of origins and age, the bulk of the 1989 vacant premises were mainly ones that had been displaced from the manufacturing sector. In many cases, they were purpose-built pottery or engineering factories and warehouses (around 50 per cent of the total) that had been constructed prior to 1918 (64 per cent) (Tables 8.2 and 8.3) and displaced during the later part of the 1970s/early 1980s contractionary phase that pervaded The Potteries sub-region (Ball 1993).

A variety of quality indicators can be used to assess the status or potential of VIPs and these range from questions of design to those of actual physical quality. This indicated potential problems in the re-use of such premises. Around 25 per cent of premises were unequivocally found to be originally purpose-built and less than 55 per cent were of multi-storey construction (Table 8.3).

Table 8.2 Vacant industrial premises in Stoke-on-Trent, July 1989: age structure

Date of construction	Number of premises	%
Pre-1900	107 (15)*	38
1901–18	72 (8)	26
1919–45	38 (6)	13
1946–60	16 (2)	6
1961–80	42 (8)	15
1981–9	5 (2)	2
Total	280 (41)	100

Note: *Figures in brackets refer to the number of persistently vacant premises in the total for each category – see text.

Table 8.3 Vacant industrial premises in Stoke-on-Trent, July 1989: number of storeys and purpose-built status

Number of storeys	Purpose-built	Non-purpose built	Total
1	31 (15)*	99 (8)	130 (23)
2	34 (8)	98 (6)	132 (14)
3	7 (3)	10 (0)	17 (3)
4	0	1 (1)	1 (1)
Total	72 (26)	208 (15)	280 (41)

Note: *Figures in brackets refer to the number of persistently vacant premises in the total for each category – see text.

The 'quality' of the 1989 VIPs can be assessed in more straightforward terms by looking at their basic condition. Around 50 per cent were classified as in very good basic condition (Table 8.4) while a modest 24 per cent were in poor condition or worse. Interestingly, the great majority of 'marginal' type premises emerged from the survey as either 'good' or 'average'. They are clearly potential industrial locations but they are usually not covered in survey work. The only problem with the figures in Table 8.4 is the disproportionate level of VIPs recording poor basic condition amongst, not surprisingly, persistent vacancies.

The matter of specific aspects of built fabric is something which confronts those charged with encouraging the re-use of such buildings and the businesses or developers who might be enticed into projects. It is the more superficial aspects that appear to deteriorate first – for example, paintwork, fittings, etc.

Table 8.4 Vacant industrial premises in Stoke-on-Trent, July 1989: basic condition of premises

Condition summary	Non-marginal	Marginal	Total No.	%
1 Good	101 (14)*	39	140	50
2 Average	51 (12)	22	73	26
3 Poor	48 (15)	19	67	24
Total	200 (41)	80	280	100

Notes: Good = available for use with little or no refurbishment or repair; Average = sound condition and available for use with only minor refurbishment or repair; Poor = available for use only if major refurbishment or repair work were to be completed.
*Figures in brackets refer to the number of persistently vacant premises in the total for each category – see text.

Table 8.5 Vacant industrial premises in Stoke-on-Trent, July 1989: specific condition of premises

Aspect of built fabric	Condition Good	Average	Poor	Total
Site	55	27	18	100
Brickwork	42	42	16	100
Roof/fittings	36	38	26	100
Paintwork	35	29	36	100
Total	42	34	24	100

Note: Percentage figures calculated by assembling grading scores for each aspect – 1, 2 indicating good, 3 indicating average and 4, 5 indicating poor quality.

Many VIPs have a high potential for re-use with relatively little essential or necessary refurbishment expenditure (Table 8.5). Once again, however, there is a clear residue of premises in rather poor physical condition.

A final representation of VIPs quality is provided in Table 8.6. This cross-tabulates two measures of potential – access and parking conditions. The accessibility of each VIP was graded using not only local access quality (i.e. site access, proximity to main road, width of access roads) but also sub-regional access (i.e. access to main trunk routes). This provided a strong indication of the likely attractiveness of at least 40 per cent or so of the VIPs, although there was a sizeable minority (25 per cent) that had not

Table 8.6 Vacant industrial premises in Stoke-on-Trent, July 1989: access and parking potential

	Parking potential			
Access potential	Good	Average	Poor	Total
Good	37 (5)*	36 (4)	30 (3)	103 (12)
Average	20 (6)	40 (7)	47 (7)	107 (20)
Poor	6 (2)	28 (3)	36 (4)	70 (9)
Total	63 (13)	104 (14)	113 (14)	280 (41)

Note: *Figures in brackets refer to the number of persistently vacant premises in the total for each category – see text.

only poor access potential but also limited parking potential. This may mean that only certain types of reoccupant are likely (e.g. those for which access and/or parking potential are not vital) or, perhaps more so, that straight reoccupation is not likely.

In general terms then, the vacant industrial floorspace available in Stoke-on-Trent in July 1989 was, on the whole, of good quality. Compared to the level in 1987 there were, of course, some marked changes in the character of the VIPs identified. Basically, there were more VIPs in 1989 (200 non-marginal against 182 in the 1987 survey) but less vacant floorspace. This reflected the greater availability of small units (about 40 per cent in Table 8.1 as against only 20 per cent in 1987) and, more discouragingly from a policy perspective, the sparsity (short supply) of medium and large premises. The former finding was surprising because the north Staffordshire local economy had been quite buoyant in the previous two or three years and demand for industrial premises was thought to have outstripped the supply. Clearly, there may be a structural problem here of one or more dimensions. Non-marketed (or even older) premises may simply not have been matched up with potential reoccupants because of information barriers – they are, without survey work such as that reported here, an unknown quantity. Just as likely – and compounding the problem – available premises may be just not suitable (in design, size, location or other terms) for the potential reoccupants.

DOCUMENTING THE DYNAMICS: VIPs IN THE MID–LATE 1980s

In addition to basic insights into the VIPs issue in a locality, it is interesting to focus on the dynamics and to isolate qualitative changes in the level of

VIPs. By focusing on reoccupations, redevelopments and persistency of vacancy over time and by considering the marketing perspective we can generate substantive insights.

Basic patterns of change

Trends in the level of VIPs in Stoke-on-Trent up until 1987 have been previously documented elsewhere (see Ball 1989a and b) and, although some aspects are drawn into the analysis, they are not discussed here in detail. The two year period from August 1987 to July 1989 (Table 8.7) recorded a reduction in vacant industrial floorspace of 51,982 square metres from 149,146 square metres to 97,164 square metres. However, this figure represents only the 'tip of the iceberg' when it comes to assessing changes in the level of floorspace. Of the 182 premises recorded in the 1987 survey, some 104 (with subdivisions, amounting to 149 units) had been reoccupied by July 1989, twenty-seven had been fully demolished and only forty-one remained out of productive use. Over the period, some 159 new vacancies were recorded (with an additional eighty 'marginal' units). Interestingly, whereas in 1987 some 66 per cent of VIPs were on the market, in 1989 the figure was a mere 28 per cent. Aggregating the persistent and new vacancies in 1989 we arrive at a figure of 280 VIPs in July 1989, representing 108,034 square metres of floorspace (including eighty 'marginal' units amounting to 10,870 square metres).

An important perspective on the issue of VIPs in Stoke-on-Trent is the geographical distribution. This is set out in Table 8.8 and in Figures 8.1 and 8.2. Figure 8.1 shows new vacancies emerging between the 1987 and 1989 survey dates while Figure 8.2 shows persistent vacancies. Both patterns reflect the traditional industrial core areas of Stoke-on-Trent with a north west to south east line of VIPs centred on Burslem, Tunstall, Hanley, Fenton and Longton.

From Figure 8.2 we can see that persistent vacancies – relatively few in number – were clustered in Burslem, Hanley and to a lesser extent in Stoke and Longton. Focusing on just one locale, between 1987 and 1989, over 30,650 square metres of vacant floorspace were reoccupied in Burslem – a measure of the greater buoyancy of the industrial property market and, to some degree, of a greater focus of attention and sense of regeneration urgency by the local authority and other interested parties, than had prevailed in the early 1980s. The Burslem Action Plan developed by the Civic Trust Regeneration Unit in liaison with many local interests is testimony to such a change (Civic Trust Regeneration Unit 1989).

In summary, considering the data in Table 8.8, it is clear that the focus of local industrial demise switched within Stoke-on-Trent in the late 1980s.

Table 8.7 Vacant industrial premises in Stoke-on-Trent: components of change, 1987–9

Component	Floorspace (square metres)	No. of units
1987 Vacant	149,146	172
Occupations	71,493	104*
Demolitions	57,618	27
Premises still vacant in 1989	20,035	41
New vacancies (non-marginal)	77,129	159
New vacancies (marginal)	10,870	80
1989 Vacant**		
(excl. marginals)	97,164	200
(incl. marginals)	108,034	280

Notes: *149 if allowance is made for the sub-division of the 1987 survey premises (i.e. seventeen original vacant premises were sub-divided into sixty-two separate units).
**Division between marketed/non-marketed as follows:

Premises still	non-marketed	13,309	
vacant in 1989	marketed	6,726	22
New 1989	non-marketed	41,238	182
vacancies	marketed	46,671	57
1989 total	non-marketed	54,547	201
vacant	marketed	53,487	79

In July 1989, the Burslem area recorded only 19 per cent of vacant industrial floorspace (38 per cent in 1987), while for Hanley the figure was also 19 per cent (against 24 per cent in 1987). There were other, marginal changes but the most noticeable differences involved the Stoke area with 24 per cent of vacant floorspace in 1989 (against 3 per cent in 1987) and Longton with 25 per cent in 1989 (against 19 per cent in 1987). Both areas also recorded high proportions of new vacancies in 1989. When we assess these figures alongside VIP reoccupation performance – at least for Stoke itself – we find starkly contrasting pictures with very few reoccupations in this area (Table 8.8). Of course, it is important to note that, aside from its greatly improved 'performance', Burslem still recorded the highest proportion of persistent vacancies.

Reoccupations

The 1989 survey results were dominated by reoccupations. In fact, some 71,493 square metres of vacant industrial floorspace, involving 149 units (48 per cent of floorspace and 61 per cent of units) were reoccupied between 1987 and 1989.

Table 8.8 Vacant industrial premises in Stoke-on-Trent, July 1989: distribution of floorspace and units by local area

Area	Vacant % by area	New % by area	Total % by area	Reoccupations % by area
Tunstall	3.2	4.9	4.6	3.3
	n=3	n=23	n=26	n=14
Burslem	35.1	15.4	19.0	43.9
	n=11	n=46	n=57	n=36
Hanley	23.8	17.9	19.0	14.9
	n=7	n=61	n=68	n=39
Stoke	22.8	24.1	23.8	2.6
	n=8	n=39	n=47	n=8
Fenton	2.1	9.8	8.4	11.6
	n=4	n=29	n=33	n=24
Longton	13.1	28.0	25.2	23.8
	n=8	n=41	n=49	n=28
Total				
floorspace	20,035	87,999	108,034	71,493
units	n=41	n=239	n=280	n=149

Notes: Vacant = persistently vacant premises;
New = new vacancies located in 1989;
Reoccupations = premises vacant in 1987 but reoccupied by 1989.

Reoccupations represent a modicum of success in the return of former VIPs to productive use. Around 46 per cent of reoccupants in 1989 were engaged in manufacturing, but relatively few were entirely new businesses (Table 8.9). Most were either local relocations from other parts of the city (and not necessarily from the same Potteries town as the new premises), location, expansions or re-openings of buildings that had been 'mothballed' some months before. The vast majority – some 76 per cent – involved premises of less than 465 square metres with relatively small numbers employed. Around 63 per cent of reoccupiers employed five or less male workers and 84 per cent employed ten or less. Clearly, most of these reoccupations involved small businesses. In manufacturing, reoccupiers employed 957 – an average of 14.5 per manufacturing business (595 males and 362 females). In total, some 1,399 jobs were created in reoccupations: 1,321 full time and 78 part time. Only 24 per cent of jobs were in the service sector – an average of only five jobs per reoccupying business. The 25 new businesses created 156 jobs at 6.2 per firm.

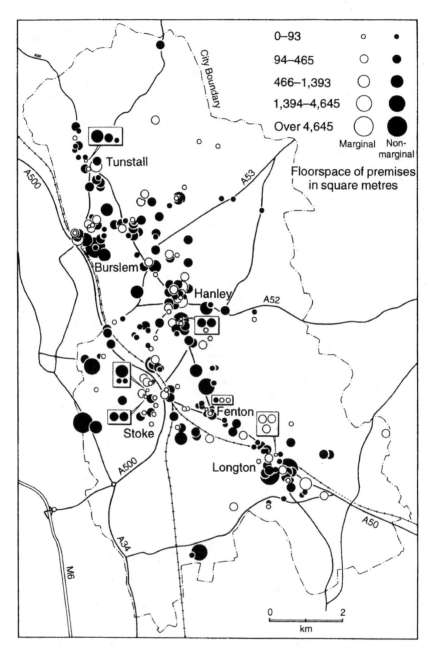

Figure 8.1 Newly vacant industrial premises in Stoke-on-Trent, August 1987 to July 1989

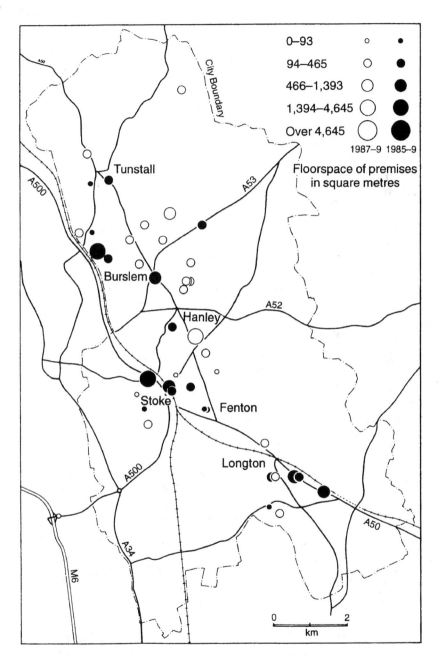

Figure 8.2 Persistently vacant industrial premises in Stoke-on-Trent, February 1985 to July 1989

Table 8.9 Reoccupied vacant industrial premises in Stoke-on-Trent, August 1987 to July 1989: reasons for reoccupation

Nature of occupiers' business (sic)	New firm	Local relocation	Others	Total	
				No.	*%*
Manufacturing	11	32	18	61	46.2
Construction	1	6	1	8	6.1
Services	13	25	25	63	47.7
Total	25	63	44	132*	100.0

Note: *Information on both aspects could not be derived for seventeen premises.

Some further insight into the nature of reoccupation can be derived by picking out examples from specific local areas. Typical businesses reoccupying small, previously vacant premises were new or expanding firms in traditional local specializations or in a range of contemporary service activities.

In the traditional pottery manufacturing towns there were numerous examples of pottery manufacturers or materials suppliers reoccupying former VIPs. This occurred particularly in Longton (eight businesses) and Burslem (seven businesses) although there were examples throughout the city. Some were entirely new businesses; others were expansions from adjacent factories; a few were firms moving back into hitherto 'mothballed' premises as demand for pottery products grew in the mid-1980s. There were also a number of general engineering reoccupiers, particularly in Burslem but also throughout the city. Outside of traditional Potteries manufacturing sectors, a substantial number of reoccupations involved locally-orientated service businesses. These ranged from the specialist retail unit – video equipment (Stoke), kitchens (Newstead), Chinese food products (Hanley) – to wholesale distribution – electrical goods (Burslem), agricultural supplies (Longton), car components (Fenton) and plastics (Hanley). There were also many examples of specialist services reoccupying former VIPs. These involved cleaning, car servicing and computer software installation (Longton), French polishing (Burslem) and printing (Hanley). Amongst the remainder was the expansion of Cauldon College into premises formerly occupied by a textile firm and certainly vacant in both 1985 and 1987. In fact, some fifty-six of the reoccupations concerned such persistently vacant premises and these also included a number of former pottery factories that in 1987 had appeared to be virtually beyond productive use. Some of these had been subdivided by developers, but some were in use – albeit with limited employment compared to their original inhabitants and often in partial occupation without obvious refurbishment expenditure.

There were numerous examples amongst the reoccupants of the kinds of small businesses that have been prominent in new enterprise growth throughout the economy in the 1970s and 1980s. Double-glazing manufacturing (Longton, Burslem and Hanley), specialist plastics moulding (Burslem), security services (Fenton) are good examples of small businesses – new or relocating to larger premises – that are typical of the 1980s and that tend to occur in industrial sectors where there are limited economies of scale and relative ease of entry into business.

In general then, there was a high level of successful reoccupation of former VIPs in 1989. These spanned a range of businesses. However, such reoccupations were not really instrumental in nurturing many entirely new businesses but rather acted to counter any dispersal tendencies amongst local firms looking for larger or more appropriate premises. Of course, how many expansions did move out of the city over the period remains an unknown, although there is some local evidence that quite a high level of dispersal – in the search for the larger available premises in good locations – has occurred.

Having identified their character, it is useful to consider the factors behind successful reoccupations, not least of all because it may help us to understand the plight of those premises that remain (persistently) vacant. Around 50 per cent of the reoccupied premises were definitely purpose-built (Table 8.10) as against 63 per cent of persistent vacancies and a greater proportion were single-storey and thus probably more suitable for small businesses. Reoccupied VIPs also compare well in terms of site potential (Table 8.11). As expected, a large majority are in locations that have good or average access – both locally and in the wider geographical sense – and parking potential, especially when compared to persistent vacancies. It is to the question of such VIPs that we now turn our attention.

Persistent vacancies

From time to time in the preceding discussion we have alluded to the problem of persistent vacancies – that is those VIPs that, even during a period of growing demand and short supply of industrial buildings, have remained vacant. Although the problem had subsided between 1985 and 1989 (see Ball 1988a, 1988b), there were still forty-one persistently vacant VIPs identified, involving 20,035 square metres of floorspace. Such figures reflect perhaps intractable problems for the local economy, especially in terms of the twenty premises that had remained vacant over the 1985 to 1989 survey period. These premises were likely to deteriorate,

Table 8.10 Reoccupied vacant industrial premises in Stoke-on-Trent, August 1987 to July 1989: number of storeys and purpose-built status

Number of storeys	Purpose-built	Non purpose-built	Total
1	28	59	87
2	26	10	36
3	15	5	20
4	6	0	6
Total	75	74	149

Table 8.11 Reoccupied vacant industrial premises in Stoke-on-Trent, August 1987 to July 1989: access and parking potential

Access potential		Parking potential			
		Good	Average	Poor	Total
Good	No.	32 (5)	33 (4)	6 (3)	71 (12)
	%	21 (12)	22 (10)	4 (7)	47 (29)
Average	No.	13 (6)	37 (7)	6 (7)	56 (20)
	%	9 (15)	25 (17)	4 (17)	38 (49)
Poor	No.	4 (2)	15 (3)	3 (4)	22 (9)
	%	3 (5)	10 (7)	2 (10)	15 (22)
Total	No.	49 (13)	85 (14)	15 (14)	149 (41)
	%	33 (32)	57 (34)	10 (34)	100 (100)

Note: Figures in brackets refer to persistently vacant premises.

compounding a problem of lost potential with one of deterioration in the built fabric, possible dereliction and visual intrusiveness.

Most of these persistent vacancies relate to old premises (71 per cent were built before 1945), often former pottery factories that were purpose-built for a production system that used much more labour-intensive methods than today and that transported most products and inputs by canal. Relatively few were in good condition (Table 8.4). In general, persistent vacancies were spread throughout the industrial areas of the city (Figure 8.2), but appeared to be particularly focused on Burslem, Hanley, Longton and Stoke, with the longer-term vacancies tending to be in the older core industrial areas. These are the most likely candidates for future redevelopment because there is clear evidence of deterioration in their condition over the intervening period between the 1987 and 1989 surveys. Some eleven of the forty-one premises had deteriorated over this period although it is perhaps remarkable that eleven should have retained their good quality status, four of them since 1985. In terms of access/ parking potential they scored relatively poorly (Table 8.6).

Although it is unproductive to dwell for too long on this component – there are rather few of them and, for a variety of reasons, they are not effectively and directly available for use (e.g. the Minton-Hollins site in Stoke or the Alexander Pottery owned by Myott-Meakin Ltd that was 'mothballed' at the time of the 1989 survey) – there is some unutilized potential. Although they record relatively modest 'potential' (Table 8.6), in only one built fabric aspect (site condition) does the relative proportion of premises in the poor condition category exceed that for 1989 VIPs. Whatever the general prognosis, there were clearly opportunities for a return to productive use for at least some of the persistently vacant premises recorded in the survey. Having said that, there was, surprisingly (Finn 1986), very little evidence of notable refurbishment of site or buildings on anything more than a small sub-set of this component.

Redevelopments

Over the 1987 to 1989 survey period some twenty-seven VIPs were re-developed/demolished (Table 8.7) and, interestingly, twenty-two of them were persistent vacancies at the time of the August 1987 survey. Although at twenty-seven this is only a modest number of units, the volume of floorspace involved (43,683 square metres in the 1987 survey) meant that this category represented a much higher proportion of the 1987 to 1989 changes in the level of vacant industrial floorspace (39 per cent) than it was over the 1985 to 1987 survey period (25 per cent). Although the redeveloped VIPs component showed no particular concentration on multi-storey, purpose-built premises, many of them were in poor condition across several criteria and few had high access/parking potential prior to demolition. As such, it is not surprising that such VIPs had been redeveloped for other uses.

The explanation for the particular redeveloped premises must, of course, be set into the context of their post-demolition use. Presumably, there is a unique set of redevelopment circumstances prevailing in each case. In the 1989 survey, retail uses seemed to have dominated the productive re-use of VIP sites that had been redeveloped (Table 8.12) and this probably meant that sites had to be cleared where refurbishment was inappropriate. Other uses ranged from residential and leisure use, to simply vacant land that was either awaiting re-use or held in abeyance by developers or other local interests.

Table 8.12 Redeveloped sites in the vacant industrial premises survey, August
1987 to July 1989: use of site in July 1989

	Number of premises
Vacant land	5
Car park	3
Vacant in preparation for retail use	7
Retail use	4
Residential use	3
Leisure facilities use	1
In process of redevelopment for offices	2
Total	25

POLICY IMPLICATIONS

In the discussion so far we have analysed the level and character of VIPs in
Stoke-on-Trent in July 1989 and investigated changes occurring over the
preceding few years. It remains now to draw out some policy implications
from these findings.

The context for VIPs policy in Stoke-on-Trent

The survey showed that the growing demand for industrial premises was
sufficient to bring many former VIPs back into productive use so that the
problem had changed from one of VIPs as 'surplus' capacity and linked to
deterioration, environmental problems and a negative image for the city, to
the rather different and more positive notion of VIPs as potential locations
for business in a 'shortage' situation. In this conceptualization, VIPs are
seen more as a form of potential. There is no doubt that the persistently
vacant premises were a much less important part of the 1989 picture.

Given these changing circumstances in the industrial property market it was
clear that the use of vacant floorspace as a potential solution to the lack of
industrial premises needed to be established as an item for policy development.
In this sense, policy needs take on a kind of dualistic nature because, in addition
to this, we need to tailor policy to deal with the problems of persistently vacant
premises – the 'traditional' contextual response to the issue.

Aside from the broad context for policy there seems little doubt that any
specific actions must be pragmatic, feasible and cost effective. Unfortunately, there were various factors which constrained any quest for
realistic actions.

Policy constraints

In seeking to develop appropriate policies for the VIPs issue in Stoke-on-Trent, the local authority was severely constrained in at least two respects. First, in terms of the nature of the VIPs 'problem', and second in terms of the financial resources and planning powers at its disposal. Most VIPs in 1989 were small units. Although there was less recorded vacant floorspace in 1989 (than in 1987), there were many more actual vacant units – meaning that the average size of VIPs had fallen over the period (from an average of 864 square metres in 1987 to 486 square metres in 1989, or 386 square metres if 'marginal' premises are included in the calculation). It may be just as difficult to launch schemes linked with small, individually insignificant buildings as it is to promote the more grandiose, large-scale but high-cost refurbishment or redevelopment of a large derelict site. Certainly, a rather different approach needs to be taken according to the scale of the problem.

Another policy constraint linked to the nature of the VIPs problem concerned the motives of their owners. Although there is a complex array of factors likely to be involved, including hoarding space and failing to dispose of small, poorly-maintained premises, as well as the sheer inability to sell or lease some premises in some areas, the survey evidence did clearly show that a large volume of available floorspace was simply not marketed. We cannot deduce the decision-making – or lack of it – which underpins such a situation, although it is quite probable that some premises are owned by companies who have overlooked their existence. However, this does severely constrain any policy that the local authority might consider to utilize VIPs potential.

A second major policy constraint concerned the peculiarly 'local' problem (at least in its intensity) of financial resource limitations. Although there was no separate policy directed at VIPs in Stoke-on-Trent, the importance of this element of the industrial landscape was clearly recognized as an issue in both land-use planning and in the economic development strategy. Unfortunately, Stoke-on-Trent is an area largely excluded from the various central government schemes, linked, for example, to Inner Area Status or Development Corporations, that have brought funds to, or encouraged private sector activity in, other 'old industrial areas' within Great Britain (see Ball 1993). It is notably disadvantaged in any intent to regenerate, improve and utilize under-used local industrial infrastructure, a fact which constrains policy action and, ultimately, directs policy into low cost areas of activity.

Policy options and survey-based policy pointers

There are basically four options available in confronting the VIPs issue. These are: a 'do little' option (retaining the status quo and relying on piecemeal activity by the private sector); a cosmetic improvement option; a policy of large-scale refurbishment; or a policy option based on extensive redevelopment. The first demands a reliance on the private sector and ultimately will lead to inroads into the VIPs problem. The second, requiring some resources, is essentially a superficial policy which would involve an alleviation of only the worst industrial degradation but which could be effective on a modest scale, certainly if operated with other (planning etc.) policies. The third, requiring substantial resources, would bring buildings back into use but at a substantial cost. The fourth, often the only feasible option from a physical perspective, and an expensive one at that, would involve the wholesale removal of those VIPs that are beyond cost-effective refurbishment. These are the broad options for dealing with VIPs. Their value partly depends on the nature of such VIPs (i.e. is redevelopment necessary or will minor refurbishment suffice?). Moreover, it is possible that some vacant floorspace is simply not being marketed for some reason even though it could be utilized with little or no refurbishment. There were certainly cases such as this in the 1989 survey and it may mean that included within the first option – 'retaining the status quo' – there is an implication for policy. This is that, perhaps, a campaign of enhanced information diffusion and promotion coupled with some encouragement to owners to 'unlock' their premises could be deployed. There is a hint here as to how the development of policy could proceed. It is unfortunate that, in the Stoke-on-Trent case, the absence of substantive financial help through national urban policy meant that local policy for problems such as VIPs was restricted to a modest combination of those policy options involving either schemes that utilized mainly local financial resources or those that the City had been able to persuade the private sector to implement. This may mean that a 'softer' style of policy is necessary. For example, given the survey findings, it seems likely that a sympathetic approach to development proposals that may bring VIPs back into productive use, even when on purely planning grounds they may not fit perfectly in with current practice, can be pursued. In addition, of course, it could be possible to lever support from the private sector for development proposals that may facilitate the re-use of VIPs, although the high concentration of small units in the 1989 survey probably requires 'smaller-scale' policy options.

Aside from the question of the size of premises, another important policy pointer stems from the finding that relatively few premises were in a very poor condition. This implies that small-scale refurbishment, if indeed any is needed, may be enough to bring such VIPs back into potential use. Given the fact that, in July 1989, only 28 per cent of VIPs were being actively marketed, there is an even stronger indication that a policy of encouragement – perhaps with the local authority seeking out absentee landlords – could bear fruit.

A particularly notable set of findings from the survey concerned those VIPs that were reoccupied between 1987 and 1989. Unlike the case of VIPs reoccupied between 1985 and 1987, where only 28 per cent had been refurbished and where there was little stated intention to carry out further work (see Ball 1988b), in the 1989 survey it was found that 72 per cent of premises had been refurbished prior to occupancy, mostly by the occupants. Some intended to refurbish to support expansion or simply to modify unsuitable aspects of the buildings. Actual expenditure on refurbishment was relatively modest – an average of £7,748. If we recalculate this figure to exclude the small number (seven) of refurbishments that involved £20,000 or more, then the (more indicative) average is reduced to £4,471. There were, of course, several re-occupations where no refurbishment spending had been made. All this indicates that a modest financial inducement could encourage businesses or developers to carry out the necessary work to bring premises in the 1989 data set back into operation or, perhaps more so, that the increased performance of the local economy had simply generated a demand for what were mostly rather modest premises.

The important role of VIPs in the local economy was evident in the kinds of businesses that inhabited them – many being new or relocating firms, most of them small. This, in effect, strengthened the case for taking action to deal with VIPs because they harboured a substantial number of expansions. Emerging new firms, relocations or simply local expansions may well have diverted out of the area if there had been a shortage of suitable sites and a policy of encouraging the re-use of VIPs may pay off handsomely in the containment of growth and jobs within the area. As such, there was clearly some potential for future policy efforts to be concentrated on the identification and marketing of premises that had characteristics similar to those successes but which remained vacant by the completion of the survey. A related implication followed from the fact that some parts of the survey area – most notably Stoke – were less successful than average in the re-use of VIPs. Clearly, policy potential varied across the area and policy could focus on these less successful areas in the future.

Other pointers for policy action stemmed from the survey findings on new vacancies in 1989 and on persistent vacancies and redevelopments over the 1987 to 1989 survey period. In the former case, it was clear that many VIPs had substantial re-use potential – indeed on past experience they were likely to be reoccupied if released by their owners. Even persistently vacant cases had been shown to contain a majority of useable buildings although some of these were old, purpose-built and multi-storey with limited access and re-use potential. A policy focused on refurbishment efforts was strongly suggested by much of the survey findings, but in this persistently vacant case the key policy option probably involved redevelopment. Presumably, there was no reason why the relatively successful redevelopment levels (and new uses) charted over the 1987 to 1989 period could not be repeated for the forty-one cases, although some active encouragement through policy – perhaps the promotion of sites for redevelopment and local planning flexibility – was probably needed. Redevelopment was certainly a feasible option, perhaps the more so when it involved a large site area.

The basis of a VIPs action plan for an old industrial area

The VIPs issue rose to prominence in the mid-1980s in Stoke-on-Trent, as it did in many other 'old industrial areas' when, following a period of rationalization in the local industrial base, large numbers of industrial buildings were discarded or 'mothballed'. It remains important in the 1990s. What should local authorities do to alleviate this problem, perhaps to make use of what is often unutilized potential?

As a starting point, it is prudent to establish some simple objectives for an action plan. Given that the re-use of VIPs will help to stabilize and reinforce a local economy by partially stemming the dispersal of manufacturing and service businesses and by providing cheap premises for new or expanding businesses the objectives of an action plan might be:

1 to encourage the productive re-use of vacant floorspace;
2 to minimize the intrusiveness and lost potential which may occur if VIPs are allowed to remain out of productive use, and;
3 to minimize blight and initiate environmental improvement.

There are a range of possible policy scenarios but, in general, and unless major public funds are available, it must be a process of subtle encouragement and low cost action that prevails. For VIPs that are in good/average condition and with adequate physical space and accessibility there are a number of tentative re-use actions. For those premises that are essentially beyond feasible refurbishment, redevelopment actions are the best course. In both cases, means of implementation must be derived as an essential component of any feasible action plan. As a first step, a strategy for the re-use of VIPs should be prepared in consultation with building owners and the local community. Within that strategy, a number of actions may be considered. Clearly, they will not apply in all local contexts. However, they provide 'food for thought' – tentative suggestions for policy action.

1 Attempt to 'unlock' non-marketed premises by contacting owners, using Valuation Office records or perhaps via the Valuation Office itself, with a view to encouraging the return of their premises to productive use. Produce a brochure to explain the potential of VIPs. Consider, where possible within government regulations, the feasibility of operating a 'tighter' policy with regards to 'void' rating in order to encourage the re-use of premises.

2 Further encourage owners through the provision of small refurbishment grants drawn from a refurbishment fund to be established by the local authority. Seek private sector and central government financial support to 'top up' available local authority funds.

3 Within the context of existing facilities, complete a feasibility study of the potential for creating one or more dispersed enterprise centres within the area. These would involve the establishment of a local enterprise office offering business advice and basic facilities in a central place around which small business premises are available. Although obviously varying by area type, such premises should be within approximately one mile of the enterprise office.

4 Develop area-based actions for VIPs concentrations in a locality. As part of a strategy for re-use, consider the declaration of small informal vacant property action areas to act as 'spearheads' for the general upgrading of those parts of the core industrial areas that suffer from high levels of VIPs, and especially from persistently vacant floorspace.

For those VIPs that appear suitable only for demolition and redevelopment:

5 Attempt to encourage redevelopment by making representations to, and producing joint plans with, site owners and development companies with a view to securing redevelopment programmes in low accessibility areas. Where there is a juxtaposition of good VIPs with less viable premises in an area, attempt to produce a mixed refurbishment/ redevelopment proposal. Available information on the range of site sizes – as produced by a survey – could be used to encourage developers to consider the feasibility of involvement.

Supplementing all these type-related actions are some more general suggestions.

6 Encourage the adoption of a flexible approach to changing land uses by the local planning authorities so that non-viable premises may be returned to productive, but not necessarily industrial use.

7 If staff resources permit, build a more up-to-date base of information on VIPs by carefully monitoring the turnover of industrial premises in the intervening periods between full-scale survey work.

8 Undertake further research work to establish the owners and other partici-
   pants involved in VIPs; and to document the processes through which major
   reoccupations or redevelopments have occurred so that successful solutions
   can be reproduced and potential bottlenecks avoided through 'lubricant'
   policies that seek to ease the processes involved.
9 In general, actively promote the view that many VIPs are as much a
   source of potential development as a 'problem' for the local economy.

CONCLUSIONS

The locality-based survey and analysis set out in this chapter demonstrate
that the issue of VIPs is important at a variety of levels. VIPs represent both
a challenge and an opportunity for local economic planners.

Basically, this chapter has produced three broad achievements. First, it
has considered the approaches to be adopted in tackling what is an underresearched and difficult survey area. Second, it has documented the characteristics and development of vacant industrial floorspace in one particular
'old industrial area', focusing not only on obviously industrial premises but
also on the variety of buildings that are often used for industrial activity.
Third, it has considered some of the policy implications, particularly as they
pertain to urban industrial economies that have a legacy of old, difficult-to-
use premises. Of course, VIPs are very much a 'live issue' in the 1990s –
especially in these 'old industrial areas'. However, more than that
'problem-orientated' approach we have shown that a focus on VIPs – as the
outcome of a much larger set of processes – may well provide numerous
insights into other dimensions of local industrial development. Reoccupations of former VIPs enables us to assess the incidence of new
activity in an area. A focus on 'marginal' premises provides some useful
insights into local property supply and needs. Moreover, the documentation
of VIPs offers a potential surrogate for the evaluation of local industrial
property market dynamics. In essence, an evaluation of VIPs opens the way
for a whole range of analyses and policy responses.

REFERENCES

Adams, C.D., Russell, L. and Taylor-Russell, C. (1992) 'The demand for industrial
    land: a north west case study', *Regional Studies*, 26(6): 586–92.
Ball, R.M. (1988a) 'Vacant Industrial Premises in Stoke-on-Trent: filling a void',
    The Planner 74(6): 31–3.
—— (1988b) *The Phoenix and the Ashes: a Survey and Analysis of Vacant
    Industrial Premises in Stoke-on-Trent*, Final Project Report, Department of
    Geography and Recreation Studies, Staffordshire Polytechnic, November.

—— (1989a) *Vacant Industrial Premises in Stoke-on-Trent: a Survey and Analysis with Some Policy Suggestions for the 1990s*, Consultancy Report submitted to the Industrial Development Unit, Stoke-on-Trent City Council, September.

—— (1989b) 'Vacant industrial premises and local development: a survey, analysis and policy assessment of the problem in Stoke-on-Trent', *Land Development Studies* 6: 105–28.

—— (1993) 'Economic and industrial diversification: policies, technologies and location', in A.D.M. Phillips (ed.) *The Potteries Region: Continuity and Change in a Staffordshire Conurbation*, Gloucester: Alan Sutton.

—— and Metcalfe, M. (1992) 'Tourism development at the margins: pits, pots and potential in the Potteries locality', in *Centre for Travel and Tourism*, Proceedings of the Tourism 1992 Conference, Durham, July.

Burnley Borough Council (1992) *Bid for Assisted Area Status*, September.

Cameron, S. and Fleming, G. (1990) 'Implications of local property markets for economic development policies: a case study of Wakefield', in P. Healey and R. Nabarro (eds) *Land and Property Development: a Changing Context*, Aldershot: Gower.

Champion, A. and Townsend, A. (1991) *Contemporary Britain: a Geographical Perspective*, London: Edward Arnold.

Civic Trust Regeneration Unit (1989) *Burslem Action Plan*, Stoke-on-Trent: Civic Trust Regeneration Unit.

Department of the Environment (1987) *Re-using Redundant Buildings: Good Practice in Urban Regeneration*, London: Inner Cities Directorate.

Finn, M.D. (1986) 'Refurbishment feasibility', *Property Management* 4(3): 209–16.

Firn, J.R. and Swales, J.K. (1978) 'The formation of new manufacturing establishments in the Central Clydeside and West Midlands conurbations 1963–1972: a comparative analysis', *Regional Studies*, 12(2): 199–214.

Fothergill, S., Kitson, M. and Monk, S. (1987) 'Industrial buildings and economic development', in W.F. Lever (ed.) *Industrial Change in the United Kingdom*, Harlow: Longman.

——, Monk, S. and Perry, M. (1987a) 'In the microchip age, there's still trouble at mill', *Guardian*, 15 May.

——, Monk, S. and Perry, M. (1987b) *Industrial Property*, London: Hutchinson.

Grant Thornton (1989) *City of Stoke-on-Trent – Gladstone Pottery Museum; Feasibility Study*, August.

Green, H. and Foley, P. (1986) *Redundant Space: a Productive Asset*, London: Harper and Row.

Lancashire County Council (1992) *Lancashire: the Case for Assistance, Submission for Assisted Area Status*, Preston: Lancashire County Council.

Lloyd, P. and Mason, C. (1984) 'Spatial variations in new firm formation in the UK: comparative evidence from Merseyside, Greater Manchester and South Hampshire', *Regional Studies* 18(3): 207–20.

London Borough of Ealing (1992) *Assisted Areas Review: Submission to the DTI*, London: Borough of Ealing.

Perry, M. (1991) 'Floorspace and commercial developments', in M. Healey (ed.) *Economic Activity and Land Use*, London: Longman.

Staffordshire County Council *et al.* (1991) *The Need for New Premium Employment Sites in North Staffordshire*, Stafford: Staffordshire County Council.

Stoke-on-Trent City Council (1991) *Stoke-on-Trent Economic Development Strategy, 1991–2001*, Stoke-on-Trent: Stoke-on-Trent City Council.
—— (1992) *Gladstone/St. James Ceramic Design Quarter: an Urban Pilot Project*, Stoke-on-Trent: Stoke-on-Trent City Council.
Wakefield Metropolitan District Council/Kirklees Metropolitan Council (1992) *Wakefield and Dewsbury Travel-to-Work Area, Assisted Area Review*, September, Wakefield: City of Wakefield MDC/Kirklees MC.
West Midlands Forum of County Councils (1984) *The Problem of Disused Industrial Buildings in the West Midlands: the Potential for Action*, Unpublished discussion paper.
Williams, H., Bozeat, N., Cook, B. and Hardy, A. (1980) *Industrial Renewal in the Inner City: an Assessment of Potential and Problems*, London: Inner Cities Directorate, Department of the Environment.

9 Property ownership, leasehold forms and industrial change

Colin Lizieri

INTRODUCTION

Despite the growing attention given to the role of the built environment in urban and regional restructuring and in capital circulation, comparatively little attention has been paid by geographers and urban social scientists to the detailed mechanics of property markets. Urban development and re-development often seem to be portrayed as an inevitable consequence of shifting economic forces and the built form as a neutral stage on which industrial and social changes take place. For example, much of the literature on 'new industrial spaces' and production linkages seems to simply assume that appropriate workshop or factory space exists in the relevant location (for example Scott and Kwok 1989; Henry 1992). Even those authors who focus on real estate have tended to underplay the role of market structures on detailed local outcomes, concentrating rather on broad trends and trajectories, aggregate statistics or cultural and architectural impacts (e.g. Beauregard 1991; Knox 1991). UK-based studies have tended to emphasise planning structures and their impact on redevelopment and urban regeneration (Healey and Barrett 1990, provide a detailed review of this literature).

By contrast, academics located within the property profession in the UK have tended to concentrate on techniques, on the 'deal', and have neglected the wider, fundamental forces that shape the property market. In particular, the interactions between occupational, investment and development markets and the key role of funding institutions are frequently understated. In part, this is a consequence of the professional structure of surveying in the UK and the imposition by the Royal Institution of Chartered Surveyors of a core syllabus emphasising conventional neoclassical economics and urban economics on exempting surveying courses. There is only limited scope for the introduction of alternative perspectives and more complex economic models.

Elsewhere, it has been argued that the institutional arrangements of the property market can create inertial forces that modify the impact of wider economic changes on the built environment and hamper adjustment to changing circumstances (Lizieri 1991, 1992). This chapter focuses on leasehold property in the UK and the development of the standard 'institutional' lease. It is argued that the persistence of the institutional lease hampers the property market's ability to adjust to changing economic circumstances. The first section examines the origin and form of the institutional lease. The chapter then assesses critiques of the standard lease and the impacts of the cyclical downturn in the property market on commercial lettings. The third section examines wider forces that might be expected to lead to changes in the forms of ownership of industrial property. Finally, the discussion focuses on resistance to change and the possible consequences of the preservation of the institutional lease.

LEASEHOLD AND THE INSTITUTIONAL LEASE

The pattern of commercial property ownership traces its lineage to the pyramid structure of feudal tenure. Megarry and Wade (1966: 39) note that 'law has preferred to suppress . . . the practical consequences of tenure rather than strike at the root of the theory of tenure itself'. There is considerable separation of ownership and occupation, with businesses as tenants paying rent but having no equity interest in the property they occupy and investors/landlords profiting from rental income and growth in the capital value of the property.

It has been argued (e.g. Massey and Catalano 1978; Fothergill, Monk and Perry 1987) that the majority of industrial users are owner-occupiers. Certainly firms have the ability to write off the cost of industrial buildings over time against tax, an advantage not conferred upon commercial property (Evans 1990). While the landlord–tenant relationship is most pronounced in the commercial (office and retail) sectors, institutional investors and property companies have significant holdings of industrial property. Around 10 per cent of the Investment Property Databank's portfolio by value is industrial property with pension funds having a significantly higher holding (IPD 1992); the precise balance varies as the yields for the three main sectors – offices, retail and industrial property – shift. Nearly 20 per cent of the portfolio used in the calculation of the Jones Lang Wootton property index is industrial (JLW 1992). The Baring Houston and Saunders (1991) survey of property funds showed a value weighting of 19 per cent in industrial property, with nearly half the funds intending to increase their holdings. Slough Estates, one of the largest UK listed property companies, owns some 25 million square feet of industrial space.

Brixton Estates and Mucklow plc provide two further examples of property companies whose growth was based on industrial development.

The separation of ownership and occupation is more pronounced with respect to industrial estates and, in particular, the more recent business parks and high-tech developments. Although the new B1 (Business) designation in the 1987 Use Classes Order has led to a switch from standard sheds with 10–15 per cent of ancillary office space to higher specification space with a much greater office content and to out-of-town office parks (APR (quoted in Houlder 1991) estimated that 79 per cent of business park completions in 1991 were office units) many parks retain an industrial/ warehousing component. For example, Rouse Associates' King's Hill, West Malling or Slough Estates' Winnersh Triangle estates are both characterized by mixed-use multiple occupancy units, while 20 per cent of the Bedfont Lakes development near Heathrow was earmarked for industrial usage – albeit ghettoized on a separate site.

The property world was slow to recognize the impact of inflation on investment values (Baum and Crosby 1988). Traditional leases were long, with no provision for regular rent increases. However, from the 1960s onwards, a standard lease form has emerged. The typical commercial lease has:

1 a term of 25 years (sometimes 15 or 20 years for industrial property) with no option to revoke the lease (break clause);
2 5 yearly rent reviews to open market value, but subject to an upward-only clause;
3 tenant responsibility for repairing and insuring the property ('full repairing and insuring' or FRI);
4 restrictions on the use of the property and the ability of the tenant to sublet or assign the lease.

This lease form, unique in the developed world, is extremely onerous for the tenant, not least because of the principle of 'privity of contract'. A lease is a contract and, as such, the first tenant remains liable for the rent of the property throughout the life of the lease. Even where the lease has been assigned, the first tenant retains a liability in the event of default by subsequent lessees. Few tenants occupy a property for the full length of the lease, yet the landlord still retains a right to claim unpaid rent.

The institutional lease does provide a considerable measure of security of tenure for tenants in conditions of under-supply. Tax structures help preserve lease length. Until the 1989 Finance Act, there were VAT implications for leases of less than twenty-one years and stamp-duty rates mitigate against longer lengths (the rate of duty rises from 2 per cent to 12 per cent for leases of over thirty-five years). However, the development of the standard lease form can be attributed more to the quasi-monopolistic position of landlords and the influence of investing institutions. As Aldridge (1992) has pointed out, a landlords' market is likely to persist, even in conditions of over-supply. The search for a specific building type of a particular size in a specific area will tend to produce a restricted choice of properties. Landlords are thus able to impose lease terms that are less favourable to tenants. Since the 1970s, institutional investors (insurance companies and pension funds) have been significant direct investors in commercial and industrial property. As risk-averse investors, they seek the long-term security of income that the standard lease provides and hence developers looking to institutional purchasers will tend to let new buildings on 'institutional' terms. Despite considerable pressures for change, the institutional lease form has been maintained through a combination of inertia and resistance to innovation.

THE STANDARD LEASE AND THE PROPERTY CRASH

The letting arrangements characterized by the standard institutional lease are not without their critics in the property industry. For example Calder writes from a landlord's perspective that the 1954 Landlord and Tenant Act 'discourages provision of easily rentable small unit commercial space . . . makes flexible short-term occupation difficult and generally confounds any principle of good property management. . . . The idea of security of tenure ossifies inefficient lease structures' (1989: 62). From the tenant's point of view, Smyth suggests that 'it is inconceivable to an off-shore tenant that they are expected to sign a lease which is effectively more onerous than owning the property' (1990: 29). Other criticisms of aspects of leasehold are reported in Higginbotham (1990), Waller (1990) and Oakeshott (1992).

The cyclical property slump that dates from 1989 and which has persisted into the early 1990s has been particularly severe, coinciding with a deep recession in the UK economy. The lack of occupational demand, combined with over-supply caused by the development boom of the mid- to late 1980s, fuelled by the widespread availability of bank and corporate finance, has created a tenants' market which has, in turn, led to an erosion of the strict terms of the institutional lease. Where lettings have occurred, lease lengths have been shorter and break clauses have become more common. Above all, tenants have been offered considerable inducements, in the form of capital contributions and rent-free periods, to take space. This is perhaps most prevalent in the office markets of London and the south east. Of deals reported in *Estates Gazette* in April 1992, some 60 per cent were for a term less than twenty-five years, a quarter included break clauses and the majority had some form of tenant inducement. The Wang UK letting of Thomas More Square in 1991 was typical: landlords Skanska agreed a twenty-six month rent free period, a capital contribution and a break clause in year seven of the twenty-five-year lease.

However, such terms may be attributed to the difficult market conditions rather than to a structural change in the nature of occupation. The majority of these deals are in the form of institutional leases with specially negotiated terms, not new lease forms or lettings outside the conditions of the 1954 Landlord and Tenant Act. The standard lease still has many defenders amongst professional advisors and institutional investors. Thus Kenny argued that 'the basic system of leasehold ownership works well and is responsive to changing market forces' (1988: 30). More recently, Bernstein and Lewis (1992) have mounted a defence of the traditional lease which, they claim, encourages investment in property. They suggest that the abandonment of the institutional lease would lead to disinvestment, reducing supply and raising costs to tenants. They advocate that, far from adopting European practices, property professionals should promote UK leasing structures abroad.

These views suggest that, although tenants can currently wrest concessions from landlords, these concessions are conditional on the depressed state of the property market and will disappear when some form of equilibrium is restored. Break clauses were comparatively common in the early 1980s (during a more shallow cyclical slump), but had virtually disappeared by the middle of the decade, when demand exceeded supply. The cyclical slumps of the property market provide the opportunity for the introduction of and experimentation with new leasehold forms, but do not seem to lead to permanent changes. However, there are forces of change from both outside and within the property market that may result in a more permanent set of changes.

FORCES FOR CHANGE

Given the cyclical nature of real estate, it seems likely that the current over-supply will, once again, be followed by under-supply, escalating rents and a landlords' market. Under such conditions, one might expect the re-emergence of the institutional lease as the standard letting format. However, there are wider forces acting upon the property market that might lead to the adoption of more flexible forms. Any categorization of forces will inevitably be an over-simplification given the complex interactions involved. Bearing this in mind, this section examines four broad factors that can be considered to impact on ownership patterns. The first is the restructuring of economic activity at a global scale, changing the technical conditions of production. Second, the last decade has seen accelerating internationalization of property markets both in terms of occupation and investment with impacts on the structure and operation of those markets. A third, and related, force has been change in the nature of financial capital and investment. Finally, the impact of growing awareness of the effects of depreciation on commercial property values will be examined.

The reorganization of economic activity across the 1970s and 1980s has been much debated. While the post-Fordism/flexible accumulation hypotheses have been subject to searching criticism (e.g. Amin and Robbins 1990; Gertler 1988, 1992; Sayer 1989), there is agreement that there have been major changes in the nature of industrial activity. Among the phenomena identified have been:

- a shift from mass production to smaller scale activity;
- a switch to speciality products and niche marketing;
- a move to more flexible, individualistic working patterns;
- rapid product innovation and shorter product life cycles;
- the internationalization of investment and production;
- new patterns of corporate ownership.

Now, these trends clearly impact on the nature of industrial premises and on the nature of property holding. The rapid shifts in product range, the changing balance between production, research and development and marketing and the patterns of rapid expansion and contraction require flexibility both in the built form and in the institutional arrangements for occupation. The creation of high-tech business space, facilitating changed working configurations and permitting a mix of office, research and production space represents a physical response to these new demands mirrored in planning terms by the 'flexible' B1 use class. In this context, the institutional lease appears as a rigid, frictional constraint to change, with its restrictive covenants preventing (or at best hampering) shifts in the type of activity, and the long lease length, privity of contract, absence of break clauses and restrictions on sub-letting and assignment hindering firms from responding to shifts in patterns of demand.

Internationalization of production impacts on the occupational property market. There are not only geographical shifts in the patterns of demand for space resulting from the globalization of production (Dicken 1992). International firms will have experienced different occupational regimes and hence be less willing to accept the rigidities of the UK leasehold structure, while changes to the organization of production (e.g. through branch-plant economies or through clusters of component suppliers servicing an assembly plant on a just-in-time basis) demand a more flexible arrangement than the twenty-five-year FRI lease. With the supply of property relatively fixed in the short term (that is supply is inelastic with respect to price), demand drives rents. Thus there should be price advantages in supplying more flexible lease terms.

Internationalization of production is paralleled by internationalization of investment, financing and funding. For off-shore investors, the twenty-five-year lease with upward-only lease terms is superficially attractive. Figures from Debenham Tewson Research (1991) show how overseas investment in direct property rose from a level of around £250 million per annum in the mid-1980s to £1.9 billion in 1988, £3.1 billion in 1989 and £2.9 billion in 1990 before falling away in the property crash. However, foreign investors have far more experience of shorter leases and break clauses and thus may take a more sanguine view than the more conservative UK investing institutions. They must also consider taxation and accounting rules which may make the purchase of long leasehold interests unfavourable – as is the case, for example, for US investors. In the current slump in the property market, high initial yields (that is the ratio of the current rent to the capital value of the building) have attracted foreign purchasers. While most overseas investors have been interested in 'trophy' office buildings in major cities, there has been a growth in interest in industrial property, particularly amongst Scandinavian investors, attracted by the higher initial yields and smaller purchase price. Such purchases aid diversification strategies aimed at reducing investment risk.

This internationalization reflects the deregulation and integration of global financial markets since the breakdown of the Bretton Woods Agreement (Lizieri 1992; Pugh 1992). Changes in the financial environment have been facilitated by the rapid development of information and communications technologies, creating a virtual twenty-four-hour global market place for equities, bonds and money. The 'hyper-mobility' of capital has a number of consequences, including:

- a tendency for annualized target (discount) rates of return to rise as circulation increases in velocity;
- a growth in the importance of short-term returns and the search for arbitrage opportunities;
- an in-built tendency for inflation and growth in indebtedness;
- rapid innovation in financial products and the securitization of existing investments;
- an increasing emphasis on liquidity and risk avoidance.

Once again, the rigidities of the institutional lease sit uncomfortably in such a context. Direct property investment's supposed advantage as a hedge against inflation must be set against its inherent illiquidity and riskiness (caused by large lot size, legal framework for disposal, absence of a central market place, imperfect information, and high transaction and marketing costs) and its (historically) low initial yields.

Property's low initial yields imply expectations of future rental and capital growth. Industrial property has traditionally exhibited higher initial yields than retail or office property, partly due to higher perceived risk, partly due to lower expectations of growth. However, in a more volatile investment market, investors may be less impressed by hypothetical long-term capital growth than by short-term income return and the ability to switch out of an investment. This reduces the advantage of the long lease as an investment vehicle. Furthermore, UK pension funds and insurance companies, for a long time the most significant investors in direct property, have become increasingly aware of the need to match assets to liabilities, and both have experienced a rise in short-term liabilities. Thus the equity (capital growth) element of property may be seen as of less value than its bond (income return) characteristics and in this context a shorter, higher yielding lease looks favourable. These changed demands have led to attempts to create a securitized property vehicle allowing direct property holding but with lower entry costs and enhanced liquidity (Rodney and Rydin 1989; Adams and Venmore-Rowland 1991a, 1991b). Deregulation has also eroded the scarcity factor created by a strict planning regime which helped to sustain capital growth: once again this points to an emphasis on short-term returns rather than the longer run investment potential of property.

Finally, there is a growing awareness of the impact of depreciation and obsolescence on the rental and capital value of property (Salway 1986; City University 1988; Baum 1990) – a factor not explicitly recognized in traditional valuation techniques. In addition to architectural fads, the value of a building can be very quickly eroded by functional obsolescence. Otherwise physically sound buildings may no longer be appropriate for the leading-edge sectors of the economy. Prime properties become secondary, the tenants prepared to occupy the buildings are confined to the less dynamic sectors, rents fall relatively, rates of return fall. To prevent this loss of value, investors need a property which is capable of adaptation and updating (the 'flexible building') and they need to be able to actively manage that property. The security of tenure provided by the twenty-five-year lease prevents the active management of a property portfolio, hinders the rehabilitation or renovation of the building and preserves sub-optimal land-use activity from an investment perspective. As a result, investment performance suffers.

These factors, then, might be expected to impel the development of more flexible lease forms: shorter leases, break clauses (options to determine), changes in rent fixing procedures (e.g. indexation, fixed percentage increases, turnover or profit rents, upward and downward reviews), an erosion of privity of contract and the principle of first tenant liability, and a wider choice in the nature of occupation ranging from owner-occupation and conventional leases under Landlord and Tenant Act provisions through to serviced premises, licences and 'easy-in easy-out' accommodation. Although the impact of the property slump has seen the emergence of some of these forms, there seems to be a considerable resistance to change and a desire to preserve the institutional lease.

RESISTANCE TO CHANGE

There would appear to be considerable advantages to be gained by both investors and tenants from the adoption of a more flexible lease form. Why then is there such resistance? Why, for example, do Arlington Securities insist on standard lease forms for Aztec West, Bristol, an archetypically high-tech business park calling for flexible arrangements? Resistance to change appears to result from a combination of institutional and professional inertia and conservatism.

The first inertial force comes from the funding institutions (both the institutions and the banking sector) who, for long-term funding, tend to insist on 'tenant with good covenant, let on an institutional lease' as a condition for provision of a mortgage or loan. This is clearly short-sighted if that lease form adversely affects the investment performance of the property and hence the borrower's ability to meet repayments and the lender's security in the property itself. Many of the innovative financial engineering techniques utilized across the 1980s to provide limited recourse funding also mirrored the standard lease form – for example stepped-coupon bonds with the coupon rate tied to the rent review pattern. The property crash has had the effect of making lenders more cautious and conservative, further entrenching the standard lease.

Lenders' conservatism tends to be matched by that of institutional investors in direct property, particularly smaller funds (who are more likely to hold the lower value industrial and high-tech properties). The ability to sell a completed and let development to an institution will typically depend on the standard lease being in place. However, the fund's ability to re-sell at an optimum price may well rest on the ability to alter the tenant mix or property functionality. Institutional requirements may thus reduce trade-ability and lower returns. As with lenders, institutions are likely to be more conservative in 'adverse' (that is tenants') markets, hampering the emergence of new ownership forms. Many institutional funds are unwilling (or do not have the resources) to engage in active property management and are content with the lower long-term returns of the 'clean' standard lease.

This institutional conservatism is matched by inertia on the part of professional advisors. The supposed advantages of standardization are set out in standard textbooks such as Enever (1989), and are thus embedded within professional training and education. Of more importance, however, is the manner in which many agency and investment surveyors approach the valuation of non-standard leases. The surveying profession's reliance on traditional valuation methods and rule-of-thumb adjustments largely prevents the potential of non-standard leases being recognized. While the academic wing of the property world has recognized the superiority of discounted cashflow techniques over traditional methods, this has not been translated into practice. Indeed traditional techniques are given legal sanction by tribunal decisions and the need to conform to the methods laid down by the professional bodies, such as the RICS's *Red Book*.

Conventional capital valuations of commercial property are based on the concept of the 'all risks yield'. This yield is determined in the market place based on comparable evidence, where this exists. For a freehold property, the estimated market rent is multiplied by the reciprocal of the all risks yield (the 'years purchase' or YP) to provide the capital value. Thus, if an industrial property has a current rental value of £10,000 per annum and comparable properties have sold on yields of 10 per cent, then the property will be valued at:

Income:	£10,000
YP in perpetuity, 10 per cent	10
Capital value	£100,000

Thus the all risks yield implicitly deals with the market target rate of return, implied rental and capital growth, the rent review pattern, asset risk, depreciation and obsolescence. A discounted cashflow valuation makes all (or most) of these factors explicit, allowing the individual assumptions to be viewed, challenged and amended.

When faced with a non-conventional property (for example an industrial property let on a short lease or with a break clause), the traditional valuation is amended by increasing the yield to account for the perceived greater risk. This has the effect of reducing the capital value. In the absence of comparable evidence, this yield adjustment is based on rule-of-thumb techniques. This essentially arbitrary adjustment then becomes a comparable for later valuations. The same process occurs with negotiations on rental levels for non-standard leases, with the premium demanded over a conventional lease reflecting the perceived additional risk for the landlord/investor.

It is possible to assess these rule-of-thumb adjustments using explicit rational appraisal techniques. These tend to suggest that the adjustments applied are out of line with those that a rational valuation would suggest. The Property Investment Research Centre has developed a number of computerized appraisal models that permit entry of assumptions on, for example, rental growth, the probability of break clauses being exercised, and the length taken to re-let a property. Values are then simulated using a Monte Carlo technique. Surveyors have been asked to supply values for the assumptions and to state what adjustments they would make to conventional yields and rents. Initial results suggest that valuers consistently apply adjustments that are greater than the appraisal models would suggest.

In one example, we examined the impact of break clauses on the value of a property. The standard 'reference' property had an initial yield of 8.1 per cent. We varied the lease by allowing a break clause at each rent review (that is every five years), assigning a 0.5 probability to the exercise of the break clause. If the option to break was exercised, a period of eighteen months was allowed to re-let the building. Most valuers questioned would have adjusted the yield on a property let on these terms upwards by between 1.5 to 2 per cent. The expected net present value generated by the simulation suggested that the appropriate adjustment to the yield would be less than 1 per cent. This was further reduced if a penalty for exercising the break clause was imposed – as is standard practice in the current market. The imposition of a break clause penalty also served to eliminate much of the downside risk. In any case, in investment terms, the building-specific downside risk associated with non-standard leases should be diversified away in a balanced portfolio.

This implies that the property industry is undervaluing non-conventional leases and demanding higher rental premia than are justified, slowing the adoption of more flexible forms. Overseas investors and more sophisticated UK investors are likely to identify and exploit this disparity – as was the case with the mis-valuation of short leasehold interests – but the impact is likely to be felt first in major urban office markets and flagship retail developments with a slow ripple out to industrial markets.

CONCLUSIONS

Changes in the world economy should have a major impact on real estate markets. Shifts in the nature of industrial production, in the location of activity and in patterns of ownership, impact on occupational markets. The global integration of financial circuits and the development of innovative funding and financing techniques alter the nature of development and investment markets. These forces would suggest that a more flexible form of occupation than that provided by the UK institutional lease is required. The twenty-five-year FRI lease, with the burden it imposes on tenants and its inherent rigidity, seems ill-suited to the changed economic environment. The current property slump has seen the emergence of a tenants' market, with shorter leases and break clauses becoming more common.

In practice, however, there is considerable resistance to the erosion of the institutional lease. Long-term development financing is often conditional on the imposition of standard leases, while investors are unwilling to purchase investment property not let on institutional terms. Above all, the professional structure of the market and the valuation techniques used to analyse property investments hamper the emergence of new forms of ownership and occupation. This inertia is important in that property is the location for all economic activity. The absence of appropriate lease forms, of flexible forms of occupation, must hamper an economy's ability to adjust to economic and technical change. For the UK, there is a further implication with the completion of the Single European Market. If industrial property is not available on appropriate terms, then firms may seek to locate elsewhere in Europe, where more favourable occupational conditions exist (Lizieri and Goodchild 1993). The industrial sectors in which the UK appears to hold a comparative advantage are predominantly high technology, flexible sectors – in information technology, communications technology and complex electronic components in, for example, aerospace. These are the very type of activity that require flexible space and flexible occupation terms.

There are also implications for research into the impact of global forces on local economies. The outcomes of this will be determined by the particular, contingent characteristics of the segmented occupational and investment markets. There are considerable frictional forces that hamper adjustment processes and create contradictions within the real estate environment, with wider ramifications for investment markets and financial capital. One key implication is that attempts to establish and forecast global (or even national) trends and outcomes by means of aggregate statistical data is likely to prove at best incomplete and possibly even futile given the existence of locally-specific institutional structures and inertial forces. This is not to argue that property research should not be informed by an awareness of over-arching economic and social forces. However, this meta-framework must be complemented by detailed consideration of the actual structures and dynamics of property markets. This integration of macro and micro levels of analysis is an important task for industrial property research.

ACKNOWLEDGEMENTS

A version of this chapter was presented to the Institute of British Geographers' Industrial Activity and Area Development Study Group's conference on Property and Industrial Development at Stoke-on-Trent in 1991. I am grateful for comments received at that conference, and from staff and students at City University. In particular, I would like to acknowledge the contributions of Piers Venmore-Rowland and Andrew Axcell. The chapter draws on the findings of a research project funded by Donaldsons, Chartered Surveyors. The views expressed here are those of the author alone and do not represent the views of Donaldsons or the Property Investment Research Centre.

REFERENCES

Adams, A. and Venmore-Rowland, P. (1991a) 'Direct or indirect property investment?', Department of Actuarial Science Research Paper 22, City University.
—— and —— (1991b) 'Proposed property investment vehicles: will they work?', *Journal of Property Valuation and Investment,* 9: 287–94.
Aldridge, T. (1992) 'Market rents – law, lore or ledgerdemain?', Discussion Paper in Property Research No. 1, City University Business School.
Amin, A. and Robins, K. (1990) 'The re-emergence of regional economies? The mythical geography of flexible accumulation', *Environment and Planning D: Society and Space* 8: 7–34.
Baring Houston and Saunders (1991) *Property Investment Report,* Issue 99, London: Baring Houston and Saunders.
Baum, A. (1990) *Property Investment, Depreciation and Obsolescence,* London: Routledge.
—— and Crosby, N. (1988) *Property Investment Appraisal,* London: Routledge.
Beauregard, R. (1991) 'Capital restructuring and the new built environment of global cities', *International Journal of Urban and Regional Research* 15: 90–105.
Bernstein, R. and Lewis, C. (1992) 'UK lease structures in the melting pot', *Estates Gazette* 9245: 108–13.
Calder, M. (1989) 'Landlord and Tenant Act 1954 – a problem for small businesses', *Estates Gazette* 8914: 62ff.
City University (1988) *Property Depreciation and Obsolescence,* London: Richard Ellis/Hill Samuel.
Debenham, Tewson Research (1991) *Money Into Property,* London: Debenham, Tewson Research.
Dicken, P. (1992) *Global Shift,* 2nd edn, London: Paul Chapman Publishing.
Enever, N. (1989) *The Valuation of Property Investments,* 4th edn, London: *Estates Gazette.*
Evans, A. (1990) 'Taxation, gross funds and the ownership of commercial property', *Journal of Valuation* 8: 339–49.
Fothergill, S., Monk, S. and Perry, M. (1987) *Property and Industrial Development,* London: Hutchinson.
Gertler, M. (1988) 'The limits to flexibility: comments on the post-Fordist vision of production', *Transactions, Institute of British Geographers* 13: 419–32.
—— (1992) 'Flexibility revisited: districts, nation-states and the forces of production', *Transactions, Institute of British Geographers* 17: 259–78.
Healey, P. and Barrett, S. (1990) 'Structure and agency in land and property development processes', *Urban Studies* 27: 89–103.
Henry, N. (1992) 'The new industrial spaces: locational logic of a new production era?', *International Journal of Urban and Regional Research* 16: 375–96.
Higginbotham, J. (1990) 'Tenants talk tough', *Chartered Surveyor Weekly, What Office* Supplement, 15 November: 35.
Houlder, V. (1991) 'Business parks', *Financial Times Survey,* 16 April: 15.

Investment Property Databank (IPD) (1992) *Annual Review 1992*, London: Investment Property Databank.

Jones Lang Wootton (JLW) (1992) *Property Index*, summer, London: Jones Lang Wootton.

Kenny, P. (1988) 'Commonhold title', *Estates Gazette*, 8812: 30–2.

Knox, P. (1991) 'The restless urban landscape: economic and sociocultural change and the transformation of Metropolitan Washington, D.C.', *Annals of the Association of American Geographers* 81: 181–209.

Lizieri, C. (1991) 'The property market in a changing world economy', *Journal of Property Valuation and Investment* 9: 201–14.

—— (1992) 'City office markets: global finance and local constraints', Discussion Paper in Property Research No. 2, City University Business School.

—— and Goodchild, R. (1993) 'The Single European Market: the impact on industrial property', in J. Berry, W. Deddis and S. McGreal (eds) *Urban Regeneration, Property Investment and Development*, London: Spon.

Massey, D. and Catalano, A. (1978) *Capital and Land*, London: Edward Arnold.

Megarry, R. and Wade, H. (1966) *The Law of Real Property*, 3rd edn, London: Butterworth.

Oakeshott, M. (1992) 'A dialogue of the deaf', *Financial Times*, 9 October: 16.

Pugh, C. (1992) 'The globalisation of finance capital and the changing relationships between property and finance', *Journal of Property Finance* 2: 211–15; 369–79.

Rodney, W. and Rydin, Y. (1989) 'Trends towards unitisation and securitisation in property markets', in R. Grover (ed.) *Land and Property Development: New Directions*, London: Spon.

Salway, F. (1986) *Depreciation of Commercial Property*, Reading: CALUS.

Sayer, A. (1989) 'Post-Fordism in question', *International Journal of Urban and Regional Research* 13: 666–95.

Scott, A. and Kwok, E. (1989) 'Inter-firm subcontracting and locational agglomeration: a case study of the printed circuits industry in Southern California', *Regional Studies* 23: 405–16.

Smyth, G. (1990) 'USA/UK practices – worlds apart', *Estates Gazette* 9033: 28–9.

Waller, A. (1990) 'How to prepare for review', *Chartered Surveyor Weekly*, *What Office* supplement, 15 November: 36.

Name index

Subject index

advance factories 11, 55
agencies 12, 26–7
agglomeration economies 11
Applied Property Research (APR) 125, 183
Arlington Securities 189

banks: conditions for mortgage/loan provision 189; environmental guidelines 71; funding of reclaimed derelict sites 72–4; lending to developers 7; repossessions 35; *see also* private sector
Baring Houston & Saunders 182
Bartlett International Summer School (BISS) 3
batch production 5–6
behavioural analysis 110–12
Birmingham Jewellery Quarter 4, 93–101
British Land Registry records 46
Brixton Estates 183
brownfield sites *see* derelict sites
Building Employers' Confederation 106
buildings: age/design data 43; B1 (business) class 30–1, 44, 86, 93, 102; flexibility 10, 107, 124–5, 188; high technology 109–10; marginal industrial potential 157–8; purpose types 109; relationship of form to activity 42; standardized units (sheds) 8, 44; warehouse units 44, 124–5; *see also* Use Classes Order
Burnley Borough Council 152
Business Monitors 41

business parks *see* industrial estates

capital accumulation 83–4, 131; flexible 5–6, 186
capital valuations 190–1
capitalism and land use 89–90
Cardiff: city centre 135–40; docklands 140–5
Census of Employment 41, 50
Census of Production 29, 41
central business districts 92–3
central government: control of land use 83–5, 88–92; environmental policies 74; floorspace information 43–5; and industrial property market 10–13, 129–31; and local authorities 130–1; property market information 29–30, 40–1, 42–8; research into role of 147–8
Central Statistical Office (CSO) 29–30; investment information 46–8
Chartered Surveyor Weekly 25
Chestertons 26
city centres: Cardiff development 135–40; and city fringe developments 92–3; socio-economic and political structures 146–7
city fringes: and industrial communities 92–3; new land uses 14–15, 83–103
City Grants 74, 75–80, 132
Coalbrookedale 4
Comedia 93
Commercial and Industrial Floorspace Statistics (CIFS) 29, 43–5, 57